Swimming

DPH SPORTS SERIES

SWIMMING

H. C. DUBEY

DISCOVERY PUBLISHING HOUSE
New Delhi-110002

ISBN: 978-81-7141-453-6

Swimming

Published by:
DISCOVERY PUBLISHING HOUSE PVT. LTD.
4383/4B, Ansari Road, Darya Ganj
New Delhi-110 002 (India)
Phone: +91-11-23279245, 43596064-65
Fax: +91-11-23253475
E-mail: discoverypublishinghouse@gmail.com
sales@discoverypublishinggroup.com
web: www.discoverypublishinggroup.com

Printed at:
Infinity Imaging Systems
Delhi

PREFACE

The need of having a sports series felt because today's situation of the world is not conducive to peace, all round there is destruction, despair, conflict and war; war if not between two nations then within the country itself. In a world where there are some 820 million people unemployed or under-employed, and where 86 million people are born every year, it is not surprising that one out of every four individuals lives in absolute poverty. The *Discovery Publishing House* by Publishing this series seeks to get positive response as—to means by which sports can promote and propagate peace and international cooperation. Sportsmen form a large identifiable cadre. We visualises a situation where a conscious efforts is made all over the world to train the sportspersons to spread the message of peace and international cooperation. Instead of peace keeping efforts through arms and army, the sportspersons may be used as soldiers of peace in a subtle manner. The effort is to make the realize the contribution of sports as a factor for sustainable development, peace keeping and international cooperation.

In developing countries, sports development cooperation is still in the need of justification and steadfast arguments. Many people ask the question "why invest in sports in developing countries for which water supply, health service and agriculture projects are much better suited? An apt reply to this question may be "for many of the people of a developing country,

Sports is the only 'Sweaty' Leisure-time activity. Sports represents a moment of joy in the midst of hard poverty-stricken and dirty everyday life. Doing sports even makes one's work go more smoothly the next day.

This series will be useful to the sports promoters, organisers, coaches and other persons related or interested in sports.

Editor

CONTENTS

1 INTRODUCTION

The most important swimming lesson that a child ever receives may well be the very first one. This first excursion into a new and exciting world may have a lasting effect. The teacher must play the paramount role in making sure that this initial 'baptism' is enjoyable as well as being gently instructive. It is up to the teacher to show that swimming is fun. When the whole class are eager to come back next time, the first lesson has indeed been a success both for the pupils and for yourself.

The first swimming lesson will probably be the most important one that the children will receive. It must therefore be a successful one, full of fun, constant encouragement, praise and repartee. The number of early activities which the class may carry out are many and varied and you will without doubt eventually formulate your own ideas as to what the introductory lesson would consist of.

The depth and temperature of the water, the size of the pool, the member and ages of the participants and the length of the lesson are the one metre of water will be most unpopular with a class of children only a metre tall! Similarly, if these same tinies are unable to stand because the water is too deep, armbands will be required in order to keep them afloat. If the water is on the cool side, the activities will need to be vigorous to keep the children warm. The size of the pool and the area of shallow water in relation to the number of pupils will dictate the extent of free movement possible.

The ages of the pupils will dictate the standard and description of the activities to be performed. The very young will love walking along in the water pretending to be 'little men and women' but a group of older children may find this a rather babyish way of getting them to immerse their shoulders in water. In this case the instruction may be given in a different way, such a warning that they should 'keep their shoulders down in the water, otherwise they will fly out through the roof!' Such The first visit to the pool should begin with some kind of introduction from the teacher. The changing-room is a good place in which to broach matters of hygiene, safety and poolside behaviour. Then perhaps a brief guided tour of a establishment to show the class where such important facilities as the toilets, showers and footbath are located and how and when they should be used. Next, the teacher should outline once more as many rules relating to safety, hygiene and discipline as are appropriate at this stage.

Before entering the water, a physical inspection of the class should be carried out. This must be accompanied by an explanation to the chilen why it is necessary to subject them to this kind of treatment.

If there is any possibility of a visual demonstration of what is required of the children, is should be used. This applies to even the simplest tasks such as getting in and out of the water and moving about. If someone is less timid than the others or has previously visited the pool, he may be used as a demonstrator.

It will undoubtedly give the pupils a little extra confidence if they can see how the long and short poles are used. The teacher must show that by holding the end of the poles the pupils are completely safe in the water. The use of the rope dividing off the shallow area of the pool can also be shown at this time. The 'ways of the water' should be carefully explained and if possible demonstrated. This should include an idea of how propulsion is created and a short land exercise to demonstrate the best way to walk along in the water, using a skiing leg movement assisted by a paddling hand action. When these short preliminaries have been happily tried and tested, it is time to get wet.

Before taking the plunge into cold water, such as the pool or the sea, the less adventurous among us like to sample the temperature by dipping out big toe in first. The best way for beginners to get used to the temperature is for them to sit along the pool's edge and dangle their feet in the water. The natural thing to do then is to kick and splash. Seeing who can the most splash' or 'splash the roof', or even 'splash teacher', usually dispels any initial inhibitions. This fun activity can set the tone of the whole lesson. One word of warning here: make sure that the children sit well back form the edge if possible: the ensuing excitement may well see some of the more vigorous participants falling in!

Most of the class will now be fairly wet, so it is time for the first entry into the pool. If there are any children who cannot touch the bottom or are extremely timid, armbands should be used. If there are narrow steps leading down into the water, a forward-moving single file is most appropriate, using any handrail which may exist as a steadier. If the steps are wide, similar to a wide staircase, the children may like to sit on the steps, slowly descending, one by one, until they are in the water.

In most modern pools, a vertical step-ladder arrangement is installed in each of the four corners. Often the steps themselves will be formed in the side wall of the pool. Both types of fitment are accompanied by two handrails, one each side of the steps. The safest method of entry is by descending slowly backwards (facing the steps) into the water, the same time maintaining a firm sliding grip with each hand on the rails. A wise move by the teacher is to tell the class how many steps there are.

Once in the water, the pupils will probably not need telling to grab hold the foot of the steps, a sideways-sliding foot movement will see them parading across the pool, sliding their hands along the handrail.

Getting safely out of the pool is an important as getting in, so, after the initial trip across the width or around the pool, an unhurried exit can be made. If there are two sets of steps in the shallow end a walk across the end of the pool from one set to the other before re-entry will help the children to get used to the safety rules relating to wandering too near to the poolside and moving at a steady pace rather then running. If there is only one set of steps available a simple adjustment to the queue-forming procedure will be required. Where there are no steps down into the water, the children should remain seated along the poolside after having their initial fun-splash. Then, placing both hands flat and side by side on the edge of the pool to the right or left of them, they can slip unceremoniously into the water, at the same time turning to face the side and grasp the handrail,. Even where there are steps for getting in and out of the water, this and sliding in' method should be tried at the first lesson: it is quicker and allows more water time. Climbing out over the side will come naturally most children, and those who are a little too tiny to clamber out in this fashion will use the steps.

The next stage is to persuade the children by bending their knees to immerse their shoulders completely below the water surface. Telling them that, with shoulder under, they won't fall over when they walk should do the trick. With shoulders immersed, the children may practise the floor-contact ski-walking action that they tried on the poolside before entering the water. The exercise may be a rail-holding one or, if the water is shallow enough, a free-moving activity. If the water is very shallow, a 'kneeling-walk' may even be tried.

It is these early exercises that give the children a fell for the water. They discover the resistance to movement which is created by the medium. Using the hands as paddles or oars, or even carrying out some elementary sculling movements, children quickly learn how to use the resistive character of the water to propel or support themselves.

If it has not happened already, the children are certainly going to get their faces wet sooner or later.

whether they like it or not. So, rather than wait till it happens accidentally, it is good practice to carry out some specific face-wetting tricks. The value of play and imagination may be seen when the teacher tells the children that 'all their faces are dirty' and need a quick wash. The exercise has a two-fold use: not only does it encourage each child to get his or her face wet, but the creation of imaginary soap-suds requires the use of two hands, and therefore they must let go of the handrail completely. There are of course many other ways of encouraging the children to release their grip on the rail, such as clapping their own efforts or singing an action song.

Taking the face-wetting exercise one step further, an experiment in face immersion and breath holding may now be introduced. By making a noise like sea lions (blowing and 'nosing' into the water), a first attempt at breath control may be made. Even at this early stage it is helpful to mention that blowing out through the mouth and nose will reduce coughing and spluttering: if air is being blown down the nose water cannot be inhaled.

The timid ones will only pretend to put their faces into the water, and the act of face immersion may take weeks or even months for some to achieve. Remember, this is only the first visit and even to get into the water is a monumental act of courage for some children. Make light of any such minor shortcomings and enthusiastically applaud their efforts, however feeble they may seem.

This is probably enough direct instruction for one lesson so perhaps some kind of game designed to increase mobility would be in order. There are many appropriate games that may be played and these have been itemised, accordance with the ages and abilities of the participants.

Finally, if there is enough time left, the lesson may end with a short period of supervised free play. The more robust characters in the class will have the chance to repeat a few of the tricks they have learnt in the new environment, while their less keen classmates will probably wish to get out and dressed.

Ensure that the steps are used correctly as the class leave the water and that there is the same number of children at the end as there was at the beginning of the lesson. The first few drying and dressing sessions should be supervised, in order to make absolutely sure that all are thoroughly dried and dressed properly.

This time you will want to the class into the water right at the beginning of the lesson. While they are changing, a quick reminder may be given regarding the use of the toilets and whereabouts in the pool the children should assemble prior to the actual lesson, and a short poolside inspection session must be carried out in case of infection, wounds, etc.

Entry into the water may be via the steps for those who feel a little unsure, while the more intrepid ones may enter by the 'sitting and sliding' method. Whichever type of entry is used, the children in the first instance hold the handrail with one or both hands once they are in the water.

To set a light-hearted tone to the lesson, a warming-up activity, such as jumping or bobbing at rail, may be carried out, possibly singing to help the 'show' along. The teacher will do well to get into the swing of things by performing a few little jumps or bobs in time with the children. The children should be encouraged to sink lower in the water after every jump, until perhaps some of the less inhibited members disappear below the water surface for a brief instant. At this stage the teacher should be prepared for a little coughing and spluttering and wiping of eyes.

The next activity, of breath-holding, should ensure that most faces are immersed. This breath-holding exercise should perhaps be a little more prolonged than that which was carried out during the first lesson. Gradually increasing an 'immersion count' from one (a quick dip) up to three or even five makes the exercise progressive. A little encouragement should be given to the swimmers to open their eyes under the water by trying to count the outspread fingers on their partner's hands, or to see the tiles on the floor of the pool.

Mimicking sea lions as a breath-control exercise may now also be sued in a progressive form, with a rhythmic pattern of short sub-aqua roars up to perhaps a count of five or six.

Further exercise in relation to balance should be incorporated into this second lesson. These may be jumping up and down while holding each other's hands or individual jumping, using outstretched arms and slightly spread-apart feet as aids to stabilisation and balance. The movements should initially be carried out in a gentle fashion, then with a little more vigour as confidence begins to soar. The teacher should watch out for the over-enthusiastic jumper who may slip on landing. The next stage in the programme may be an attempt to assume a handrail-supported, face-down, prone, floating position. The horizontal mode may be achieved by the swimmers merely placing their faces in the water while grasping the rail firmly, either allowing their legs to float to the surface or kicking their feet up and down (front-paddle fashion) to bring them to the surface. This exercise naturally leads to a brief interlude of leg kicking at the rail. The finer points of technique can be dispensed with at this initial stage, the main aim of the exercise being to 'splash the roof with straight legs and floppy feet'.

Those who have difficulty in elevating their feet to the surface should try undergrasping the handrail and applying a little pressure between the elbows and the wall.

A partner-assisted kicking exercise may be performed by arranging the class in small groups and joining hands in chain fashion. The 'anchors' at the ends of the chains may each hold the handrail with their free hand, thus forming a half-circle away from the rail and back again. Alternate 'links' in the chain now attempt to raise their legs to the surface and kick on either front or back, their adjacent partners standing to provide the necessary support. A further development of the of the exercise is for the two 'anchors' to join hands, thus forming a full circle.

Leg kicking to the untrained can be rather exhausting: thirty seconds of the kicking as a single spell would be adequate, this being followed by a short period of rest. (Supporting struggling partners also tends to make the shoulders ache.)

Regaining the feet after performing a short kicking exercise will be achieved by most children without really thinking about it. Those experiencing difficulty in elevating their legs will find little trouble in standing once more, while the swimmers whose limbs display some degree of buoyancy (probably the girls), may easily regain a standing posture once more by applying a downward pressure on the handrail or on their partners' hands and assuming a slight tuck at the same time.

This is an introduction to the skill of regaining the feet and, before any free and unassisted kicking or swimming exercises are carried out, the particular prone or supine-related standing-down procedure must be taught. The teacher must make a special point of emphasising how this is done every time the floats are used in these initial lessons.

Before using the floats as a practice aid to regaining the feet, however, they may be utilised in order to provide some degree of physical and movement. Some of the more adventurous members of the class may even be inspired to 'take off' for a few brief moments. The more timid children may be fitted with armbands at this stage if they are not already wearing them.

Practice in regaining the feet from a prone position may now be carried out with the intention of learning the front glide in the next lesson. The standing-down skills are necessary before an attempt is made to introduce this new feature in the syllabus.

Towards the end of the lesson, a short game should be a popular move, followed by a similar period of supervised free play before the class climb out of the water (preferably over the side). After the inspection and detection session, the class may enter the water either down the steps or over the poolside; some brave ones may even feel like jumping in by now, and a brief warning should be given to them to bend their knees before landing in the water.

Once they are all in, a quick 'jumping bean' activity will serve to accustom them to being in the water. The first exercise may be a brief interlude of rail-supported face-down floating. This is a repetition of one of the second-lesson activities and is carried out in preparation for the ensuing theme.

Armbands may be used at this stage and the class may be grouped into perhaps two ability sections. The glide activities may commence with a little jump from the bottom of the pool in order to perform a float-assisted glide to the handrail before standing down.

The next exercise is similar to the first, except that the swimmers push off the wall before carrying out the glide and standing down once more. Partner-assisted one: the partner, standing a short way from the wall, assists the swimmer by grabbing the float as it arrives and holding it firmly while a standing position is regained. Both these activities may be tried in head-up and head-down modes.

After these important practices the swimmers should be sufficiently confident to attempt their first swimming stroke, namely the front or dog paddle. The practices should be carried out in a logical sequence.

The lesson can again end with a game followed by a few minutes of supervised free play.

A plan of campaign is always useful, and a few suggested plans for thirty-minute periods are given in the table below. The teacher is advised to formulate a personal set of lesson plans and be prepared to modify them according to circumstances. It is worth remembering that ideal lesson circumstances are very rare indeed and the times that are given are simply a guide. It may be necessary, for instance, to repeat an exercise many more times than anticipated, thus throwing the whole schedule out of gear. On the other hand, you may get a class of budding champions! So keep an open mind and be prepared to change your plans.

2

SWIMMING AS A SPORT

DEVELOPMENT OF DIFFERENT STROKES, STARTS AND TURNS

Strokes

There is evidence in literature and other forms of act handed down from centuries before the Christian era proving that strokes resembling our present swimming techniques were used in antiquity. The oldest descriptions of swimming on record and some pictures from antiquity suggest that strokes similar to those used today were used for propelling the body through the water. In *Homer's* "Odyssey" the author describes how "Odyssey spreads his arms in water" in order to propel himself. This suggests that he used a technique resembling the breast stroke. The crawl in use today is also described in records handed down to us from the past. In can be assumed that the backstroke was also used in antiquity, but no records or drawings describing how the stroke was executed have been found to date.

In Germany, the breaststroke technique is mentioned for the first time in 1538 by *Nicolaus Wynmann* in his book "Colymbetes". It is assumed that the movements used in the breaststroke as described in the book imitated those of frogs in the water. As the sport developed in Europe the process of differentiation of the techniques of swimming progressed. The first reports about the *"side stroke"* came from Great Britain in 1840. The legs executed a scissors kick while the arms moved the water. Later on one arm was swung forward above the water. In 1873, *Trudgen,* an Englishman, brought new technique to Europe from South America in which the scissors movement of the legs is retained but the swimmer propels himself through the water through alternate overarm movements. This stroke gave rise to the development in Germany of the technique Known here as the overhand strode in which the swimmer used the alternate overhand movement but in which he executed the breaststroke kick, *Healy,* an Australian, showed a *new crawl technique* during a swimming festival in Hamburg in 1906. He coordinated the alternate overhand movement with the leg kick, which he also executed alternately, raising his calves above the water. This last major improvement in the crawl was made in 1912 by *Kababamoku.* He executed the alternate kick, which became known as the flutter kick, with both legs completely immersed in water. This technique has survived without any fundamental changes up to this day. The *backstroke* has developing along with breaststroke since the 18th century. Guts Muths taught both in the course of his 30-odd years of swimming tutorship at Schnepfenthal. The movements made while the swimmer lies face upward, especially the kick, resemble those used with the breaststroke kick, the arms are brought outward and sideways in the which is still known here as the "popular backstroke", has evolved into the old English backstroke. The kick remained unchanged, but arms were later thrown back from the shoulders and pressed towards the thighs to be swung back again simultaneously above the water to repeat the cycle. As crawl stroke became known at the beginning of the 20th century the *back crawl. Hebner,* an American, showed the new technique for the first time in Europe at the Olympic Games in Stockholm in 1912. His winning time was clocked at 1:12.2, which put him 1 second ahead of *Fabr,* a German swimmer, who still used the simultaneous stroke. The back crawl stroke was used more and more in competitive sports. The old English backstroke became one of the forms of popular swimming. The simultaneous kick is particularly important in life-saving work. The basic features of the back crawl stroke have remained unchanged since that time. The development of *butterfly stroke* started in 1930. Athletes and coaches sought new ways to improve the breaststroke technique in order at achieve better time. The development of the butterfly started when swimmers moved their arms down to their thighs and then swung them forward toward the wall above the water before turning and before reaching the finish. This series of movements was repeated and the new butterfly stroke came in being. At first the was used only over short distances-mostly at the beginning or in the final sprint-in breaststroke events. This technique was given official recognition by FINA on 1 January 1935. But improved methods of training enabled swimmers to swim increasing distances with butterfly in breaststroke events and there was the danger of the traditional breaststroke disappearing from the programme of competitive events altogether. Another change was made in the rules of competition to halt this development. The breaststroke and the butterfly became two independent strokes. Further efforts were made after the FINA resolution of 1935 to improve the butterfly technique. Jack Seig, a swimmer from the University of Iowa tried a new leg movement in 1935 by kicking his feet up and down at the same time in a manner resembling the movement of a dolphin's tail Working together with *Armbruster,* his coach, he was able to tie this kick in with the butterfly arm movement. He swam the 100-yard event in 1:00.2.

Fejer and *Tumpek,* both Hungarina swimmers, played a major role in developing butterfly stroke in Europe by introducing the so-called dolphin movement.

The dolphin movement was co-ordinated with the butterfly stroke and became an independent swimming style. The use of the dolphin movement in competitive events was approved by FINA in 1953.

The basic features of the breaststroke technique hardly changed at all in the centuries that passed since it was rediscovered by *Wynmann.* The sequence of movements was slightly improved only in 1925/26. The long sideways pull of the arms gave way to a *short pull of the arms,* which enabled a faster sequence of movements to be introduced. The wide straddle kick was replaced by the *lower leg swing movement.*

This improvement, just as the butterfly stroke mentioned earlier, came into being as a result of efforts to achieve better times within the constraints of existing rules of competition. After the decision had been taken by FINA at include the two independent swimming styles in the competition programme, efforts were continued to raise the speed of the breaststroke by improving the technique, Prompted by Japanese swimmers, who dived over considerable distances in competitive breaststroke events, athletes in almost all countries in which there was competitive swimming practised the *underwater breaststroke* Japanese style). After diving the swimmer pulled his arms down to his thighs and then recovered by moving them up close to his recovered by moving them. The leg action remained unchanged.

This modification meant a further change in the orthodox breaststroke. From May 1957 FINA prohibited prolonged swimming under water and introduced stricter rules on the breaststroke under which the swimmer was allowed only one dive stroke after the start and after each turn, the rest of the time the swimmer's head had to stay above the water.

In the breaststroke just as in all other fields of competitive sports efforts to improve performance are continuing by modifying the technique within the framework of existing rules of competition and by improving training methods. There are also other in tractions between the training method and swimming technique.

Experience gathered in raising the stroke frequency in alternate-stroke swimming styles was made use of in the breaststroke. In some cases the stroke frequency was in creased to the point where the gliding phase so typical of the breaststroke disappeared almost entirely. There are several technique variants between this from, in which the arm movement is more vigorous and the legs are thrust back in short calf movements directed more towards the rear rather than being swung out so far, and the old orthodox form characterized by the long passive gliding phase, shorter arm movements and wide swing. It is only natural that the trend towards faster stroke frequency has asserted position at the end of each stroke cycle

Starts

The start has also gone through a series of evolutionary phases before it reached in present from In the old days of competitive swimming the swimmers stated from a swimming position. In Germany, the racing dive was introduced for members of the "Deutscher Schwimmverband" in 1912. Swimmers organized in the "Deutshce Turnerschaft continued to use the old push off start in swimming position until 1920. While swimmer belonging to the "Arbeiter-Wassersport-Verband" used the racing dive start, except in the case of the backstroke, which they also started form the swimming position. The racing dive from the edge to pool was used with all swimming styles in Germany from 1920; four years later the start in backstroke events was changed back to the swimming position.

The starting command has also experienced numerous changes. Today the command is only an acoustic signal or a flag signal (in the case of deaf athletes) preceded by the starter's command "Take your marks!" At the 1952. Olympic Games in Helsinki some athletes started by pushing off from the gutter. It resembled a backward jump start. But the international rules of competition (FINA) put a stop to this and prescribed he backstroke start used today in which both feet must be fully immersed. The start from the starting block has been in general use in all other swimming styles since the Olympic Games of 1936.

Turns

The internationally valid standard lane length is 50 metres. Records are recognized only if they are swum in lanes of this length is 50 metres. Records are recognized only if they are swum in lanes of this length. Lanes are usually shorter in most indoor swimming pools (33 1/3 metres, 25 metres or even less). In most events the distance to be swum is a multiple of the standard lane length, which means that the swimmers must change their swimming direction by 180 degrees one or several times in the course of race, i.e, they have to "turn" A 1500 metres event, for instance, involves 29 turns. This fact stresses the importance to *turns* This fact stresses the importance of *turns* in swimming competitions Each badly done turn costs time. Changes in pool design (pools shallow on one side, beam borders, pools of even depth, etc) have had a telling effect on the on the development of turn styles and turning techniques. A wide range of factors, which have been taken into account in the rules of competition, have played a role in the quest for more effective techniques from the stand-up and beam turns used years ago to the deep turns used today. The swimmers must touch the wall with onc or both hands, depending on the swimming style, or only with any part of the body (in the case of freestyle). Between the time they touch the wall with their hands and push off with their feet they may execute any movement or turn. The push-off from the wall must be executed with both legs. The turns authorized for all swimming styles can be classified into three groups. The main feature of the turn is the position of the head in relation to the surface of the water during the turn. Thus depending on the head position, turns are grouped into high turns, flat turns and deep turns. Any of these turns can be used with the four swimming styles and with set-style swimming. But since there is still plenty of room for improvement in turning technique, the sequences of movement used in turns will continue to be subject to frequent changes in efforts to improve records.

BASIC SWIMMING INSTRUCTION

Objectives of basic swimming instruction The object of basis swimming instruction is to teach people how to swim. i.e., to enable them to feel safe in water and to propel themselves through water in the desired direction. This instruction will give the learner the fundamental skills and abilities, which he can improve or his inclinations of objective requirements in a special field of area of application. To achieve this objective the learner must undergo a comprehensive programme of swimming instruction consisting of *two stages, between* which three is no fixed delineation but which differ in the subject matter of instruction. In the *first stage* the novices are taught the five basic swimming skills (diving, jumping into the water, gliding, locomotion and breathing), which give the beginner a sense of security in water and which form the basis of the art of swimming. In the *second stage* the techniques used in swimming styles, starts and turns are in the foreground. It is essential that the conditions under which swimming instruction is to be given are checked to make certain that the learners are not endangered in any way; this applies to all forms of tuition (continuous instruction over an extended period or training courses), of the athletic facilities available (indoor or open-air swimming pools, deep or shallow water) and to all ages and both sexes of learners, The following "organizational notes are designed with this objective in mind.

Organizational notes

All advantages and beneficial effects of swimming are forfeited unless good sense and discretion are used. Over exertion lack of discipline can bring disastrous consequences not only to those concerned but also to others. The following is a summary of the basic rules to be observed in bathing and swimming:

Swimming rules

1. Do not swim by yourself.
2. Cool off by wetting face, armpits and chest before immersion.
3. Do not stand still move around vigorously when in water.
4. Do not stay too long in the water; blue lips' violent shivering and goose pimples are indications to came out.
5. Dry well after swimming take off wet swimming suit and put on warm up the body again.
6. Do not bathe or swim if you so not feel well.
7. Do not into the water on full stomach.
8. Do not overexert yourself.
9. Do not scream or romp in the water. Do not call for help in fun; do not dip or push others into the water.
10. Do not leave the area marked off for bathing.
11. Always obey the instructions of persons in charge.

But the instructor (sports or swimming in instructor coach, trainer) must know more than just these rules. It his task to help educate young people in the spirit of our educate young people in the spirit of our social developments, in which the communist education of the young generation is particularly important. His duties include feeling responsible for the lives of young people entrusted to him. If he or she fails to meet these obligations he or she will have face the full consequences.

Instructor's duties

Under the legal liability stipulations, the instructor is responsible for the safety of his pupils. The instructor is expected to use all his physical and professional abilities, the most progressive methods of education and to have the highest sense of responsibility in order to avert any possible danger to the learners.

All teachers assigned to watch over the safety and skills in the field of life saving and in resuscitation and they must constantly try to improve them. Analogously this also applies to all persons in charge who accompany groups of children on excursions, hikes go swimming or bathing with them. In addition to the basic briefings which the person in charge should give the young athletes before commencing swimming training the following should be taken into account:

1. The state of health of pupils entrusted to an instructor must be checked by a physician (school medical officer of sports physician). Special attention should be paid to the heart and the ears. Persons with contagious diseases, skin rashes, festering wounds are not allowed to swim. If the

instructor neglects his obligation over the children's safety and if it is proved that a disease is aggravated as a result of a learner being exposed to water or that other persons are contaminated he can be made liable.

2. Preliminary familiarization with the swimming pool, checking and repairing equipment and aids are part of the preparatory work that must be done before starting swimming instruction.

   This means:

   — swimming zones in lakes and rivers and in the open sea should be marked off;

   — the non-swimmer zone should be clearly marked;

   — all sources of danger (water plants, reeds, bog, rocks, rubble, etc) should be removed and the condition of the site (sand, rocky ground, gradients, abysses, etc.) should be equipment, such as dressing-rooms, toilets and showers emergency and first aid facilities diving boards, swimming zone limits and rescue equipment should be checked to make sure that they are in order.

3. Before commencing swimming instruction the learners must be briefed on how they should behave during swimming instruction, when dressing, in the shower-rooms (thorough drying after swimming especially of the ears and hair is particularly important), near and in the water. The danger of slipping in indoor swimming pools is great and should be stressed.

4. Discipline and good organization are a cardinal rule in swimming instruction. The intensity and success of a swimming lesson and prevention of accidents largely depend on them. If possible a class should consist of no more than 15 learners, bigger classes are difficult to keep watch over. The instructor should know at all times how many learners were present at the beginning of a lesson and he must be able to account for all learners during and especially after the lesson. Organizational forms in and out of the water should be-well-thought out. Suitable organizational forms make it possible to conduct swimming instruction efficiently and safely (this is particularly important in diving). The exercises and the standard of performance required should be adjusted to the pupil's age and to their performance capacity.

Beware of overexertion!

Children who have just recovered from a serious illness should be treated with special care. This also apples to people suffering from diseases of the eyes and ears. Teacher's instructions should always be obeyed. If a pupil is told by the teacher to come out of the water as result of breach of discipline, shivering, not feeling well, etc, the pupil should put on some dry clothes without delay lest he or she could catch cold. It should be checked to make sure that such pupils comply with these rules. The swimming instructor should wear a swimming suit or sports clothing in order to be able to help immediately should the need arise, A bathing gown or a sweat suit and appropriate footwear should be worn as protection against cold (the teacher should take good care of his own health as well). He should be near the edge of the pool or at some other elevated point in order to be able to see and be seen by his pupils at all times. If he demonstrate movement patterns in water himself, the children should get out of the pool and line up in an orderly manner along the pool to watch the demonstration. All learners should be instructed not to separate from the group without asking the teacher's of instructor's permission. If a child is found missing, it is imperative that the person in charge should consider the possibility of an accident. In such a case all pupils must be ordered by the swimming instructor in charge to get out of the water. A search party should carry out a search of the toilets, shower rooms and adjoining rooms and of the bath superintendent should be informed immediately, Life saving swimmers, if present, should immediately start searching in water.

Significance of objective conditions for success of basic instruction

Successful swimming instruction depends to a considerable extent on the objective conditions, which include the state of the training facility and of the available training equipment and the air and water temperature. Often the person in charge of swimming instruction will have little if any influence on these conditions. In such cases he should carefully devise a plan of instruction that would enable him to adapt methodically and organizationally to the existing conditions. But the teacher or instructor should not came to term with all conditions. In many instances existing training conditions can be improved through initiative or with support from such quarters as the local mayor, headmaster, pool superintendent or sports official and the efficiency of training can be raised considerably.

1. If training instruction is given while the swimming facility is open to the public, the training area should be marked off in agreement with the pool supervisor in charge and no persons other than those belonging to the class should be permitted to enter the area.
2. All detrimental influences coming from without such as loud noise or unruly behaviour on the part of bathers (this applies particularly to public baths) should be eliminated in order to create a proper atmosphere for the swimming instruction. Other wise the pupil will not be able to concentrate properly and will feel hampered and anxious as result. To reduce these difficulties to a minimum the instructor should, in cooperation with the pool supervisor and, if the need arises, with the headmaster or the local district committee for swimming, consider all relevant factors in order to work out the best possible time schedule for conducting swimming instruction, Swimming instruction sessions should be held before the bulk of the public turns up.
3. The instructor's methodical work is facilitated by swimming aids (swimming and diving hoops, reach poles and gliding boards, swimming rungs, cf, Swimming aids). He should see to it that such aids are procured. Most equipment of this kind is not very expensive.
4. Efforts should be made not only to obtain swimming aids but also to erect push off walls at every bathing place, including bathing resorts on

lakes, rivers and along the Baltic coast. Such a wall can be built by boarding up the side of an existing pier facing the bathing place only a few boards being required for this purpose. It is important to make sure that there is enough room between the edge of the foot-bridge and the push-off wall for a secure hold. If there are no gangways, them provisional gangways of push-off should be built, from which the teacher can watch and instruct his pupils. In this way the bathing place gets a fixed boundary to one side, which makes for a higher measure of safety and better organization. Swimming facilities have also been built on open water with good results by using pontoons.

5. The duration of a person's stay in the water depends on the water and air temperature. The principle that effective instruction cannot be conducted when the learners are cold should be borne in mind. The younger the learners, the more important it is to have higher water temperatures to achieve good results. This is due to the fact that the adaptability of their circulatory system to cold water has not yet reached the level of development of that of adults; the subcutaneous layer of fatty tissue in young children is still much thinner in relation to their body weight than in adults. The best water temperatures for children of pre-school age ad for younger school children are 25 to 27 degrees.

The instructor can often tell when it is time for individual members of his class or for the whole class to get out of the water by their bluish lips, paleness, goose-pimples and in sufficient concentration. It is not possible to fix a generally valid length for the period of instruction. However, empirical values show that even 5-to 6-year-old can stay in the water for up to 60 minutes if the water temperature is around 27 degrees and if the proper method of instruction is used. It is imperative that the children be given an opportunity to warm up by doing suitable exercises or playing games before and after swimming if the water is colder; some times a swimming training by such exercises and games. The question as to *how often* training sessions are to be held has been clearly answered numerous studies, Frequent training within a definite period of time produces better results. The best result are achieved through regular daily instruction.

A *duration* of 30 instruction units under favourable weather and water conditions is recommended, for instance, for children in older per-school age brackets in order to develop in them a feeling of confidence in water and swimming ability. There training sessions per week has brought good results. But four training sessions a week or even daily training is possible without overexerting the children. Such a training complex is given in the from of a course. Hole day swimming courses play an increasingly important role in instructing children living in areas without suitable training facilities, Such courses should last for at least three weeks, and at two training sessions per day, the total length of instruction at the end of this courses is about 35 hours, which is about the time prescribed for the first instruction complex under the curriculum presently in force in our comprehensive polytechnic secondary schools. This period of instruction is sufficiently long to enable the child to learn the basic skills of diving jumping, gliding locomotion, movements involved in an alternating stroke style (back or font crawl) and in the breaststroke. Experience has shown that a learner from the first age bracket onward should attend at least two training sessions a week in order to complete the course of instruction successfully on an extracurricular basis. In the case of adults the duration of their period of basic instruction will depend a great deal on their degree of confidence in water and on the amount of experience they have in movement. But with them too the best results are achieved by attending a course of instruction with daily training sessions. As a rule a two-to three week course is sufficient for adults.

DEVELOPING BASIC SWIMMING SKILLS

Tasks and contents of first stage

A person wishing to learn how to swim should fist adjust himself to the water as a new element in his experience. The body is propelled through the water in a nearly horizontal position using both the upper and the lower extremities and utilizing the physical properties of water. To learn this method of locomotion in the water the beginner must collect new movement experience, which differs completely form his or her previous experience on land.

It is very important to know the physical properties of water in older to be able to move about in it. One should not only know them, but also feel them. This is particularly important with regard to specific gravity, Archimede's principle, cohesive force of water molecules, low compressibility of water and pressure conditions in water. Getting used to moving about in water involves a lengthy process of differentiation and development of reflex reactions in response to the external forces and conditions encountered in water. Such external forces are first and foremost the *force of gravity,* which one hardly feels in the water as a result of the relations of specific gravity existing in that element, *water resistance,* which on the one hand, must be made use of in order to propel one's body through the water and which, on the other hand, must be overcome because it impends motion, but *moment of inertia,* which requires other muscle concentrations in the water than on land, and the *forces of friction,* which offer a much firmer support for pushing off on land than in water, while friction in the water is greater than in the air. The learner must also overcome unconditioned reflexes, notably the labyrinthian and balance reflex, which elicit contractions in the throat muscles via the vestibulary system in order to move the head into a position in which the crown of the head is at the top. He must also learn to control the eyelid reflex whose function normally is to protect the eye from harmful influence by closing the lids at the slightest excitation of the eye. But the swimmer should be able to orientate himself also under water, which means that the unconditioned reflex must yield to a conditioned reflex enabling the swimmer to keep his eyes open under water.

To feel safe and to act in the water in line with requirements one should meet the following minimum demands: One should be able to jump water without feeling any fear, dive beneath the surface open his eyes to find his bearings, assume a swimming position (breaststroke or backstroke position) and swim in a specified direction by using one's extremities covering a distance of about 25 metres and breathing rhythmically in the process.

To be able to do all these things at the same time, one must have the following basic skills:

Swimming with open eyes under water, *jumping into deep water* from a point above the water level, *gliding* in prone and supine positions, *locomotion* by using arms and legs, *breathing*—deliberate regular inhalation and exhalation. One can see from this list of skills that more is involved here than just "getting used to water" in the usual sense.

Swimming under water

To feel sate in water it is important that one should be able to *swim under water*. Whoever has learned to swim under water to get his bearings under water and swim towards a specified goal, will in most cases be able to act in an appropriate manner even if he should suddenly find himself under water unexpectedly.

In addition to the labyrinthian reflexes and eyelid reflex, the human body reacts to the carbon dioxide concentration in blood, which increases the longer one holds one's breath under water and which acts as a stimulus on the respiratory centre. As a result one tries to get one's head above the water as soon as possible in order to be able to breathe.

Through proper demonstration and explanation, which should be adapted to the level of development to the learners, it should be shown that one should not press the air child swimming under water and that one should let the air out gradually. The instructor should choose coaching forms in which stimuli, to develop conditioned reflexes, which can be voluntarily controlled, there by enabling the pupil to stay under water longer. In the course of further training the beginner learns to move about under water, to orientate himself and to find and carry objects under water. Usually the ability to swim under water is developed in conjunction with other founds mental swimming skills, especially with jumping into the water and with gliding after push-off of racing dive.

The beginner also experiences the buoying force of the water. It takes an effort to dive down to specified depths in order to retrieve object or to move in water at a specified depth. In the process the beginner gathers valuable experience in counteracting buoyancy or utilizing it in swimming. There is also a close interaction between swimming under water and conscious breathing. These multiform relations between basic skills should be taken into account in deciding on the structure and system of training sessions.

Jumping into the water

Jumping into the water is an important part of instruction because it helps the beginner build up confidence in water. It promotes the formation of such valuable character traits as resolution, will power and courage and gives the novice an opportunity to be come aware of the influences exercise his body when it suddenly enters the water from certain height above water level. Friction, water research, water pressure and buoyancy act on his body in the process. The first jumping exercises are carried level into hip or chest-deep water. This variant of jumping is an extension of the basic skill of jumping which child normally acquires in his or her third year of life. In executing these jumps the beginner touches bottom with his feet and his head comes up above the water once he straightens out. The learner feels that the water brakes the fall and prevents a hard impact.

Gradually the learner is taught to jump into increasingly deeper water reaching up to his neck, his mouth and his eyes. At this stage the learner often does not touch bottom at all or only slightly so. The buoying force of water forces him up, enabling him to keep his head above the water. The sense of buoyancy, which is developed through other exercises, is reinforced in this manner. The learner's sense of buoyancy is further consolidated by jumping into deeper water. As the learner learns to jump into deeper water he is also gradually conditioned to jump into chest-to neck-deep water, head first form steps, ladder rungs or from the gutter using the "frog leap" or "fall-in" technique. Concrete objectives, such as retrieving objects from the bottom or diving through a hoop helps learners, especially children to execute the dives. This also helps to inhibit the posture and balance reflexes and to develop the gliding position after pushing off and after the racing start.

The instructor must take the necessary steps to make sure that those practising jumping and those already in the water are not endangered, this is especially important in deeper water.

Jumping is important not only for getting used to the physical conditions of water, for forming correct habits in the water, for developing positive character traits but it also produces positive emotional influences. If the skills of jumping into the water are developed in accordance with "didactic principles", the learners will derive a great deal of enjoyment from these exercises, which can be varied time and time again to make them more exciting; there are also many in formal diving forms which can be used.

Gliding

The decisive step in the transition from being a non-swimmer to being a swimmer is made when the learner learns to push himself off from the pool wall or from the ground of a lake or river and to glide through the water in a horizontal position. Having learned this the beginner can now proceed to use his extremities efficiently to propel his body in the water. "Gliding", which is one of the basic skills of swimming, is taught in stages.

First of all the learner should learn to assume a horizontal position and to balance his body in this position in the water. He experiences *static buoyancy* by practising the "outstretched float", which he is required to know how to do in prone and supine positions.

In the second phase of training the learner is acquainted with *dynamic buoyancy*. He feels how the buoying force is strengthened when the body is propelled through the water by assistance from others (reach pole, partner) or by the thrust produced from his own push-off. Through this training the pupil learns the most appropriate body position for gilding through the water in outstretched prone and supine positions. In this position the learner must stretch his body from finger to toe, hold his arms stretched out, the hands are folded together flat, the head is kept between the upper arms, the legs are kept close together.

Once the learner has successfully experienced

gliding through the water he can start learning the swimming movements which propel his body through the water. We should like the stress that under no circumstances should the pupil omit learning the basic skill of gliding or fail to learn this skill properly before going on to the next stage of instruction. Gliding remains an essential exercise throughout the process of learning to swim and in subsequent athletic training: it is the basis for learning the different styles of swimming and of the different starts and turns.

Locomotion

Unlike on land, where man moves about almost exclusively with the aid of his lower extremities, *locomotion in the water* is effect by using one's *arms and legs,* the arms being even more important than legs in most swimming styles (crawl, backstroke and butterfly). Owing to the fact that the physical conditions in the water differ completely from those encountered on land, the beginner must elaborate new reflex complexes to enable him to respond to the influence of the new external forces through new forms of co-ordinated arm and leg action.

There are numerous ways of using one's extremities to propels one's body through the water. Currently four forms of locomotion predominate in swimming, known as swimming styles. They are crawl, back crawl, breaststroke and butterfly stroke. Efficiency, economy and speed were the main criteria which determined their dominant position. The pupil should learn all four swimming styles in the course of swimming instruction to get a good basic training. The sequence in which they should be learned depends largely on the specific objectives set and on the age of the learner. Young people being instructed in the People's Army should first be taught the breaststroke, because this is the most suitable style for overcoming water obstacles in combat conditions without causing much noise and carrying one's field pack. On the other hand children of pre-school age and of early school age should start with the crawl stroke.

The reason are:

Firstly, the alternating pull action of the arms is more beneficial for the mobility of the spinal column and for proper body posture than the simultaneous arm movement in the case of the breaststroke.

Secondly, alternating movements and transverse co-ordination (crawling, toddling, walking, climbing, running) predominate in the process of development of locomotion in babies and small children. Thus it is easier for a child to learn the alternating movements used in the crawl stroke.

Thirdly, by exercising the complementary crawl technique in prone and supine positions the pupil learns the essentials of two swimming styles and the way is paved for teaching him the butterfly stroke with dolphin kick, which has many characteristics in common with crawl.

Fourthly, the greater importance attached to the alternating stroke in competitive swimming (freestyle and backstroke account for over 70 percent of the Olympic events) should also be mentioned in this connection.

An elementary training programme in water polo and in synchronized swimming can also be built up on the basis of alternating stroke forms of locomotion in water.

Owing to the fact that at present swimming instruction is given mainly to children (and this will probably be the case in future as well), we shall concentrate our attention on teaching with the aid of alternating stroke patterns in the first phase of instruction dealt with in the following.

Despite the fact that leg action contributes less to propelling the body in water than does arm action in most swimming styles, the principle of teaching the leg movement sequence first, followed by arm movement and then by the co-ordinated arm and leg movement has asserted itself in modern swimming instruction. The flutter kick in prone and supine positions, which is relatively easy to learn, propels the body continuously through the water. It enables the swimmer to keep his body in a streamlined position, in which the chest is somewhat higher than the abdomen. A good hydrodynamic position adjusted to the speed is important to enable the swimmer to swim his arms forward above the water and to work his legs in the water at an appropriate depth.

For this reason the beginner is first taught the kick. He should learn to use his legs and feet well enough to be able to cover a distance of 20 to 25 metres.

There are also a number of exercises designed to prepare the learner for the alternate arm stroke movements. In this connection it should be pointed out that teaching the crawl technique by way of the "dog-paddle" technique is unpractical and tends only to prolong the learning process. For this reason it is important to make sure that the learner raises his arms properly out of the water. The beginner learns this technique in its elementary form at an early stage. At the end of the first phase of instruction the beginner achieves a certain measure of coordination between the arm and leg movements, but at this stage he should not be expected to co-ordinate his breathing rhythm to this as well.

Breathing

Proper, effective *breathing* is important in all sports if good performance is to be achieved. This is particularly true of sports requiring a great deal of endurance. Proper breathing is even more important in swimming, because of the increased metabolic activity, of the pressure the chest is exposed to in the water while inhaling and of the resistance that has to be overcome when exhaling into the water. An optimum rhythmic movement can be maintained over prescribed distance in the cyclic sequence of movements used in a given swimming style only by suing a perfect breathing technique executed automatically. That is why it is important to pay attention to a learner's breathing from the very first lesson. The integration of breathing processes into the movement pattern of individual swimming techniques is a complex process, which as a rule takes several years of systematic practice to stabilize.

Owing to the specific conditions under which a swimmer practises his sport, he should get used to *inhaling only through the mouth.* Due to the fact that the swimmer's head is constantly in the water the swimmer is likely to get water into his sinuses through the nasal cavities, which would interrupt his rhythm of movement and could result in disruption of the entire movement co-ordination.

On the other hand, *exhalation* should be through the *mouth* and *nose,* in this way any water that might enter the nose despite oral inhalation is blown out. Controlled exhalation should be practised during basic instruction. This is done by forcefully blowing e.g. at small balls, floating plastic objects, etc., against the water and underneath the surface. Later on, this exercise is linked with controlled inhalation through the mouth.

In the course of his further training the pupil learns to link the rhythmic inhalation and exhalation to the cyclic arm and leg movements. The learner practises turning his head sideways when preparing for the crawl stroke. Already at this stage sufficient attention should be paid to co-ordinating breathing with the movement cycle.

At the end of the first phase of swimming instruction the learner should be able to make integrated use of his newly-acquired basic skills. He should be able to enter and come out of deep water without assistance. At this stage a swimmer should not be expected to meet certain standards in any given, swimming technique, but he should be taught the basics for learning the different swimming styles. For children it is recommended to start with crawl and back crawl and then proceed to the dolphin or breaststroke styles. But this rule should not be applied dogmatically; the main thing to bear in mind is to make sure that the learner learns all swimming styles if possible and that he does not neglect the other fields of swimming.

Methods and means used in the first phase

The objectives outlined in the foregoing make it necessary for the learner to get used to the new conditions encountered in the water and to gather experience that will enable him to propel himself through the water. This process of teaching the pupil how to act and move about properly in the water is facilitated if the pupil is assisted by an experienced swimming instructor.

By knowing the routine of the learning process in the three characteristic phases of elementary co-ordination, fine co-ordination and stabilisation of movement (after *Meinel)* the instructor is able to organize swimming instruction in such a manner that the learner becomes consciously aware of the proper way of acting in the water by actively coming to grips with the new element.

New tasks are set in conformity with good teaching principles, taking into account the principles of instruction according to a certain plan and system, of clear and understandable presentation and of reinforcement of skills already learned.

The methods and means of instruction should be chosen in such a way as to ensure that the skills of movement and physical abilities are developed in the shortest possible time and that they become permanently assimilated.

The best way to introduce the pupil to a new movement is to demonstrate it to him. If the pupil is properly motivated he will be receptive and the demonstration will help him to form a visual idea of the movement. The demonstration should be immediately followed by practice, because the concrete idea of the movement takes shape in the course of a pupil's own execution of it in the water through the kinaesthetic motor analyser in conjunction with his optical and tactile perception. Explanatory and corrective remarks, adjusted to the pupil's level of mental development, supports this process.

The method using practical exercise help to develop movement skills and to form co-ordinative and conditional abilities. For this reason both aspects should be taken into account in planning each instruction unit. Repetition of the exercises within a specified length of time should be properly balanced between the load and the relaxation phases and adjusted to the level of development reached. The use of certain forms of competition are the principal way of raising the level of physical abilities and of further improving the quality of movement control.

The instructor uses various means to implement the methods in practice. This shows that methods and means are directly interdependent. The method is the route by which a certain aim is to be achieve, while the means are designed to complete the process successfully and as quickly as possible.

The means in the wider sense include styles and exercise forms, routines of exercise complexes (e.g., in the case of the interval method: standard distance sections, relaxations sections, break organization) and aids which help the learner directly, such as optical or acoustic signals (they also include pacemaker systems, brake clock, telemetric equipment, walkie-talkies and other equipment used in competitive sports training).

Use of equipment aids

Equipment aids play an important part in promoting the learning process in the entire field of athletic training.

They are an adjunct to the methods of the instructor. Methodical aids proved themselves in practice a long time ago and they have become indispensable in instruction.

1. They support the acquisition of complete and correct ideas of movement.
2. They promote the development of movement skills.
3. They help achieve a faster rate of performance improvement.

In most cases they resemble preliminary exercises, which make it possible to learn difficult movements routines. They enable the learner to concentrate more on the exercise to be performed, and since they are especially useful in helping the inhibited child overcome fear they are an important educational factor.

They enable the teacher to add variety and excitement to instruction, to stimulate the learners interest, to raise the intensity and to achieve better performance.

Selection and use of aids

The following swimming aids have proved useful time and again for basic training:

— Little plastic boats or floating animals, soap-boxes, little balls and similar floating articles

— Hoops

— Objects to be retrieved by diving

— Gliding poles

— Multi-purpose swimming rung devise

— Floats

We should like to point out once again that the purpose of these aids is to support swimming instruction, and *support* does not mean that this should be the only methodical approach. It would be wrong to assign aids a central position in instruction and to confine tuition to the possibilities offered by such aids. But the aids can be very useful if used wisely. They are used for teaching swimming under water, diving, gliding, locomotion or breathing and solving individual organization tasks. One should choose the most suitable aids.

Game and exercise equipment is used with a view to achieving certain results, such as getting the learners used to a certain *order.* For this purpose the pupils should be familiarized with the intended organizational forms and their terms while they are still on land. Another purpose is to get the learners *adjusted to water* with the aid of games adapted to the age group in question. Concentration their attention on the game or exercise device helps them overcome their initial fear of water and makes it easier for them to get used to their new environment. In addition, the use of toys stimulates their intensely felt need for movement. In this playful process they learn to execute movements which they could not learn at all or only to a very limited extent otherwise.

Methodical aids are also used to help the learner to develop *self reliance* in water and to *learn movement routines.* The successes experienced in the process boost the learner's self-confidence and are a source of continuous inspiration to make fresh efforts. It is amazing how much patience and endurance even children of pre-school age have in practising certain movement routines. And finally game and exercise devices are used for movement training. They are useful in teaching certain important movement components.

The *use of swimming aids* (cork belts, inflated pockets, etc.) such as *artificial buoyant aids* (worn at the body's centre of gravity) is rejected in modern swimming instruction. "Athletic movements are more than just a mere bio-mechanical process, they are a complex manifestation. They are purposive functions which make demands one person, they are forms of a person's actively coming to grips with his environment".. The philosophy underlying our modern instruction is based on this realization. Applied to swimming this means that the necessary conditions must be created for the learning process. The novice should be familiarized with water before commencing movement exercises in order to enable him to cope with the new physical conditions and to get him accustomed to new stimuli such as cold, water pressure and more difficult breathing conditions.

To start the learning process without meeting these conditions would mean limiting success to a minimum. Getting adjusted to water by being in water and especially experiencing and feeling the upward buoying force cannot be, replaced by examples, lucid explanations or industrious land exercises. The adjustment phase cannot in any case be using floatation devices or replaced by them. It is also possible to teach swimming by using floatation devices or replaced by them. It is also possible to teach swimming by using floatation devices, and regrettably many swimming instructions still resort to this method. The upward buoyant force is enlarged by wearing a buoyant aid on the trunk enabling the learner to execute movements in swimming position which he learns on land. As the novice acquires more and more experience, the swimming movements become automatic and enable the learner gradually to do without the flotation devices. But these "swimmers" are not swimmers in the true sense of the word. Often they feel insecure and are unable to cope with situation arising in the water. Many of them never get rid of their fear of water and of drowning. Experience has shown that if a movement is not learned in the active process of coming to grips with one's environment then such a movement will very rarely meet requirements in practice.

In using flotation devices the learner puts his trust in these aids but not in the water. He is not given a chance to feel the buoyancy. The increased buoyancy the swimmer gets from the buoyant aid facilitate his breathing and does not force him to get used to normal breathing in water. But "swimming is breathing-those who fail to learn to overcome to new conditions of pressure when exhaling into the water will always feel insecure, they will never feel "at home" in water. Moreover, they will not learn to balance their body in the water, a skill movement. Plenty of examples can be given of the importance of maintaining one's balance in water. If the novice is unable to cope with the shift in the centre of gravity in the water he will not have the necessary confidence to feel comfortable in the water in outstretched position, his movement in water will either be tense or he will not be able to execute them at all. The pupil can learn the outstretched position only through the intensive practice of the five basic skills. This often requires a great deal of patience on the part of the instructor. But if through instruction is sacrificed for a fast teaching pace, the learner will be unable to learn the swimming movements properly.

Artificial aids

1. Small floating articles, etc.

   These objects are normally used in the first few lessons, in which it is important to help the beginner adjust to water. They help him to overcome inhibitions and they prepare him for learning how to swim under water and how to breathe properly. Games adjusted to the learners age help them to develop their concentration and reaction, to enjoy the lessons and to add variety to the instruction.

2. *Hoop:* The gymnastics hoop made of aluminium tube is a multi-purpose aid. It is easy to hold, wear resistant, waterproof and it is hold, wear resistant, waterproof and it is hygienic. Coloured plastic bands can also be used in a variety of ways, but they are more prone to damage. The hoop is especially useful in facilitating the organization of instruction, especially in the early stages of tuition. The learners get used to a certain formation and order, which makes instruction not only easier but also safer. It also promotes the feeling of being part of the team among members of smaller groups. The hoop's many uses help to develop confidence in the water. The various exercises which can be

preformed with the hoop cover all aspects of the 1st phase of instruction ranging from the most elementary jumping and diving exercises up to gliding.

The hoop gives the instructor a number of ways in which fun and variety can be added to instruction. The more exciting the task to be accomplished by the novice, the more sustained his concentration on its execution.

3. *Diving objects:* No limits are set to the instructor's creativity here. Any object that is convenient to hold, has no sharp edges and is not too heavy for a pupil to carry in water can be used. Colours should be chosen to provide plenty of contrast at the bottom of the pool. The special value of such objects is that the children get used to keeping their eyes open under water.

4. *Reaching pole:* The reaching pole is an indispensable helper in the initial phase of training. The best material to use for the reaching pole are aluminium, plastic or bamboo. Wooden poles have a limited utility. They get waterlogged after a while, lose their buoyancy and finally start to rot. Lengths of 3.5 to 4.0 meters and diameters of 3 to 4 cm have proved most suitable. The ends of such an aluminium or plastic tube are sealed and a bright coat of paint should be applied. Learners should be familiarized with the pole on land in the same way as with the hoop, preferably on a meadow or lawn. All forms of organization, games and exercises that are to be done in water should be practised on land first. This saves the instructor a great deal of time explaining things to children while they are

standing around in the water. If the instructor manages to capture the beginners' interest and arouse their enthusiasm on land they will be much more receptive in the water. Exercises that are a lot of fun to do on land are then done with equal enjoyment in the water. It goes without saying that minor difficulties will have to be overcome, but this technique has brought very good results. The psychological boosts children get from doing such exercises substantially help to promote instruction.

5. "Swimming rungs"-Multi-purpose apparatus.

   It consists of Vinidur or flexible exercise rods and Ekazell boards whose sides are 22.5 cm long (different from the dimensions of the familiar flats). The thickness of 8 cm is sufficient for drilling holes in the boards into which the exercise rods are stuck. Some short connecting pieces also have to be cut with the aid of which the Ekazell boards can be joined together.

This apparatus offers the following advantages:

It is intended for instructing mainly children in kindergartens and school-children. One of the many advantage of this board, which is very stable and buoyant in water, is that the instructor can do without an assistant, which is particularly important in teaching children of kindergarten age.

The board is relatively inexpensive to make. Sixteen boards of the width mentioned can be obtained from a standard Ekazell board (light synthetic material).

The parts can be joined together or taken apart as

required. The components are very light, so that even children can help carry and assemble the board in the required form. Little storage space is required.

The following apparatus can be assembled from the component parts:

(a) Swimming runs,

(b) A reaching pole, although a pole made from a single piece is better than one made of several exercise rods.

(c) The square,

(d) The diving bridge,

(e) The merry-go-round.

Float

Little Ekazell floats (30 x 25.5 x 4 cm) have replace the heavy, cumbersome wooden boards. They feature good buoyancy and are convenient to handle, the material is light, resistant to wear, waterproof, and free from splinters. They are available in all sporting-goods shops.

Apart from its use for various games-in lieu of the pole, the gutter or the swimming rung-this apparatus is also suitable for teaching the proper leg movements. At the same time it makes considerably higher demands on the child than other aids. Unlike the pole, which the beginner can hold on to firmly, the child is forced to learn to make do with the relatively unstable board in the water. He has to rely more on his own strength and skill.

Methodical routines

"The principle of graspability used in teaching means

that we should take into account our pupils' individual as well collective, age-related, physiological and psychological idiosyncrasies in such a way that the subject matter at all times corresponds to their abilities and their development." This teaching principle is based on the logical order of instruction, in which the student proceeds from the elementary to the complex, from the known to the unknown, etc. The methodical routines described in the following should be seen from this point of view. They should serve the instructor as a guideline and help him to be creative in the broadest sense of the word. They do not relieve him of the responsibility to scrupulously examine his teaching situation, to choose the right subject matter and to decide on the right and best methodical approach.

In the following are contained brief instructions with regard to the sequence of the individual forms of exercise in the different complexes involved in developing fundamental swimming skills. "Organization" here connotes not only the formation and the fixed exercise routine but also the use of methodical aids, presented in an outline form. All objectives mentioned subsequently have been tried out on six-year-olds (1st objective 10th exercise unit; 2nd objective 20th exercise unit; 3rd objective 30th exercise unit). The learners should be expected to achieve these objectives at progressively shorter intervals corresponding to their age and level of development.

Swimming under water

Jumping up and down with the hoop, jumping into shallow water, the first breathing exercises and a number of other elementary exercises are preliminaries leading up to underwater swimming exercises. The aim of systematic training should be to enable the learner to submerge his body completely in water, to feel the pressure difference and to overcome it gradually and to open his eyes under water in order to find his bearings. The instructor should make sure that the learner opens his eyes only *after submerging* his head, because if he does so beforehand he will experience an unpleasant sensation when his open eyes contact the surface of the water.

The process of learning to swim under water should be started in shallow water. The learner starts by touching the water with his face for short periods; gradually the complexity of the exercise is increased.

a) *Simple submersion with and without the use of hands for stabilisation*

— Organization:

All apparatus mentioned are used; exercises can be executed in a circle, with a partner or individually. The instructor should see to it that the learner inhales properly before submerging; by and by the head should be fully submerged; the duration of submersion should be extended and the learner should exhale under water;

The aim should be to enable the learner to swim under water without aids or assistance from a partner.

— Games and exercises:

Ring-a-rosy, oranges and Lemons, diving underneath the reaching pole (hoops, ropes, swimming rungs or diving bridge can also be used for this purpose), alternate breathing and diving lane, move down ladders in hang position and allow oneself to float up.

b) Swimming under water with open eyes

— organization:

Learners should practise with the help of diving objects, partners can also assist in the exercises.

Exercises should always be coupled with a concrete task.

— Forms of exercise:

Watching one another under water, "making faces" under water, "talking" to one another, counting fingers, identifying objects in one's partner's hand, counting tiles, retrieving objects out of the water (in conjunction with moving under water and carrying objects).

c) Diving head first

— Organization:

Using diving objects.

Preparatory exercises should be practised before diving into deep water. The instructor should also show the learners how they should hold their extremities.

— Forms of exercise:

Preliminary exercise: handstand position (should be done in shallow water, the instructor should demonstrate the technique), dolphin jumps, head first dives from edge of pool from sitting position with feet resting on the gutter (make sure the water is sufficiently deep).

d) Performance standards for diving as par of basic swimming instruction programme

1st objective: The learner should be able to submerge his head completely under water and dive a certain distance.

2nd objective: The learner should be able to keep his eyes open under water, he should retrieve two to three rings or plates.

3rd objective: The learner should be confident when diving into deep water (the dive should be executed from a jump).

Jumping into water

Beginners should be accustomed to jumping into the water from the first swimming lesson onwards in view of the fact that jumping considerably helps to strengthen the child's confidence when in water. Most novices take to this exercise with enthusiasm. The instructor should make good use of the children's willingness to do this exercise, because it helps the learner to develop his breathing and diving skills. Jumping into deep water enables the beginner to feel the upward force of buoyancy, to reinforce this feeling and to enhance his confidence. The first jumps should be taken into hip-deep water. Jumps into chest-and shoulder-deep water can follow in quick succession. Subsequently learners can jump into deep water.

The following sequence of instruction has brought good results in practice:

a) Jumps into shallow water with assistance

— Organization:

The assistance can be provided with the aid of a pole or direct by the learner's partner.

The learner's toes should always grip the edge of the pool when jumping into the water in order to prevent slipping. It is important to pay attention to knee flexion when jumping into shallow water.

— Forms of exercise:

The learner should hold on to the pole (Partner) first with both and later on with one hand, jumping for the pole held in the water, broad jumping (pole or partner. should be further off the edge of the pole).

These exercises need be used only with children who are afraid.

b) Jumping into shallow water

These jumps are executed into chest-to shoulder-deep water without assistance.

— Organization:

The learners can jump individually, in Paris, as groups and in chains; numerous variations are possible by using hoops, reaching pole and swimming rungs.

— Forms of exercise:

The learner should jump into the hoop without touching it; over a large ball, a swimming rung, a reaching pole, to wards a pole, etc.

— Variants:

Jumping into the water and then swimming under a pole, swimming rung, etc.; jumping through the first hoop and coming up through the second hoop; climbing over the aid after jumping and swimming back under water, etc.

c) Jumping into water of shoulder depth and deeper

— Organization:

A reaching pole should be kept ready to assist learners in deeper water if the need arises.

The learner should be encouraged to open his eyes under water. The instructor should brief the learner on how he should move in the water and use his arms and legs effectively.

It is important that the instructor should wear swimming trunks.

— Forms of exercise:

Jumps outstretched, squat, pike, straddle dives right a twist, tuck dives, back dives, jumps with partners, obstacle jumps, followed by transition to swimming position.

d) Head first dives

— Organization:

Individual dives, group and chain dives.

Care should be taken with exercising in shallow water. Learner's toes should grip the edge of the pool-deck, head is held between the arms, which should be lowered somewhat, then the learner should jump off with a powerful thrust of his feet. He should jump off horizontally to the surface of the water if the water is shallow. The instructor should indicate where the entry is to be made. Transition to swimming position should be exercised as often as possible.

— Forms of exercise:

Jumping off from a sitting position from the edge

of the pool, placing feet on the gutter or on the starting bar, later on diving exercises should be practised from the starting position or fall-in dives from tuck position, etc., (especially if the edge of the pool is very high. Otherwise beginners should be taught the normal racing dive from the start).

e) *Standard diving performance expected during basic swimming instruction*

1st objective: Forward feet-first jump into water of shoulder or chin depth.

2nd objective: Forward dive from 1 metre into deep water.

3rd objective: Head-first front dive from 1 metre into deep water or feet-forward dive from 3 metres into deep water.

Gliding

The experience of "swimming" represents a decisive phase in the systematic development. Special attention should be paid to it because success or failure in the learner's further swimming career will depend largely on the success or failure of this phase.

The reaching pole is particularly well suited for exercises in preparation for gliding in the prone and supine positions.

a) *Exercises in preparation for gliding in the prone and supine positions*

— Organization:

The reaching pole or the swimming rung should be used or the learner should be assisted by a partner.

Prone position, outstretched position, head held between outstretched arms, air should be exhaled into the water. Supine position, hips are kept high, head on the water.

—Forms of exercise:

The learner holds on to the pole while being pulled. Moving in a circle = merry-go-round (suitable only for gliding in supine position).

b) Outstretched prone and supine flats

— Organization:

The children should be positioned in such a way as to make sure that they do not get into each other's way. Partners can be assigned if necessary for the first exercises who are to help learners recover.

The learner falls into the prone or supine position from straddle position, arms stretched out laterally. Prone position: head between arms, face in the water.

Supine position: head on the water, hips kept high.

— Recovery:

Recovery from the prone position is by pressing one's arms vigorously downwards, legs are drawn up and the trunk is brought into the vertical position.

Recovery from the supine position: The torso is brought into the vertical position by drawing up one's legs and effectively using one's arms.

c) Porpoise glide by pushing off from the bottom of the pool

The learner starts by gliding to something he can hold on to which is within reach, for instance from the edge of the pool to the reaching pole and back. The learner can be supported by a glide board.

d) Gliding by pushing off from the edge of the pool

— Organization:

The learner should be assisted by a partner if there is no edge to push off from or reaching pole.

The beginner should start by pushing off with one leg. Later on he can use both legs. Recovery should be assisted at first, subsequent recovery without assistance.

— Forms of exercise:

Learners should be motivated to improve their performance by holding contests to see who can glide longest, who can glide up to the tip of the pole, who can glide underneath the pole and the diving bridge without touching them, etc.

e) Gliding standards for basic swimming instruction

1st objective: Pushing off and gliding in prone and supine positions.

2nd objective: Improving the gliding positions and lengthening gliding duration in prone and supine positions (glide diving underneath the diving bridge).

3rd objective: Extending the gliding distance in prone and supine positions (through contests.

Locomotion in water

A child responds in a perfectly natural manner the first time he is allowed to hold onto a pole or onto the edge of the pool and to let his feet touch water: He starts thrashing the water with his feet. This activity corresponds to the child's urge to move. The instructor makes use of this urge by letting the child carry out tasks designed to help the child gather experience and to develop his swimming skills.

Owing to the fact that in the first phase of the learning process the child's movements are still very inefficient and that a great deal of concentration and persistent practice is needed to reinforce the beginner's unsteady movements, appropriate aids are recommended for practising certain movements.

The learner should assume a streamlined position in the water to ensure good results in practising swimming movements.

Attention should be paid from the very beginning to co-ordinated leg movement and breathing; air should be exhaled into the water.

a) Front crawl leg movement

— Organization:

Swimming rungs, reaching pole or floats should be used as aids.

Legs should be stretched out at all times, but they should be kept loose.

— Movement tasks:

Vigorous splashing, fast splashing, diminished splashing, executing movements under water, exhaling air into the water at regular intervals all the while.

b) Back crawl leg movement

— Organization:

Same as above.

Knees should not be raised above water level when splashing.

— Movement tasks:

Due to the fact that leg movement in back crawl is almost identical with the leg action used in front crawl, the movement tasks are the same.

Arm movement should also be developed and subsequently co-ordinated with the leg movement.

c) Arm movement in front and back crawl

— Organization:

The learner can move his legs slightly to stabilize the position of his body.

The hands should push vigorously before starting overwater recovery. Hands should continue their push down to the thighs, in the overwater recovery phase the arms are kept loose and relaxed.

— Forms of exercise:

Preparatory exercises carried out on land with a view to improving shoulder joint flexibility: Windmill rotation forward and backward. The movements of the arms and hands should be controlled consciously when walking forward and backward. At first the arm action is performed without co-ordination with breathing, later on arm action and breathing are linked.

d) Complex movement pattern in front and back crawl strokes

Leg action starts after the push-off, followed by arm movement coordination, especially in the case of crawl stroke, is performed without linking with breathing.

The elementary form of crawl learned during the first phase of instruction forms the basis for further refinement.

e) Standard of locomotion in the water in basic swimming instruction

1st objective: Preparation of flutter kick and alternation arm stroke in prone and supine positions.

2nd objective: Flutter kick in prone position using a gliding board; in supine position without the aid of a gliding board; locomotion by means of leg and arm movements.

3rd objective: Improvement of the leg and arm movement pattern; locomotion over a certain distance by means of complex movement.

Breathing: Breathing exercises are initiated by having the pupils move objects such as little toy animals, soap-boxes or little balls by blowing at them. The object here is to get the learner used to intensive breathing, which comprises short, deep inhalation and slow, forceful exhalation into the water. The instructor should demonstrate the breathing pattern.

a) Deep air inhalation followed by slow exhalation

— Organization:

Little toy animals, soap-boxes, little balls.

— Forms of exercise

Blowing away objects. The exercises should be varied by having the pupils blow the objects up to a goal line, through a passage formed by hoops, etc.

b) Blowing a "hole" in the water

— Organization:

Hoops, reaching pole

The mouth is kept just above the water surface, the emphasis is on forceful exhalation.

c) Bubbling

— Organization:

Hoop's reaching pole, multi-purpose apparatus-edge of pool, circle, partner.

The mouth is kept in the water. Who can bubble loudest? Who can bubble and splash most vigorously? Children should be reminded not to rub their eyes when they take their heads out of the water.

d) Deliberate exhalation into the water

— Organization:

All aids, especially the board, can be used.

The face should be fully immersed when exhaling. The instructor should make certain that the pupils inhale and exhale rhythmically, first five, then ten times in a row. The mouth should be open and ready for inhaling as it is raised above the water surface; not even "the last rest" should be exhaled above the water.

— Forms of exercise:

Inhaling and exhaling in standing position, walking forward and in conjunction with locomotion, e.g., leg movement in prone position.

(e) Side breathing

— Organization

Mainly with the aid of reaching pole, board, swimming rung, edge of the pool deck or support from the partner.

Preparatory exercise for the crawl stroke: The head is turned to one side for inhalation in such a way that one ear is submerged, then the head is turned in the other direction after inhaling. The head should not be raised in the process. The instructor makes sure that the learners exhale vigorously into the water.

— Forms of exercise:

The exercises should be performed bilaterally and linked with the arm or leg movement and with the complex movement.

f) Breathing-in-water standard for basic swimming instruction

1st objective: Rhythmic inhalation above and exhaling into the water, the breathing cycle being repeated ten times.

2nd objective: Inhalation and exhalation while raising and lowering the head and inhalation and exhalation while turning the head in both directions linked with locomotion in the water.

3rd objective: Inhalation and exhalation in conjunction with the combined movement in prone and supine positions (elementary co-ordination).

Use of all acquired basic swimming skills

The basic skills of swimming under water, jumping into the water, gliding, locomotion through the cyclic action of the arms and legs and controlled breathing are taught simultaneously and systematically. There are a variety of ways in which they can be combined with each other. There are many things in common, e.g., between jumping into the water and diving, gliding on the surface and under water, gliding in and prone and supine positions and the corresponding forms of locomotion as well as between breathing, diving and locomotion, etc. The quality and quantity of instruction is measured by the learner's degree of mastery of the complex movement.

Some examples:

— Head first front dive from 1-metre spring board;

— Deep dive and exhalation into water;

— Surfacing and orientating oneself in relation to given object;

— Swimming to said object, which is about 10 metres away, and breathing regularly in the process;

— Carrying said object to the edge of the pool using one's feet for propelling one's body through the water.

Using this method children of pre-school age were expected to execute this series of movements after 30 units of instruction and almost all of them passed the test.

Special factors to be taken into account in carrying out the first stage of instruction is deep water

Owing to the fact that numerous swimming pools are being built which are 1.80 metres deep or deeper at all points, the need to modify the 1st stage of basic swimming instruction is being increasingly felt. Field studies conducted in Leipzig, Neubranden-burg and elsewhere have shown that buoyant aids worn on the trunk can be dispensed with also for instruction in deep water. This holds true also for group instruction (school swimming instruction, preschool swimming classes, extracurricular swimming training).

On methodical routines

The teaching of basic skills in underwater swimming should be given priority if swimming instruction is given in deep water, especially in the early phase of instruction.

With the help of suitable aids the beginner should first practise complete feet-first vertical immersion, holding on the gutter or other suitable objects at first. Soon he will realize that the water's buoyant force does not allow him to sink lower so it will not take much effort to persuade him to let go of the gutter and, by pushing himself off, to dive to a greater depth and allow himself to be raised to the surface by buoyancy. These exercises should be combined with all exercises which encourage the beginner to open his or her eyes under water. Maximum importance should be attached to beginner being able to orientate himself under water from the very start.

Exercise designed to let the novice experience static buoyancy should be started immediately after, and in the further course of instruction in conjunction with, the diving exercises. At first the best way to execute these in the form of the "extended float" in prone position, the beginner holding on to the gutter. Holding the arms slightly spread to the sides and the legs spread out help the beginner in this phase to develop the skill of balancing his body in the water. He will soon be able to let go of the gutter or the object and to float freely on the surface. The process of experiencing buoyancy is reinforced by the "turtle float" exercise, in which the learner's body is rolled up into a compact bundle and in which part of the pupil's back protrudes above the surface of the water once its position is stabilized following a little initial forward and backward rocking (the exercise should be demonstrated first).

Once the learner has become aware of the static buoying force he can start with his first jumping exercises by practising the *feet-first-jump*. The learner's confidence should be kept up at all times by using a pole (see section on jumping into the water). These jumping exercises also the serve to help the pupil feel the static buoyancy.

Head-first jumps are introduced in much the same way as the jumps into shallow water described earlier, except that additional precautions should be taken by using such aids as the pole, lane markers, safety zones etc., to ensure the learners' safety at all times. The dive from a sitting position is a good way to introduce the *front glide*. This exercise too should at first be arranged in such a way that the learner can get a firm hold of an object at the end of the glide. Once the learner has gained the necessary measure of confidence he can start practising free glide forms from a standing dive and by pushing off from the pool wall. Experience has shown that if is best to start with the extended float and with the *back glide* in deep water only after the beginner has acquired a good command of these exercises in a prone position. It is particularly important to have him consciously experience the kinaesthetic sensation associated with the complete extension of his body, because a certain measure of insecurity can easily cause the learner to flex his hip joint, thereby assuming a "cradle" position in the water. Supporting exercises can also be performed on land: raising oneself, with the help of the instructor or the partner, from a stiff lying position to stand upright the learner maintaining his out-stretched posture by tensioning his muscles.

The following preliminary exercises are recommended before practising locomotion: Having the pupil move hand over hand along the gutter or a similar object offering a firm hold with a view to letting him experience the resistance of water: doing the flutter kick while sitting on the edge of the pool deck; executing the flutter kick in a prone position while holding on to the gutter or another object providing a firm hold; practising the flutter kick lying in the water in a supine position supporting one's neck on a lane rope or a pole.

Numerous other exercises can be performed with the aid of the swimming rung. The rung can also be used in combination with the gutter or with the lane rope.

Not all the *breathing exercises* described for shallow water can be practised in deep water, because some of them can be performed only when standing in water of hip or neck depth. But then the learner can be assigned exercises which he can perform on his own in a bath-tub or wash-basin and which can complement and help him master the technique, which he can improve with the help of the gutter or other aids.

On choice and use of artificial aids

The reader will have gathered from the remarks

concerning the methodical routines that the success of basic swimming instruction in deep water hinges on the wise use of aids. The "gutter" as an aid deserves to be mentioned first. It gives the beginner the security he needs in the first few lesson to learn the fundamental swimming skill.

But owing to the fact that the large area of a 25 by 12.5 metres swimming pool could not be used economically by beginner groups if the gutter were the only aid offering a firm hold, *Lewin* has developed in Neubranden burg what are known here as "safety zones". They consist of aluminium pipes about 40 mm in diameter sealed at the ends and joined together by Ekazell blocks (450 mm x 450 mm) in the same way as the swimming rungs mentioned earlier. They are used to mark out parts of a swimming pool for use as exercise areas, their size being adjustable to the learners' level of proficiency. "safety zones" make it possible not only to use various forms of organization and for the teacher to keep better track of his class but also give more pupils a chance to practise all the forms of exercise that in the past could be done only with the aid of the gutter or lane ropes (moving in a hanging position with hands only, alternate floating, leg movement in prone and supine positions, breath control exercises, etc,).

Lane ropes, which are used to divide up pools into longitudinal or transverse lanes, are also very useful as aids. As soon as the learner begins consciously to feel static and dynamic buoyancy he can use the lane rope to hold on to or as a goal in glide exercises. Another very important aid is the "reaching pole" (aluminium, plastic or bamboo about 2.5 to 3 metres in length). The teacher supports pupils in their first attempts at jumping into the water with the aid of this pole. The pupil can grab hold of the pole after diving or later on after surfacing; goal markers can also be used in the initial phase, by drawing back the rope the learner can be encouraged to dive greater distances. Diving exercises are performed by placing one end of the pole on the pool floor and holding it in a vertical position (the pole can also be secured in this position if necessary); learners practise by "climbing" up and down the pole. Coloured markings spaced half a metre apart can be painted on the pole to help learners judge the depth (this encourages them to go deeper and to open their eyes under water).

Solid rubber rings: Which can be suspended on ropes from safety zone bars or fastened to swimming rungs, can also be used for diving practice and as a means of encouraging the learner to open his or her eyes under water. The depth at which the rings are suspended can be varied by altering the rope length. By using this aid the learner can be system artically accustomed to greater depths and to greater degrees of difficulty until he is able to retrieve the rings from the bottom of the pool. All other aids described in the section on swimming instruction in shallow water are also used in deep-water swimming instruction, the importance of the role played by the different types of aid varies from case to case. The most versatile and for this reason the most important artificial aids are the *swimming rungs* and the *floats.* To conclude the chapter on the special features of the first phase of basic swimming instruction in deep water it should be stressed that the teacher has a greater measure of responsibility for his pupils that in shallow-water instruction. This should not deter the teacher from teaching the basic skills in accordance with the recommendations set forth in the foregoing, but it should encourage him methodically to plan his instruction, to choose the most promising forms of organization of exercises and to use and aids in the most expedient manner.

Basic standards of good swimming instruction

1. Learners should be accustomed to certain strict forms of organization from the very start (to ensure order and discipline and thus to intensify instruction).
2. Transition between different forms of organization and between different parts of a lesson should be fluid (they should be safe and orderly and there should be no less of time).
3. Pupils should be kept moving to prevent them from getting cold too early (the pace of exercise can be speeded up to keep the pupils warm).
4. The instructor should pick a good vantage point to be able to survey his group properly.
5. Acoustic cues or sign language should be used during instruction.

Forms of organization in shallow water

Intended mainly for beginners:

Row, alley, circle-with all forms the instructor can decide whether the pupils should hold hands with members of the group or partners or not. Beginners should be positioned in such a way that they can stand securely and that they can at all times get a firm hold of the edge of the deck, of the rope or other object used to mark off the swimming area, or of artificial aids such as hoops, reaching pole, multi-purpose device or partner. With growing confidence the beginner learns to get by without these aids.

Lining up the pupils along the edge of the pool deck or along other pool bounds and letting them swim or glide to the opposite side or to another goal in groups is a good way or beginners to practise pushing off.

The "exercise lane" is a form of organization which makes it possible to make maximum use of the available swimming area and which enables the instructor to control the intensity and frequency of exercise.

Jumping into the water-pushing off from the pool wall in supine position-back crawl flutter kick up to first mark-dive under rope (1st time)-back crawl complex movement up to 2nd mark-dive under line (2nd sign)-back to the edge using back crawl flutter kick-climb out report for assignment of 2nd task-repeat exercise.

These and similar forms of exercise are designed to give children a chance to move about in water, a thing they are fond of doing anyway, and to develop their endurance.

Organizational forms for deep and shallow water

Suitable for basic swimming instruction and training: Swimming across the lane exercising in groups "flow line" exercise. The instructor splits up the class into groups of learners of equal performance level in order to prevent those who are still unable to do this exercise properly from getting in the way of those who have already mastered it. But the instructor should keep trying to get the weaker learners to improve their performance so as to enable them to take part in normal group exercises.

If the class is very large and the exercise unit limited, then it is recommended to have the learners swim in one direction individually, in twos or in groups. Once the learner has swum one lane he gets but of the water and walks back to the starting point again. This technique is also used in interval training and in spurts.

SECOND PHASE

The main aim of the second phase of instruction was outlined in the introduction to the section basic swimming style techniques, including starts and turns. Swimming styles are the strokes which are used in swimming events held at present in accordance with FINA rules and regulation: breaststroke, backstroke (using the back crawl technique) free-style (using the front crawl technique) and butterfly with the dolphin kick. There are also numerous variants of these swimming techniques which are used for such specific purposes as transporting objects, rescuing people in distress, overcoming obstacles, etc. They are used as "general means of training in water".

To achieve greater versatility two or more swimming styles are taught in the second phase of basic swimming instruction, depending on how much time is available for this phase and on the level of performance of the learners. In compulsory school swimming instruction, which consists of two complexes covered in a total of about 60 lessons, most of the pupils learn the elementary co-ordination of three swimming techniques: back crawl, front crawl and breast-stroke. But if for some reason only one instruction complex consisting of about 35 lessons is available, then most of the pupils manage to master the elementary co-ordination of only two swimming strokes, e.g., back crawl and breaststroke.

If time is available for instruction on an extracurricular basis the learners can be taught the butterfly stroke. The following views on the teaching approach should be seen in this light and applied in practice. Scientific advances in the fields of biomechanics, hydrodynamics, sports physiology and sports psychology have not only revolutionized training methods, but they have contributed to the evolution of the different techniques of swimming and of starts and turns. The breaststroke is a good example of this development. The early forms of "breaststroke" with their long glide phases after each movement cycle have evolved to become a "simultaneous stroke technique" in which the cycles of movement are executed almost without intervals.

The efficiency of movements depends on the laws of physics, on the athlete's anatomical make-up and on the specific movements of his arms under and over the water.

To get a better general picture we shall first analyse the *common feature* of the techniques of the *freestyle* (crawl), back crawl, butterfly (dolphin) and *breaststroke* style.

We shall use the front crawl stroke as a basis for studying these common features. It is important to bear in mind the characteristics of movement of this swimming style.

This will be followed by an analysis of the specific technical questions involved in the other three swimming styles.

Crawl

On the body's position in water: The swimmer should lie in a relaxed prone or supine stretched out position in the water. The shoulder line should be raised slightly above the water surface, the pelvis should be deep enough below the surface to permit convenient leg action beneath the surface. In this position the longitudinal axis of the body runs at a slight angle to the water surface to give the body a good hydrodynamic position. The position of the head has an important bearing on the body's position in the water. The head's steering function should be developed with a view to ensuring that the body is propelled through the water in as straight a line as possible.

The swimming style, the distance to be swum, the swimmer's constitution and the speed a swimmer develops should be taken into account in deciding on which is the best body position.

Leg movement: The leg action gives the swimmer an upward drive and forward propulsion and balances the body in the water (this is especially the case in the alternating stroke styles). A general comparison of the front crawl, back crawl and dolphin leg action patterns shows that they have many basic features in common. In all three styles the movement commences at the trunk and continues sequentially along the thighs, knees, lower legs, ankles and toes. The leg action is in the vertical plane and the kick amplitude varies between 30 and 50 cm, depending on the constitution of the swimmer, the beat rhythm and the frequency.

Both the upswing and the downswing of the leg help propel the body. The foot assumes a pigeon-toed (inverted) position during the upswing. The efficiency of the legs' propelling action depends, among other things, on the speed of the swing reversal, on the extension of the foot joint and on how relaxed the feet are kept. The leg movement in the crawl techniques are largely analogous. Leg us examine the front crawl leg swing to get a clearer notion of the leg action.

3

PRINCIPLES OF TRAINING

In a trained athlete all the physiological mechanisms involved in exercise appear to function more effectively. Although the details of this process of adaptation are not yet fully understood, many specific effects are now well substantiated.

Broadly stated, these include

1. Increased cardiac output and reduced pulse rates for any given workload, as well as increased muscular capitalisation and more effective oxygen utilization and energy expenditure mechanisms;
2. Increased local (skeletal) muscular strength and endurance; and
3. Improved neuromuscular coordination and greater mechanical efficiency for any given work load.

THE OVERLOAD PRINCIPLE

The overload principle accounts for the general phenomenon of adaptation to stress. *Overload* refers to a work load greater than to which the body is accustomed, or more precisely, one for which the oxygen intake is inadequate to supply the needs of the body. The overload principle states that increases in muscle size (hypertrophy), strength, and endurance result from an increase in work intensity within a given time unit.

Hypertrophy occurs only when a muscle performs work at an intensity greater than usual. An increase in the work duration without a corresponding increase in intensity produces no effect. In general, training effects are specific to the work load. For example, an increased training effect cannot be obtained merely by prolonging the activity; the speed of the activity must also be increased to produce a training effect.

Progressive overload is the gradual and progressive increase in work load in accordance with the body's capacity to resist stress. To improve performance, training should aim at progression, but always within the individual athlete's fund of adaptive energy.

Adaptation is the gradual process of the body overcompensating to overload stresses, during which the body undergoes various functional and constitutional changes. In making these adjustments to increased stress the body draws on its fund of "adaptation energy."

Failing adaptation is the body's inability to cope with overload stress. It can result from any number of causes, particularly a too rapid increase in the training work load based on a seriously misjudged ideal balance between volume and intensity, but also from such "hidden stresses" as inadequate rest or nutrition, emotional stress, or the inexorable demands of growth.

Forbes Carlile was the first to apply the work of Hans Selye, author of *The Stress of Life*, to swimming training. Selye's ideas provide a scientific basis for applying the training work load; his "general adaptation syndrome" proposes quite specific agents not only have their own quite specific actions as parts the organism but also have stereotyped nonspecific effects.

The body makes certain adjustments and changes in adapting itself to prolonged stress. Coaches must be able to recognize differences between individuals in this respect. Applying the proper volume and intensity of exercise stress will produce the optimum amount of specific adaptation for each person.

Failing adaptation may be countered by reducing the work load-by swimming at a slower pace, increasing the amount of rest, or reducing the distance swum in training. Excessive local stress requires complete rest. Diversion can consist of varying both the format of the training schedule and the strokes swum in training. In extreme cases where diversion is inadequate to counter failing adaptation to stress, the athlete may require complete rest from both training and unnecessary daily activities. Some swimmers have been shown to benefit from bed rest immediately before a big meet, but an intelligently planned training program will not require such extreme measures.

Specificity of training is a fundamental principle of training, but one that was only vaguely understood in the early days of formal training programs. People realized that to be able to swim fast athletes should practice swimming fast and that to have endurance they should practice swimming long distances, but the principle of specificity is far more complex than merely following these two concepts.

Training effects are specific to the type of work load placed on the body. Brouha studied this concept of training and reports that athletes in one sport require considerable time to adapt to and reach maximum efficiency in another sport, even when equally skilled in both activities. Indeed, specificity applies not only *between sports* but also *between events within sports;* it applies not only to learning the precise skills and paces of a sport but also to conditioning the body to perform at maximum capacity in the different events within a particular sport.

According to Selye, specificity refers to a few units within a system, implying that training should be planned according to a specific purpose, whether it be to establish desired physiological effects by training the appropriate energy systems of the body, to form skills, to swim a race at a certain speed, or to use certain strategies and paces in competition. Within a single daily work-out, appropriate time should be allocated for training specific aspects of the body. As the season progresses the emphasis given to specific physiological requirements should gradually change according to the swimmer's improving fitness and the event(s) competitive swimming program requires a certain balance between speed and endurance, which naturally varies between individuals.

Specificity does not refer merely to preparing for a particular competitive event, nor is the establishment of general physiological fitness the only "specific" requirement; rather, specificity takes the form of whatever particular quality is being emphasized during any phase of seasonal activity, whether it be endurance training or specialized training for the season's important competitions. A swimmer should thus first build a broad base of endurance. Once this base has been established, the program gradually changes in format to include a carefully planned balance between duration and intensity of effort. These considerations are vital because can result in failing adaptation to the exercise stress; in fact, training at very high levels of intensity should form only a small percentage of the seasonal activity.

ESTABLISHING A TRAINING EFFECT

Different types of work produce different physiological effect. The different systems of the body do not adapt to training at the same speed. An increase in capitalisation, for example, may take place within a matter of days, whereas heart muscle takes years to condition properly. The "establishment of effect" is a loose term used to describe specific adaptation resulting from training.

Training has an accumulative effect. The positive effects of training do not appear the very next day after a work load has been applied. Adaptation to the stress of training is a gradual process and requires time to produce the desired biological changes.

INTERVAL TRAINING

Interval training superseded the older type of training in which swimmers did long continuous distances at a comparatively slower pace. The originators of interval training found that by breaking up the training into comparatively shorter periods of activity with intervening rest periods of varying duration, it was possible to place a greater training overload on the swimmer. Swimmers were found capable of withstanding much greater work loads than hitherto believed possible.

Interval training involves swimming fixed distances at a fixed pace with fixed rest intervals, thus providing control of the duration and intensity of effort. Increased quality of effort should result when a longer rest period is provided between swims. Generally speaking, the higher the quality of a set of interval swims, the fewer the repetitions that can be accomplished. Conversely, it is possible to produce a greater quantity of work when shorter rest periods are set between longer sets of interval swims. The prolonged activity reduces the intensity of effort.

The two options are as follows:

1. *Quality swimming* involves long rest periods, which permit high-speed activity but the intensity of which limits the duration of the activity.
2. *Quality swimming* involves short rest periods, which permit only submaximal speeds to be maintained. The reduced speed enables the activity to be prolonged, thereby enhancing development of the endurance factor.

The preceding sketches the ideal criteria for producing specific training effects, but the human factor-the individual swimmer's level of motivation, drive, and dedication-will contribute to the success or otherwise of the activity. Various training effects can be achieved by applying different work: rest ratios. There are four basic types of interval training.

1. Sprint training
2. Repetition training

3. Fast interval training, and
4. Slow interval training

SPRINT TRAINING

Sprint training consists of short distances swum at top speed. Although speed starts to fall off after about 50 meters has been covered, distances up to 100 meters are commonly called sprints and are treated as such for the purpose of speed training. Sprint training is usually done in multiples of 25-,50-, or 100-meter sets. The heart rate should be allowed to recover to 100 beats per minute or below after each swim.

Work: rest rations from 1:5 to 1:10 should permit adequate rest to enable training to emphasize speed. The ratio chosen will depend on what percentage of top speed the swimmer wishes to attain. In sprint training the swimmer on occasion may attempt to swim at 100% of best time, especially over 25s and 50s. Sprint training attempts to develop speed and muscular strength as well as the ability to tolerate oxygen debt.

Basic examples of sprint training sets are as follows:

1. 8 x 25 (2 minutes rest)
2. 4 x 50 (5 minutes rest)
3. 4 x 100 (10 minutes rest)

Repetition training consists of simulating the race pace by swimming distances shorter than the racing distance at a pace than the pace of the total racing distance. However, any kind of training in which the heart rate is permitted to recover to approximately 110 to 100 before the next swim may be classified as repetition training.

When performed at high enough speeds, repetition training will accustom the swimmer to *anaerobic exercise* in that there is an increase of oxygen debt and an accumulation of higher levels of lactate in the working muscles. Repetition training also increases speed and muscular strength and power.

The work: rest ratio should be at least 1:3 to permit speeds approximately 90% to 95% of a swimmer's racing speed. To develop a high level of blood lactate it is essential that a swimmer exert close to 100% effort. The heart rate also should reach maximum, somewhere in the range of 190 to 200. So that the swimmer can maintain a high enough level of work intensity, the distances used in high-lactate repeat swimming ideally should not exceed 250 to 300 meters. Because high-intensity repeat swimming can be very stressful and send a swimmer into failing adaptation, the training set should not exceed a total distance of 1,000 meters or be presented more than twice a week in the work-out schedule.

Basic examples of repetition training sets are as follows:

1. 15 x 50 (3 minutes rest)
2. 10 x 100 (5 minutes rest)
3. 6 x 150 (5-10 minutes rest) (The last two 150-meter swims should be faster than the swimmer's 250 split recorded on the swimmer's fastest 200-meter swim.)
4. 4+250 (10 minutes rest) (The last two 250 repeats

should be faster than the swimmer's 250 split recorded on the swimmer's best time for 400 meters. The swimmer's time at the 200 mark will usually accord with the 200-meter pace recommended to the swimmer by physiologists for the purpose of high-lactate training.)

Applying items 3 and 4 twice weekly during the hard training season can be particularly effective in improving a swimmer's times for the 200-and 400-meter events, respectively, possibly because a swimmer becomes accustomed to tolerating the higher levels of lactate that probably start to accumulate around the 150 mark in the 200 and the mark in the 400.

FAST INTERVAL TRAINING

Fast interval training consists of work: rest ratios of about 1:1, permitting the swimmer to develop speeds approximately 80% of best pace. At least theoretically, this ratio enables the equal development of speed and endurance.

Fast interval training introduces a significant element of speed to any prolonged activity. It simulates to a high degree the type of stress experienced in racing events, which makes great demands on both aerobic and anaerobic endurance. In fast interval training the heart rate after each swim will be around 160 to 190. The heart rate should be permitted recover to approximately 120 to 130 before the next swim.

Although the rest period in fast interval training is shorter than that permitted in sprint and repetition training, it is much longer than in slow interval training. Fast interval training develops heart muscle and the ability of skeletal muscle to tolerate oxygen debt.

Basic examples of fast interval training sets are as follows:

1. 30 x 50 (30-60 seconds rest)
2. 15 x 100 (30-120 seconds rest)
3. 8 x 200 (1-3 minutes rest)
4. 4 x 800 (3-5 minutes rest)

SLOW INTERVAL TRAINING

Slow interval training consists of relatively slow activity designed to improve aerobic endurance. It is based on the endurance development principle of prolonging the activity and gradually trying to increase the speed of the prolonged activity as the season progresses. Slow interval training involves swimming at speeds ranging from approximately 60% to 70% of best pace for the distance. The speed of the swims is also limited by the short rest periods. The activity continues for at least 20 minutes to ensure that the intensity of effort is kept primarily hours when used to lay the early season endurance foundation. The heart rate after each endurance approximately 160 to 170, but the recovery will be in the range of 150 to 160.

Basic examples of slow interval training sets are as follows:

1. 30 x 50 (10-15 second rest)
2. 15 x 100 (10-15 seconds rest)
3. 8 x 200 (10-20 seconds rest)
4. 8 x 400 (15-30 seconds rest)
5. 4 x 800 (15-30 seconds rest)

Various applications of interval training

Interval training can be applied in many ways. A few of these variations follow.

Straight sets. A straight set is a series of swims done at near constant speed, for example, 16+100 in 62 seconds) with 30 seconds rest.

Descending sets. A descending set is a series of repeat swims in which each subsequent swim is done progressively faster, for example, 20 x 50 (30 seconds rest) descending (first 50 in 35 seconds, twentieth 50 in 28 seconds). A variation of the method is to post the work-out item on the board as 20+50 (30 seconds rest), 1-4 descending. This means that the swimmer will decrease the time over the first four 50s and repeat the process four more times until 20 swims have been completed.

Yet another variation of descending sets is to decrease the average time for each set of repeat swims by starting each subsequent set with a faster first 50 than in the preceding set and then continuing to decrease the second, third, and fourth 50 accordingly.

In this type of training, however, the first repeats in a set sometimes are swum too slowly to warrant intervening rest periods. In the previous example, namely, 20 x 50 for a total distance of 1,000 meters (or yards), it might be better to swim the first half of each set continuously without rest intervals and then complete the second half of the distance as a descending set of equal multiples.

For example, the athletes would perform a 250 continuous swim at a fast pace followed immediately by 5 x 50 descending (30 seconds rest), repeating the set for a total of 1,000 meters.

Broken sets. A broken set is a series of swims in which the total distance is broken into sectors with short rest intervals between them, for example, 400 meters broken at each 100 with 10 seconds rest. At the end of the swim, deduct 30 seconds (the total amount of rest) from the gross time to obtain the actual swimming time.

Broken swims are highly motivating and can be used to break up all training distances. Several broken swims can be used to form a training set by providing a long rest after each swim, thus combining repetition training and interval training. Another interesting variation is to perform a set of broken swims in a descending series, reducing the gross time for each subsequent swim.

The following are some further examples:

1. 8 x 400 broken at the 50 with 10 seconds rest and 5 minutes rest after each 400
2. 8 x 200 individual medley broken at the 50 with 10 seconds rest and 3 minutes rest after each 200 medley
3. 2 x 150 going straight through into 2 x 50 (a broken 400 with 10 seconds rest between each sector) and 5 minutes rest after each 400
4. 8 x 100 with 10 seconds rest after each 100, and 5 minutes rest after each set, and sets 1 through 4 descending

Pyramid. This format consists of a set of swims divided into irregular distance sectors and rest periods. The swimmer may either keep the same pace in each swim or vary the pace by going faster on the shorter sectors.

Three examples follow:

1. Swim 50, rest 10 seconds
   Swim 100, rest 20 seconds
   Swim 200, rest 40 seconds
   Swim 400, rest 1 minute
   Swim 200, rest 40 seconds
   Swim 100, rest 20 seconds
   Swim 50
2. Swim 400, rest 3 minutes
   Swim 2+200, rest 2 minutes
   Swim 2+100, rest 1 minutes
   Swim 2+50, rest 30 minute
3. Swim 400 medley, rest 5 minutes
   Swim 200 medley, rest 5 minutes
   Swim 100 medley, rest 1 minutes
   Swim 200 medley, rest 3 minutes
   Swim 400 medley

Permutations. Permutations are swims broken at irregular sectors of the total distance. The following are examples of permutations of 400 meters in a 50-meter pool (8 lengths of the pool to complete 400 meters). The work-out items are posted on the board as 4 x 400 meters (perm) (5 minutes rest after each 400).

1. 2-2-2-2 (10 seconds rest)
2. 4-2-1-1 (10 seconds rest)
3. 1-2-3-2 (10 seconds rest)
4. 4-1-1-1-1 (10 seconds rest)

The pace is kept constant on 3-or 4-length

segments but increased on the 1-and 2-length segments.

We developed and use this methods. It is effective for developing a swimmer's ability to change pace or accelerate tactically at any stage of a race; alternatively, the pace can be held constant for all sectors. It can also be used for teaching "negative splitting". Whatever procedure is used, permutations, or perms, provide an opportunity to practice a variety of paces.

Simulators. The simulator is a method used to simulate the desired pace of a specific racing distance. Basically, the procedure is to cover half the racing distance at the desired pace before stopping for a short rest that will permit the heart rate only a slight recovery. The swimmer then covers half the stopping for distance already covered before stopping for another short rest. The pattern continues until some arbitrarily small segment remains for the total to equal the racing distance.

For example, suppose the racing distance being practised is 400 meters.

Swim 200 meters, rest 10 seconds
Swim 100 meters, rest 5 seconds
Swim 50 meters, rest 5 seconds
Swim 25 meters, rest 5 seconds
Swim 25 meters

The rest interval is reduced in this example from 10 to 5 seconds before the shorter segments of the racing distance.

Negative spilt. Swimming the second half of a racing distance faster than the first half (usually 2-3 seconds faster) is known as a "negative split". Its purposes are to delay the onset of oxygen debt and to teach evenly paced swimming. The negative split also in sense "pays back" the momentum of the starting dive in the first half of a racing distance.

Other types of training

Many of the following options provides unique training benefits as well as add variety to the training schedule.

Overdistance swims. Broadly stated, overdistance swims are twice as long as the distance for which a swimmer is training. For example, a swimmer whose specially is the 100-meter event would practice overdistance swimming by doing 200-meter swims.

Locomotives. Locomotives provides pace variations over different segments of a total non-stop swim. They are an excellent early season conditioning exercise and a useful diversion during the stress of hard mid-season training. The following is one example.

Swim 1 lap fast, 1 lap slow.
Swim 2 laps fast, 2 laps slow.
Swim 3 laps fast, 3 laps slow.
Swim 4 laps fast, 4 laps slow.
Swim 3 laps fast, 3 laps slow.
Swim 2 laps fast, 2 laps slow.
Swim 1 lap fast, 1 lap slow.

Time swimming. Time swimming is an effective method of developing increased endurance; it basically consists of increasing the distance a swimmer can cover within a prescribed time, which, after all, is what speed swimming is about.

Fartlek. Fartlek was adopted by swimmers as an informal early season conditioning exercise. Used this way, most of the distance is covered at an easy pace with intermittent bursts of speed using such devices as changing stroke and pace after a certain number of lengths. However, chapter 6 describes how to use fartlek training to greater purpose and effect by setting more definite requirements.

TETHERED SWIMMING OR SPRINT-RESISTED TRAINING

Tethered swimming was first used 50 years ago at the Chicago Towers Club when Stan Brauninger, coach to 1936 Olympic backstroke champion Adolph Kiefer, attached canvas belts with long elastic bands around the midriffs of his swimmers. In the 1940s, coach Harold Minto of the Firestone Country Club, Akron, Ohio, trained the first postwar Olympic 1,500-meter champion, James McClane, in a canvas harness connected to several yards of elastic aircraft shock observer cord. In the 1950s, Robert Kiphuth suspended scores of elastic stretch bands from the balcony of the Yale University pool for the use of his swimmers in the water below. In similar vein, Santa Clara's George Haines had his swimmers use latex surgical tubing (type 202) for stretch cord exercises on land.

In the later 1950s and the 1960s the use of tethered swimming became sporadic, but it was revived in the mid-1970s by Randy Reese, the renowned University of Florida coach. Reese experimented with several new in-water drills using 1/8-inch thick surgical tubing that had a 3/32-inch inside diameter and was cut into sections of 18 to 22 feet. He repopularised the use to tethered swimming throughout the world.

Tethered swimming (also known as sprint-resisted training) was used originally to improve the muscular power necessary for sprint swimming, but research suggested that swimming against an increased resistance actually slowed muscle speed instead of increasing it. In light of this, Counsilman used this method for aerobic training of *distance swimmers only*. He prescribed selected periods of activity such as three minute segments with 1-minute rest intervals and cut rubber stretch cord to approximately one third the length of the swimmer and the elasticity of the cord.

Speed-assisted training (SAT)

Like so many other swimming training methods, the concept behind speed-assisted training came from track-in this case, the use of such methods as towing, downhill running, and treadmill sunning at accelerated speed. Ernest Maglischo refers to a variation of the use of tethered swimming for improving sprint swimming speed. He describes how leading coaches Randy Reese and Nort Thornton each used this method in their programs. The swimmer, and then allowed it to snap back on the return, thus assisting the swimmer to swim at a faster speed than would normally be possible. Counsilman developed a system of an-aerobic lactate training by having the swimmers use repeat swims such as 10 x 50 on 2 to 3 minutes or 5 x 100 on 3 to 5 minutes while attached to stretch cords. He instructed the swimmers to swim diagonally across the pool to avoid becoming entangled in the cords when returning down the pool. The method was not practical in a 50-meter pool because the cords would not stretch tightly enough and the course was too long for sprinting.

Counsilman devised another variation of the method wherein the sprinter pulled themselves along the lane markers to the other end of the pool and then rested before allowing the taut stretch cord to snap back and give a speed-assisted sprint back to the starting point.

During the 1960s, we experimented with the use of a 16-2/3-meter course at the Hillbrow Club, Johannesburg (6,000 feet altitude), when preparing swimmers for international competition in the standard Olympic 50-meter course. One of the swimmers in the group, Ann Fairlie, swimming in Benziers, France, 7 days after completing 3 months of continuous training solely in this 16-2/3-meter course, succeeded in breaking the world 100-meter backstroke record, which had been set by all-time great Cathy Ferguson when she won the 1964 Olympic title. Other swimmers on the team appeared to derive similar benefit from training in this ultra-short course.

In 1959 Devitt had told that how he had trained for the 100-meter event by marking off on the wall of the pool intermediate distances of 60, 70, 80, and 90 meters and then trying to reduce his time for each of these marks, which enabled him to learn the exact stage of the 100-meter race at which his speed would start to slacken off. In this manner, Devitt trained himself to maintain his initial speed farther and farther into the full 100-meter distance.

Faced with the lack of a suitable training venue and remembering the method explained to me by Devitt several years earlier, we encouraged our swimmers to improve their speed over each of the following intermediate distances on the way to the 100-

meter mark: 16-2/3 meters, 33-1/3 meters, 50 meters, 66-2/3 meters, 83-13 meters. In preparing for the 200-meter event, the distances swum were extended to include 100 meters, 116-2/3 meters, 133-1/3 meters, 150 meters, 166-2/3 meters, and 183-1/3 meters.

This method of training appears to have the following advantages:

1. When swimming 16-2/3-meter sprints a swimmer can achieve the *highest possible rate of speed* while at the same time learning to improve starting time off the block as well as the importance of accurate timing of the first few strokes of a race.
2. By improving speed over smaller increments of the total racing distance the swimmers learn a greater refinement of pace than would be possible in a larger training pool. One reason is that these conditions allow easier detection of the exact stage of the race at which speed starts to deteriorate.
3. The increased number of turns provides extra turning practice, improving the speed of the turn and the muscular strength and power specific to performing it.
4. The method enables the introduction of different breathing patterns into practice routines, with the swimmer using a different pattern on each length of the pool.
5. The method provides a particularly rugged and arduous form of training and is therefore an excellent conditioner when used judiciously. Short sets of repeat swims, such as 4 x 400 meters with 5 to 10 minutes rest, can be done with great benefit 40 to 3 weeks before tapering for a major event.

PERIODISATION OF THE TRAINING PROGRAM

Varying the intensity and duration of the work-outs from day to day and week to week results in a long-term cyclic application of the training program. The days of easy, moderate, and hard work ought not be planned more than one week in advance; even then a coach may decide to change the intensity of a work-out based on the-spot observation of a swimmers reaction to a previous work load. Work-outs are monitored by means of measuring blood lactates in only a few teams, and for most programs, this phase of coaching remains an art instead of a science. When a program is under the direction of an experienced coach, however, it is often remarkable how a well-balanced pattern of easy, moderate, and strenuous sessions will appear consistently over a period of many weeks.

Several researchers, notably Kindermann, Matveyev, Harre, and Berger, have studied the periodisation of the training program. As a result, it is common in Eastern Europe for training preparation to be viewed in the context of three distinct cycles, namely

1. Motorcycle of 1 week duration,
2. Mesocycles of 3 to 7 weeks duration, and
3. Macrocycles, one to four per year up to 4 years.

Spirals and mesocycles

During the 1960s and 1970s several leading programs, mainly in Europe, adopted a new terminology to describe the various phases of seasonal training. For example, Igor Koshkin, coach of the great soviet 1,500-meter world-record holder Vladimir Salnikov, described a typical training years as being divided into five *spirals,* each having a duration of 8 to 12 weeks, and ending with a 1-to 3-week competition period.

Each spiral comprises 2-week development stages called *mesocycles.* Each mesocycle concentrates on developing specific qualities in the swimmer. During the last mesocycle-the preparation for major competition-the aim is to integrate all the specific qualities developed in the four or five preceding mesocycles.

THE SEARCH FOR A SELECTIVE METHOD OF APPLYING THE TRAINING WORK LOAD

The introduction of the interval training method in the 1950s soon showed that the *quality* of the overload stress was the determining factor in producing a desired training effect. What is the proper proportion of quality work? How much is too much and how much is too little? This was the question that continued to puzzle swimming coaches as they sought the ideal balance between quality and quantity in designing training work loads for their athletes.

In the second half of the century, sport doctors in the former East Germany, realizing the importance of determining the stage of the work-out at which the athlete arrives at the lactate\ventilatory threshold, introduced their now famous method of regular blood lactate analysis. Previous to the introduction of blood lactate testing, however, many talented coaches as well as swimmers were able to judge intuitively when the lactate\ventilatory threshold had been reached and to adjust the pace of the work-out according to the training quality they wished to develop.

The East Germans, under the direction of Lothar

Kipke, Alex Mader, and other, developed a very practical method of blood lactate analysis. One method for determining the lactate\ventilatory threshold involves timing evenly paced swims at 200 or 300 meters, some of which are done at an easy pace. The pace is then slightly increased to a moderate intensity just above the lactate\ventilatory threshold. Finally, much faster swims at almost 100% of maximum effort are performed.

As few as two blood lactate concentrations are plotted against the velocities of the test swims, and the lines joining them are extrapolated to cut the 4 mmol/l blood lactate level. The estimated velocity at 4 mmol/l is read off to predict the exercise intensity for each individual swimmer's lactate/ventilatory threshold.

East German coaches regularly used the 10 x 200 anaerobic test on their swimmers. Studying the nature of the lactate velocity curve helped them assess at regular intervals the changing aerobic and anaerobic capacities of individual swimmers throughout the training season. In addition, they were able to determine a swimmer's ability to reach a high lactate level with maximum effort performance. The purpose of the procedure was to test a swimmer's "mobilization capacity," or the highest level of blood lactate the swimmer is able to generate. The East Germans maintained that this scientific approach to training enabled them to make very accurate judgments concerning the training condition of each individual swimmer right through the season, up to and including the final pre-competition tapering-off period.

Should all swimming coaches use lactate testing?

In 1983, Counsilman told me that he believed lactate

testing to have limited applications and that too much depends on where and how lactate measurements are taken. He added that just from normal observation a coach will know the training load better and that it is not a good measure because a swimmer can get the same high lactate level by doing a few strenuous 50s or a moderate 30 x 50 series.

According to Counsilman, a study of pH would, however, show something quite different. He said that the pH factor is important and also that physiological researchers had failed to test many other possibilities. To continually test VO_2 max and all the other popularly tested things is a waste. He cited the need for new approaches that would involve a little creative thinking and cooperation with coaches, saying that in the United States the coach and scientist had not worked together.

Counsilman says that during the spring of 1983 at four swimming clinics he asked over 1,000 coaches whether they had ever used blood lactate measurements to help them evaluate their training programs. Only two people raised their hands. Counsilman says that at Indiana University he took blood lactate measurements off and on since the era of Mike Troy and Chet Jastremski (the mid-1960s). The procedure was expensive because of the necessary equipment, personnel to draw blood, intention to continue to take blood lactates for research purposes but not as a means of evaluating his swimmers' progress, adding that even the East Germans test for blood lactate only with their elite swimmers. According to Counsilman, all these reasons render it unlikely that the method will become common practice.

TAPERING FOR COMPETITION ORIGIN OF THE TAPER

In the early years of competitive swimming swimmers took little if any extra rest prior to a major competition other than retiring earlier on the previous night. It was not uncommon for training, such as it daily practice, often resting 5 minutes after swimming "300 yards easy." Individual swimmers were thought to vary in their ability to swim distances between 1,000 yards to mile and a half. The emphasis in daily practice was on stroke improvement. Training swims were kept to moderate speeds so as not to interfere with maintaining good stroke mechanics and accurate timing.

Swimmers were cautious about training too strenuously because coaches constantly warned them about the danger of over exertion. A common dictum in the day's coaching parlance was "training should be *training* and not straining!"

The tendency was for training intensity to be increased rather than decreased during the 10 days prior to a championship meet. In the 1940s it was common practice to do repeated time trials in one's speciality events as late as 10 days before the meet. Coaches and athletes believed this method would provide ample time to do specialized training for an event, particularly if the swimmer was behind in preparation.

This "specialized training" took the form of having the sprinters swim three fast 100-yard swims with a 20-minute rest between them. The distance swimmers and backstroke and breaststroke swimmers (there was no butterfly stroke then) were advised also to attempt the middle distance schedule but with a 45-

minute rest period instead. In the early 1950s swimmers began to increase the distances covered in training. As the quantity of work increased they found they could swim faster. At this time, the tendency was to swim long, unbroken mileage with "wind sprints"- usually a series of 50s interspersed with rest periods- performed at the end of a work-out to introduce an element of speed.

Some thought that if a lot of mileage gave good results, then more would give even better; of course, this was not always true. What they found was that swimmers often carried considerable residual fatigue over long periods. They saw that they needed an adjustment to the training regimen that would enable swimmers to produce their best performances in important competition.

The introduction of alternation "easy" and "hard" training days was an attempt to permit a measure of adaptation in the midst of strenuous training, but swimmers still did not obtain sufficient rest to perform at their best. Nevertheless, the idea of alternating days of easier and harder work was to lead to experiments with even longer rests.

Basic concept of the taper

Carlile's interest in Selye's concepts of stress combined with his own studies of failing adaptation to stress prompted him to provide his swimmers with far more rest before competition than was previously thought necessary. This period of reduced activity became known as the *taper*. The beneficial effects of tapering on performance became clear to coaches once they learned to taper swimmers skillfully.

During the 1970s and 1980s the tapering process grew more complex for several reasons, one of them being the increased frequency of top international competition. Often, radical changes had to be made to already busy regional and national schedules. Preparing swimmers to compete successfully in series of top-flight competitions became a fine art-and only partially a science. Many swimmers chose to "swim through" (either not taper or use a reduced taper) for some meets and then taper completely to swim at a higher level in others. In addition, many lower-ranked swimmers tapered in mid-season attempting to meet required qualifying times for entries to championship and major meets.

Principle considerations in tapering

Before a major competition swimmers gradually reduce their heavy work load and increase their rest. This period is known as the taper or tapering off. The transition to easier work causes the adaptive processes of the body to overcompensate as the swimmer prepares for maximum effort. The word "taper"-diminishing toward the end-aptly describes the process. Its use in training was coined by Frank Cotton, professor of physiology at University of Sydney, Australia, and his understudy at the time, forbes Carlile, now the dean of Australian swimming coaches.

These two pioneers discovered that for physiological adaptation to occur, arduous training must be tempered with adequate rest. The concept of tapering is based on this realization, and over a period of more than 30 years, it has proved to be one of the most significant contributions to the progress of competitive swimming. Tapering was first described in the literature-and in detail-by Carlile. Not only the concept but also the term was quickly accepted and employed worldwide.

A successful taper results from good judgment and careful planning. The taper should be planned carefully for each individual swimmer. It is rare that a swimmer will taper in exactly the same way every time. Variations in the taper will arise from different factors that have acted on the swimmer during the period preceding an important meet, several of which must be considered on every occasion. Planning an effective taper requires of the coach not only technical skill but also an acute insight into the state of individual swimmers, particularly their reaction to pre-competition anxiety.

The taper should be relevant to the work done in the preceding months. Its duration and the amount of rest it provides should allow complete recovery from accumulated fatigue. The body will then overcompensate in its adaptation to stress, enabling a superior performance.

During the taper, attention should be given to every aspect of preparation-mental as well as physical-including mental attitude, physical conditioning, stroke technique, pace, and strategy. Finally, the effects of rest on adaptation should be understood. Rest is a vital determinant of performance and just as important as an ideal balance between different levels of work intensity.

For young swimmers, the excess energy levels that result from tapering often cause a tendency to indulge in horseplay. The coach should forewarn the team against wild or unruly behaviour—calling it "excessive exuberance"—that could cause injury and the consequent waste of a whole season of preparation.

The entire season should be mapped out in advance and major and minor meets decided. The program design should include the duration and emphasis of each training cycle with adequate time for the final taper.

General guidelines on tapering

What worked last season may not work as well—or at all—this season. Any number changes in conditions can cause this, including alterations in the annual program of competitive events, the available time for work-outs, absenteeism, conditioning emphasis, swimmers' levels of development, temperament, and many other factors. Although a coach may recognize recurring situations, it is wise to be alert for new sets of circumstances likely to influence tapering decisions.

Before identify situations that need special attention in the tapering decisions, it may be helpful to provide a few general guidelines.

1. The shorter race, the longer the taper; conversely, the longer the race, the shorter the taper. Distance swimmers and sprinters need different tapers.
2. The more races to be contested, the shorter the taper.
3. The younger the swimmer, the shorter the taper. Younger swimmers have a higher level of vital energy; moreover, they tend to lose the feel of the water quickly if they taper too soon. Conversely, an

older swimmer may need a longer taper. Swimmers who have competed for many years appear to need a longer taper with each successive season.

4. Nervous athletes need a shorter taper.
5. Large, well-muscled athletes generally need a longer taper.
6. Swimmers with an adequate background of hard work will usually obtain good results if tapered fairly early. Those who have been over-stressed in training will show dramatic adaptation and recovery from accumulative fatigue after a long, well-planned taper.
7. Swimmers who have done only a moderate amount of work through the season often will not show great improvement when tapered because they lack the background training.
8. Seasonal goals should be established at the start of the training program when the coach should identify and outline to the swimmers the type of work and the duration of each training cycle necessary to achieve these goals. Early on, the coach should decide which meets the swimmer will enter and the level of importance to be accorded each competition. More important meets require more complete tapers (major taper). The importance of the meet and the stage of the season will determine whether to use major, minor, or mini tapers.

A meet may be used to check the progress of the team as a whole toward its established goals or to provide opportunities for certain individual members. In particular, the coach may decide to rest a swimmer will who lacks confidence so that the swimmer will be able to record a morale-boosting fast time. It is sometimes necessary for an up-and-coming youngster to record a fast swim to encourage continued dedication to a demanding program of hard work.

9. An ideal psychological "climate" should be nurtured and every effort made to foster a positive team spirit. Physiological and psychological preparation should keep apace of each other throughout the season and into the tapering period, resulting in a well-conditioned athlete with a strong, positive mental attitude.

10. An ideal taper, from the physiological standpoint, is when a swimmer has had just the right amount of rest. Sometimes a swimmer will appear unaffected by the taper and show no improvement in speed. There is not much to do in such a situation except be patient and wait for the taper to take effect.

    It is just as possible to have too much rest as to have too little. Usually, a swimmer who has had too much rest will lack the conditioning to finish a race strongly; conversely, the swimmer who has had too little rest may not have sharp speed initially but may still be able to finish a race strongly. If competing in a 3 to 4 day meet, for example, the under-rested swimmer may improve over the subsequent days as a result of having more rest. The outlook for the over-rested and underworked swimmer will not be as optimistic, however, as there obviously would be insufficient time to become conditioned.

Preparing a basic plan for the taper

A basic plan for the tapering period should be mapped out at the beginning of the season when the number of training days and competitions leading to the major meets first become known. The plan should include an outline of each phase of the season together with the duration of each training cycle, as well as adequate time for the tapering period.

Nearly all coaches will agree that tapering is a complex phase of the season—in fact, the word "complex" seems most readily to spring to mind in any frank discussion of the topic. The challenge, then, is for the coach to ensure clear communication on all the important aspects of the planned taper with individual swimmers and the team as a whole. Team meetings and clearly drawn charts will help explain the tapering plan to swimmers at all levels. Not least of all, the coach should warn the swimmers about overeating and becoming overweight as a result of the reduced energy demands placed on the body. The importance of early bedtimes and adequate sleep should also be stressed.

Super-adaptation

At some stages of the season, many swimmers work so hard that they are unable to approach their best times in training or competition before they taper for the season's most important meets. Counsilman calls this phase of training "the valley of fatigue" and considers it necessary for what he terms super-adaptation. The reasoning behind its use is that when the work load is finally reduced in the taper period, the body's adaptive mechanisms will continue to overcompensate at the same high level even though the unusual stress of the hard training period has suddenly been removed. If the taper is well planned, the result is a superior performance.

THE WARM-UP

The benefits of the warm-up procedure include the following:

1. The resultant increase in body temperature and pulse rate, combined with dilation of blood vessels in the muscles, takes the body from its "resting state" to the physiological level needed for the competitive event.
2. It loosens the muscles and increases flexibility.
3. It familiarizes the swimmer with the pool conditions in which the competition will take place.
4. The swimmer gets into stroke rhythm and feels out the required pace of the race.
5. Muscle fatigue occurs later in the race after adequate warm-up.
6. A muscle that is warmed and stretched prior to maximum exertion is less likely to sustain injury.
7. The warm-up induces a sense of well-being.

During the work-outs of the hard training season, a swimmer should cultivate a feeling for how much swimming is sufficient for warm-up. This will significantly aid a swimmer in tapering and warming up before meets.

In some teams, the amount of swimming needed to warm up in daily training sessions is the amount of swimming used in each session during the taper period. The swimmer does just enough work to be able to swim at pace. This is usually followed by some short, sharp work, a loosen-down swim, and practice in starts and turns.

Warm-up procedures vary according to a swimmer's racing events. Short distance swimmers and sprinters will include some short speed work-mostly 25-meter and 50-meter efforts-whereas distance swimmers will establish their race pace by covering a few 100-meter sections.

The warm-up should last 20 to 45 minutes, and the swimmer should be out of the water at least 20 minutes before the meet starts. A swimmer preparing for morning competition may need more warm-up time to "wake up." In the evenings, before swimming in the finals, a shorter warm-up usually will suffice because of the swimming done earlier in the day.

After warming up, a swimmer should don warm, dry clothing, gloves, socks, and shoes. The swimmer should stand up and become active just before the race starts by walking around and doing mild stretching exercises.

As the season progress, each swimmer should determine his or her best "basic" warm-up. Every competitive session should be preceded by a warm-up and followed by a loosen down; this helps eliminate stiff or sore shoulders, hips, knees, and ankles.

4

TEACHING TECHNIQUES

It is the aim of this chapter to help the teacher develop a good and sound teaching technique. Above all, safety must be the paramount factor, whatever swimming or diving activities are being performed.

ESTABLISHING A GOOD TEACHER/PUPIL RELATIONSHIP

Sometimes this is rather difficult when you remember what little so-and-sos they were during the last lesson, but it is worth trying once more. You can often 'beat the system' by just rising above it. Be firm in your decisions but, on the other hand, don't be too restrictive, as this tends to incite mutinous feelings among the older pupils. Don't down' on your class, look at' them. Keep a sense of humour flowing through the lesson. Remember, swimming is fun: let it be so at all times. With the younger swimmers, the teacher must develop a rapport with the class, always encouraging, coaxing, gently chiding, kindly mocking and generally crating a light and enjoyable atmosphere, ensuring finally that they want to come back again.

TEACHING POSITIONS

It is always necessary for the class to be able to see the teacher (by rolling over in the water or by turning around), and it is always advisable for the teacher to be able to see every member of the class. When giving a demonstration, the teacher must be positioned in such a way that all the pupils are able to see his or her movements and, at the same time, they should be able to hear clearly what is being said.

The position the teacher takes on the poolside when the class is in the water is largely dependent on the size of the class. For instance, with a them, while they are in the water either standing or holding the rail. On the other hand, if the class is large enough to stretch the whole length of the pool, it is best that the teacher stands on the opposite side of the pool. The only disadvantage in taking up this position is that the swimmers must always return to the far side of the pool, away from the teacher, before the next instruction can be successfully given.

Another popular teaching position is at the end of the pool, with the pupils standing, or in the water holding the rail, along the length of the pool. A disadvantage of this position is that the pupils at the end of the pool farthest away from the teacher stand less chance of hearing the instructions. On the other hand, the teacher is able to wander across the end of the pool, back and forth, always being in the position to stop the exercise and deliver the next instruction. This position is ideal for a medium or small class and where there is an unobstructed walkway across the with of the pool.

With beginners in the shallow end, the teacher may stand to the side or at the end of the pool, taking care to stand well back from the edge, in order that the class may be addressed with a minimum of head turning or lifting.

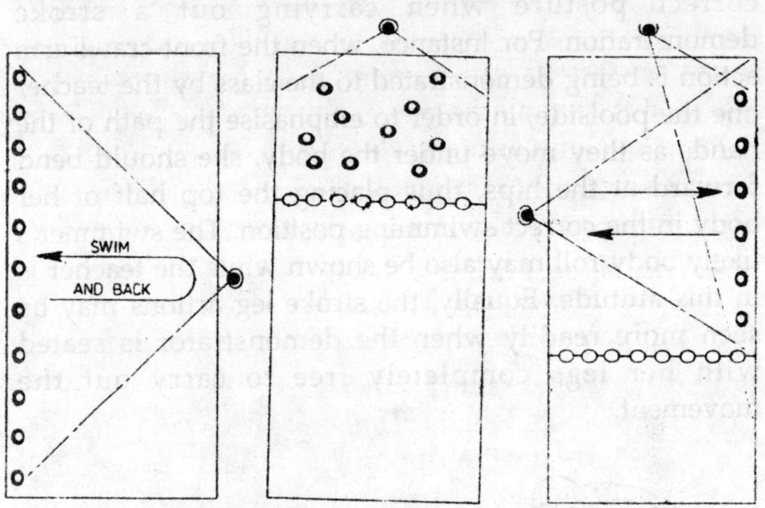

Teaching positions

The teacher should always stand erect when delivering instructions and never squat or kneel or lie down flat! This upright stance gives all the pupils a chance to see and hear what is about to take place. Never turn resist the temptation to talk to the backs of their heads. Often, one sees a teacher sending a class swimming away from where he is standing at the poolside, delivering unheeded instructions to the backs of their heads.

Another bad practice is that of delivering an oration to the class while walking away from them across the end of the pool. This often happens when the teacher is anxious to get on with the exercise in hand.

It is very important for the teacher to assume the

correct posture when carrying out a stroke demonstration. For instance, when the front-crawl arm action is being demonstrated to the class by the teacher one the poolside, in order to emphasise the path of the hands as they move under the body, she should bend forward at the hips, thus placing the top half of her body in the correct swimming position. The swimmer's likely body roll may also be shown while the teacher is in this attitude. Equally, the stroke leg actions may be seen more readily when the demonstrator is seated with her legs completely free to carry out the movement.

Demonstration positions

Generally speaking, the teacher must choose a teaching position according to the size of the pool the size of the class and the particular topic being taught. Experience will show where and how to stand and how to deliver instructions to the best advantage.

Finally, when addressing a class, talk to the whole class and not to a small group or individual, except, of course, if someone is misbehaving. Try not to show favouritism, and avoid sacrificing the whole of the class for the sake of a few. Each pupil or group of pupils must constantly be kept constructively and gainfully occupied.

DELIVERING THE INSTRUCTIONS

When addressing a class of swimmers, the teacher should speak slowly and clearly, using words and phrases suited to the standard of the children.

The amount of instruction given at one single time should be limited. It is absolutely useless to issue a class with a multitude of teaching points all in one breath, like: 'Put your hands in the water in front of your nose, fingers together, hands flat, then pull down in the water, underneath your body and, at the same time, bring your other arm out and over the water, elbow high and hand low,' etc. Could you take this in yourself at one go and think about each individual point during the ensuing swim? Keep each individual instruction short and simple.

It is important to avoid issuing instructions in a negative way, saying 'Do not do this' and 'Do not do that.' By giving positive instructions, you are suggesting to the pupils only one way-the right way.

VISUAL AND SPOKEN ACCURACY

One of my golden rules of the teaching of swimming is: 'Be visually and orally correct'. Children are the best imitators in the world and, if a particular demonstration is incorrect, so will be their performance. If you are in doubt as to the visual correctness, stand in front of a mirror and practise the motions until you are sure that you have it right. Enlist the aid of a colleague in order to check, if you're still unsure.

Probably the prime examples of incorrect movement are to be found in the front-and back-crawl arm actions. One often sees the teacher demonstrating the elbow' recovery of front crawl, waving his hands high in the air, then wondering why the class are also waving their hands higher than their elbows on the recovery. Similarly, when demonstrating the recovery movement of the back crawl, best performed with the arms is a straight and vertical mode, quite a high percentage of teachers seem to carry out the action with anything but a straight arm. Needless to say, the children copy the movements beautifully.

As a teacher of swimming, become knowledgeable about swimming and all its associations, and always sound authoritative. At all times be in complete control of your voice in order that you may say what you mean and mean what you say.

Frequently, throw a little humour into your teachings; this helps to build up a good working relationship with the class.

Be enthusiastic and try to inject some form of competition into the lesson: children are great competitors.

Talk to the whole class as a group, look at them all in turn while you are talking to them. Make each individual feel as though he or she is an integral part of the class.

Use your sense of imagination in your instructing. For instance, back-crawl leg kicking may be likened to the class swimming like little boats with propellers churning merrily away at the back ends. Children are also great ones at the imagination game, as we all nostalgically recall.

Never be hesitant in encouraging any individual in the class. But contrast, never encourage individuals who are successful in their endeavours to the detriment of those who try very had, but just cannot make the grade. Conversely, if there is a group of keen and enthusiastic swimmers, be sure to set them a full programme of work to keep them busy and involved. Never neglect those who can for those who cannot. Remember, encouragement for trying is as important as encouragement for getting it right.

THE SYLLABUS

For every educational course of swimming instruction, there should be a planned syllabus of activities.

The programme itself may be defined by the local education authority, or alternatively it may be left to the teacher to establish a suitable plan of campaign.

The ultimate aim of any syllabus must be to promote the art of swimming and to foster all its many associated skills. Throughout the syllabus, the water-safety feature must predominate, but, as secondary features, the demanding skills of watermanship, competition swimming, diving, life-saving, personal survival, synchro and waterpolo are all important aquatic activities which may be included. The teacher must therefore be equipped with adequate knowledge to deal with most, if not all, of these.

THE VALUE OF GAMES

All children love playing games. So if each little activity is treated as a game, an exercise which in the cold light of day is a chore becomes quite pleasurable. A fine example of this is a game of 'tag' or 'touch'. Walking through the water in order to catch his or her 'victim', the prospective swimmer unwittingly develops a feel for the water and how it affects movement. The 'victim' also learns to walk forward or sideways during the pursuit and, when contact has been made, both participants need to turn around in the water in order to reverse the situation and continue the fun. What a fine way to establish mobility and the feeling of balance and control. There are many other games to be played, some with apparatus such as a ball, a piece of rope or a hoop. They may be graded according to the age ad ability of the swimmers and should always be supervised. A list of suitable water games is given on page 89.

WHAT TO TEACH FIRST AND WHEN TO TEACH IT

Opinions vary widely as to which aquatic-based activity should be taught first. Perhaps we should first acknowledge the fact that when we plunge into water, we enter an alien environment. Therefore our first concern must be to teach people to survive in the water.

Just being able to swim a basic stroke is not really enough to make one safe in the water. For instance, consider someone who has been taught how to perform a version of breast stroke (or any other stroke) during their first lesson. Nothing else, just that!

How can they start off? A push and glide would help, but they haven't been through the rituals! How do they stop? They probably can't regain their feet. What happens if they wander accidentally or, through a false sense of security, into deep water and are then forced to stop? They probably can't trend water in order to remain stationary. If someone swam across their path or got in their way, how could they manoeuvre their way around them, if they've never been taught to swim other than in a straight line?

So perhaps there is a little more to swimming than merely being able to swim, and perhaps we should give consideration to some of the basic watermanship activities before attempting to teach the more formal styles.

This does not mean that any basic stroke teaching should be entirely neglected until all are able to push and glide or twist and turn. Indeed, if any stroke-related limb movements or combinations of movements can be practised in pursuit of some other activity, this can only enhance the teaching. For instance, our little swimmers playing shallow-end 'tag' would probably find that an alternate arm-padding action (not unlike a front-crawl movement) assisted them in their endeavours to catch one another.

THE PLANNED LESSON

Each individual lesson should have a definite objective and a carefully planned progression of activities by which this objective can be achieved. The activities must be practised in their correct sequence, for attempting to perform activities for which the swimmers are not ready may result in everyone just going round in circles and getting nowhere.

So, before taking a lesson, we must ensure that we have a definite plan in mind, and to formulate this plan the following facts must be ascertained:

1. The number of pupils in the class.

2. The ages of the pupils.
3. Whether it is a mixed group of boys and girls who may need segregating: teenage boys and girls sometimes lose concentration when they are mixed.
4. Their watermanship abilities: there may be a need for an assessment and grading session.
5. The pool requirements, availability of facilities and water temperature.
6. What equipment is available, such as robes, armbands, floats, diving blocks, submersed rings for survival practices, etc.

Now to the lesson itself. The individual practices should not be beyond the swimming abilities of the children, but, at the same time, they should become progressively more difficult so that the pupils are always slightly stretched. As previously mentioned, for new classes a grading session will probably be necessary.

As has already been stated, each individual lesson plan should form an integral part of an overall educational teaching syllabus containing a series of definite objectives. Each objective should be directed towards improving the children's watermanship and their swimming skills.

THE BASIC LESSON PLAN

The lesson may itself be divided into several parts, each part fulfilling a purpose. The basic constituents are outlined and, after a very brief poolside description of what is about to take place, the following format may be adopted.

1. *Introductory activity:* This brief and controlled activity is introduced mainly as a warm-up to the lesson. It allows the pupils to 'get themselves wet' and can set the tone of the ensuing lesson. The teacher may decide on a specific theme for this initial burst, or elect to give the pupils freedom of choice.

2. Recapitulation of the previous lesson (if it is related to the current one) A quick recap on the main theme or objective of the preceding session will serve as a useful link between the two.

3. Main activity (based on the main theme or objective of the lesson) This is the major feature of the whole programme and should be allocated the maximum amount of time. This particular feature may not be quite so evident during the initial lessons for beginners. The associated practices should be progressively phased and accompanied by the relevant teaching points. (See the various chapters on teaching the strokes.) The teacher should be aware of any faults which may occur during the practices and be able to apply the necessary corrective measures. Faults and their correction are to be found at the end of the chapters relating to the various skills.

4. *Contrasting activity:* In order to give the pupils a break from intensive learning, a short activity may be introduced into the lesson which, while being a complete contrast to the major theme of the lesson, bears some relationship (however slight) to the practices that have been performed.

5. *Supervised free time:* The lesson should end with a

short free period in which the pupils can 'do their own thing'. This part of the lesson should be supervised, because, when they are released from the restrictions of the compulsory part of the lesson, children sometimes become a little wild. Strict control is necessary, therefore, in order that any dangerous activities may be curtailed.

Times should be allocated to each part of the programme according to the importance of each activity, although circumstances may often cause the teacher to adjust the length of each period.

TEACHING THE SKILLS

For the purpose of teaching, the elements of each basic swimming skill may be categorised in the following manner:

1. *The complete skill* — Front crawl
2. *The associated activities*
   These are the component skills or part-practices which may be performed individually and, when combined, form the total skill. — Legs only
3. *The teaching practices*
   These are the various methods of practising the activity. They are usually progressive in terms of difficulty and are designed to establish the basic stroke movements or combinations of movements.
   (i) With two floats
   (ii) With one float

(iii) Unassisted

4. *The teaching points*
   Each teaching practice should be accompanied by a set of definite instructions as to how the various movements are to be performed.
   (i) Kicking movement originates at the hip
   (ii) Loose ankles

By sub-dividing each skill in this fashion, the teacher should be able to plan a lesson constructively. The activities, together with their attendant teaching practices, may be used during fault analysis and correction sessions and also during periods of training.

THE TEACHING SYSTEM

When learning a new aquatic skill, pupils will benefit greatly from watching it being performed. If the main theme of the lesson is the teaching of some new skill, it is advantageous to commence the activities with a visual demonstration of that particular skill, whilst describing it verbally.

The class may then be invited to attempt the skill themselves, and the resulting performance should enable the teacher to assess precisely what kind of task he or she is faced with.

Following the initial whole-skill performance, the programme of individual part-practices should be carried out. These may be itemised as follows:

1. Leg-kicking practices
2. Arm-stroke practices
3. Breathing practices
4. Timing, rhythm and stroke co-ordination practices
5. Variations of the whole stroke

6. Return to part-practices for fault correction whenever necessary

The teaching therefore follows a whole/part/whole pattern, repetition of the various skills and part-skills being necessary throughout.

WHICH STROKE FIRST?

The pupils having attempted the two basic mobility strokes, namely front and back paddle, the teacher must now decide which particular style should be taught as the next major activity in the syllabus.

Probably the paramount stroke feature which dictates progress in the watermanship skills is the act of breathing. After all, if a swimmer cannot breathe adequately in proportion to the energy being used, he or she cannot possibly proceed very far without becoming very quickly exhausted.

Many traditionalists choose breast stroke as the starting stroke (even before the two basic mobility strokes) because it may be performed in a leisurely fashion with the head held high and face clear of the water. Consequently, providing conditions are favourable, a swimmer is able to breathe quite easily regardless of the overall stroke timing. Similarly, a swimmer may perform the back crawl stroke with the face clear of the water and again breathing presents no problem. Timing the breath is of no real consequence during the very early teachings.

Proceeding to front crawl, we encounter a problem. In order to perform the stroke correctly in its flat and horizontal mode, the swimmer's face must be placed into the water and some breathing discipline becomes necessary.

The butterfly stroke, with its particular breathing technique, is usually attempted after one or more of the previously mentioned skills have been accomplished.

Let us examine a few of the other factors that should be taken into account if the teacher adopts the 'easy breathing' approach. First, consider the breast-stroke leg action. What an odd combination of movements this is! To the learner, there is nothing natural about the limb tracks whatsoever. Good breast strokers are rare: it may be that good breast strokers are born rather than made and that they achieve the required symmetry of kick through natural ability. There is a school of thought which suggests that if the breast-stroke leg kick is taught as a first water movement, the swimmer stands much less chance of developing the 'dreaded screw kick'. This is very difficult to prove or disprove.

If we condemn the leg actions of front and back crawl as begin detrimental to a good breast-stroke kicking movement, we must also take into account the fact that the natural walking action itself is very similar to the alternating and vertical movements of the crawls. This being so, most swimmers will have articulated their joints in this natural walking fashion, many times before they even enter the swimming pool. Consequently, if the movement were really detrimental, the number of good breast strokers would be much less than at present. Considering these arguments, perhaps breast stroke is not after all such a good 'starter' as it has been made out to be.

The back crawl also has its problems as a starting stroke, despite the 'natural' leg kick and face-up attributes which are considered to be advantageous. The vertically biased arm-recovery action tends to sink the less adept swimmer, and a large majority of learners feel insecure lying on their backs in the water. The teacher therefore must also have reservations about back crawl being the first stroke.

There remains what might be described as a 'democratic alternative'. This is to allow the swimmers to try out three, or even four, different strokes successively and to let them make their own particular choice regarding which style (or styles) sits them best. The amount of instruction during such an exercise may be quite minimal. This popular method of teaching is known as 'multi-stroke' and is generally considered to be highly successful. Of course, it does not in any way absolve the teacher from teaching the related stroke progressions, but it does provide opportunities to divide the classes (and the pool) into sections, whereby differing styles may be simultaneously practised. As stated above, basic watermanship exercises up to and including the front and back paddles will already have been attempted, and these two skills readily adapt themselves to the front and back crawl strokes respectively.

It should be stressed, however, that the four competition strokes, i.e. the front and back crawls, butterfly and breast strokes, should not be regarded as the ultimate in stroke teaching. There are other styles that should be included in the syllabus, such as the various forms of back and side strokes. These movements may be practised in connection with life-saving and survival, or performed simply for pleasure.

Swimming is one of the most pleasurable and

beneficial activities that exists and it is for this reason that the ancillary strokes should form an integral part of the overall programme.

ANALYSING THE STROKES

It is rare for a skill to be performed reasonably correctly by the whole class during their first attempt. Aquatic techniques are very exacting and demand considerable practice and concentration. It is an essential part of teaching therefore to be able to identify stroke faults, analyse their causes, and apply the necessary remedies. Technique can be analysed according to the following guidelines:

First impressions

Does the stroke look right? Is the movement disjointed and uncoordinated? The swimmer may seem to be working extremely hard and getting precisely nowhere. The effect may be picturesquely described as 'having no feel' for the water.

On the other hand, there are the gifted ones who make it all look so very simple and, apparently without effort, glide through the water with ease and grace. These performers seem to be in complete harmony with the water, caressing rather than fighting it. But, should the former situation prevail, as is more than likely, we must learn to examine each of the various stroke features in order to discover precisely what is wrong.

Body position

The swimmer should lie as flat and horizontal in the water as the stroke technique will permit. His position should be observed first from the side, and then from the front, from behind and also from above. Only then do you gain a total appreciation of the swimmer's basic body position. Of course, a swimmer may vary his body position slightly during the stroke cycle in accordance with the style being swum. (The undulating effect in the butterfly movement is a good example.) His faults may be related to a characteristic of the stroke.

Leg action

Each stroke displays a different pattern of leg movement. The observer must decide whether the particular action is propelling, stabilising or elevating. Or does the leg movement contribute a proportion of each characteristic towards the overall effect? Are the various contributions sufficient?

If the stroke is of the simultaneous and symmetrical variety, is the movement being performed correctly and within the requirements of the stroke law?

If there is a definite recovery and propulsive phase, is the recovery movement being carried out with a minimum effect on propulsion? Remember that the recovery movements of both arms and legs contribute nothing towards propelling the swimmer forwards.

Any incorrect movement may affect the swimmer's basic body position in the water.

Arm action

In most swimming strokes, the arm movements provide the major contribution towards propulsion. Each complete arm cycle may be divided into two basic phases, recovery and propulsion. Recovery must be performed economically in terms of energy dissipation and with a minimum effect on propulsion. As soon as a limb has finished its propulsive phase, its profile should be minimised. Alternatively, it may be removed from the water so as not to create unnecessary resistance. If the recovery is over the water, the inertia effect of the swinging arms should not disturb the swimmer's natural body alignment causing him to zig-zag.

Are the arms being lifted completely clear of the water during their forward movements?

Are the hands entering the water in the correct position or are they too wide or too near to the face? Is there a 'cross-over' taking place?

Is the swimmer over-reaching and contributing in this way towards distorting the body alignment? As the result of an excessively fast, over-the-surface recovery, does each hand crash into the water setting up unnecessary turbulence? This is not conducive to propulsion.

Is the propulsive phase being carried out efficiently? Are the swimmer's fingers together or almost together? Are the hands flat or cupped? Is the propulsive pressure being directed backwards or is there too much sideways tendency? Is the propulsive phase too short or do the hands tend to 'feather'? It must be remembered that for the best results in stroke efficiency, the thrust which is generated by the arm movement must be projected directly backwards for as long as possible during the propulsive phase.

Breathing

Breathing out into the water is not a natural function, but is sometimes necessary. Lifting the head to breathe when it should be turned, or vice versa, can cause streamlining problems to the swimmer. (It usually results in sinking of the legs.) If there are obvious breathing difficulties, the method, type and rate of respiration should be investigated.

Is the swimmer using the best method of respiration for the stroke being performed? Sometimes it is best to exhale simultaneously through both mouth and nose into the water explosively. Sometimes a slower ejection is required, perhaps through the nose only, in a trickle fashion. Beginners sometimes find it easier to breathe out through their mouths, but there may be a problem of water entering the nostrils. A good point to remember here is that, if air is flowing down the nose, water cannot be flowing up it!

Is the type of breathing appropriate? There are many kinds of stroke-related breathing:

Unilateral	—	breathing to one side only
Bilateral	—	breathing on alternate sides
Regular	—	a constant respiratory rhythm
Irregular	—	unevenly spaced intakes of breath
Frequent	—	once every one or two stroke cycles
Infrequent	—	the breath is held for periods
variations in timing	—	breathing either early or late in the stroke cycle

Each individual type or combination has its own particular merits. For instance, a swimmer who is fresh and swimming front crawl with a rapid cycling rate does not necessarily need to take a breath at every stroke. At the start of the swim, the type of breathing that would most probably be used would be infrequent and explosive. He may breathe to one side only on the first lap in a unilateral fashion. On the second lap, he may wish to view the opposition in adjacent lanes, so he breathes bilaterally in order to have a quick glance to both sides. Towards the end of the swim, he is requiring more oxygen to cope with the sustained effort and therefore requires to breathe more often. The pattern then becomes more frequent and regular, but he is still probably using the explosive method.

During a training swim, breathing will probably be regular and in trickle fashion.

Breath-holding, owing to a fear of breathing out into the water, should not be confused with any of the above types. It is very common amongst beginners and can easily be identified by severe breathlessness, the occasional blue face and popping eyes!

Co-ordination

in very swimming style, the arm, leg and breathing movements should be in complete harmony with each other. The swimmer's stability, balance and propulsion in the water depend on the co-ordination and synchronisation of the arm and leg movements.

Similarly if air is taken in at the wrong time, the timing and rhythm of the stroke may well be affected, giving it a jerky and less aesthetic appearance.

These are the basic stroke features and each should be examined carefully when forming an opinion of an individual's performance. It is worth remembering also that we are all built differently, both physically and mentally. Therefore, something which occurs when a particular swimmer carries out a certain action may not necessarily happen when someone else performs an identical movement. Be prepared to judge each stroke performance on its own individual merits in order to make the final analysis.

STROKE CORRECTION

At the end of each chapter relating to specific strokes, competition and otherwise, will be found a comprehensive section on faults and analysis relating to that particular style.

Individual stroke faults can often be difficult and sometimes even impossible to correct. A case in point is the 'dreaded screw kick' among aspiring breast-stroke swimmers. Patience, perseverance and concentration on the part of both swimmer and teacher, are needed to overcome this problem. More often than not, if the screw has developed, it stays for good. A swimmer who swims or trains regularly, can repeat a recently developed stroke fault many thousand times in a very short period so that it becomes deeply integrated into the overall movement and hence extremely difficult to correct. This problem shows the importance of correct initial teaching, together with the ability to recognise quickly the many and various stroke faults and understand their causes.

One tried and tested method of remedying faults is 'over-correction'. For example, a swimmer doing front crawl and entering his hand into the water too near to his face is instructed incorrectly to over-reach. He then attempts to stretch his arm further forward at the end of each recovery movement. He feels he is over-reaching but in reality he is probably entering his hand somewhere near the correct point.

Many other faults, such as excessive rolling, head lifting and recovery defects, may be corrected in the same way.

Fault correction is important and requires an extensive knowledge of the behaviour of the human body in the water. The teacher should attempt to gain experience in this field whenever possible.

GROUPING THE CLASS

Unless they have been specially pre-selected, a class of swimmers will usually exhibit a fairly wide range of aquatic capabilities The teacher may choose to subdivide the class into manageable groups to do ability-related tasks in order that each swimmer's interest and enthusiasm can be maintained. Boredom during a lesson usually leads to distraction and disorder. The number of groups will depend on the range of ability and the number of pupils in the class.

There are various methods of employing the group system. For instance, at the commencement of a lesson, it may be advantageous to teach the class as a whole before resorting to group teaching. Alternatively, if the class has been working in groups it may sometimes be desirable to bring them together in order to point out and correct some common underlying fault.

Group teaching may also be employed at particular stages during the planned lesson. For instance, during the 'contrasting activity' period, several variations on the life-saving or survival themes may be practised simultaneously in group form.

Should unqualified buy knowledgeable help be available during the swimming lesson, such assistance may be quite usefully employed in group work. The assistant should, with the help of some verbal and/or written instruction, be able to manage a group of swimmers and keep them occupied during the lesson. The teacher, of course, should always be in complete control of such an arrangement and frequent visits to such organised groups around the pool should be made during the lesson. It must be realised that an unqualified assistant will often the unprepared for an emergency situation calling for rescue or resuscitation.

Group work has many advantages, a few of which are summarised as follows:

1. A class of varying abilities may be taught more effectively.
2. With good planning the whole class may be kept fully occupied and interested for the entire lesson.
3. Progress of the more capable swimmers is not inhibited by the less skilful performers
4. Special and personal attention may be directed when and where it is most needed.
5. No individual need be neglected.
6. By relating individual capabilities to the depth of the pool, a certain degree of safety may be ensured.
7. Many differing aquatic skills may be practised during one single period.
8. When suitable poolside assistance is available, it may be utilised effectively.
9. Upgrading (and downgrading) may be carried out by simple transferring swimmers from group to group, and, of course, changes of practice may also take place by the transfer method.

10. Smaller groups of swimmers present fewer problems to the teacher where instruction is concerned.

Partner assistance

It is sometimes helpful and always enjoyable for children if they share their water work with a friend or partner. In the shallow end of the pool one partner supports the head, shoulders or feet of the other. It is often a useful activity whether both physical and moral support are necessary initially to establish some kind of swimming movement.

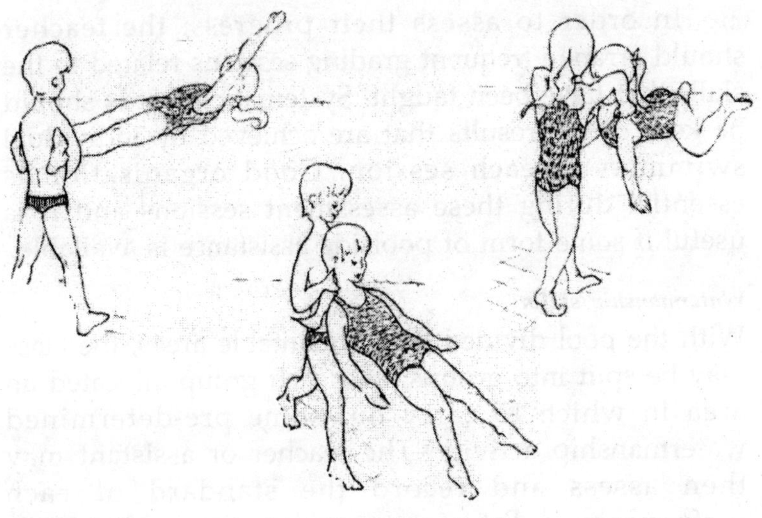

Partner assistance

The carrier can learn from watching the performer, but the main disadvantage of the system is that when one member of a partnership is working, the other is resting and hence effective lesson time is halved. There is also the problem of the resting pattern getting cold.

The teacher must, from personal experience assess the value of partner assistance by taking into account class standards and current environmental conditions. However, if partner work i to be introduced into a lesson, it is advisable to restrict it to short period sin order to avoid inactivity and boredom.

The grading session

Children are quick learners and, especially if they attend the swimming pool in their own time as a recreational activity, their watermanship abilities will soon manifest themselves.

In order to assess their progress, the teacher should arrange frequent grading sessions related to the skills that have been taught. Systematic records should be kept of the results that are achieved by individual swimmers at each session. Good organisation is essential during these assessment sessions and it is useful if some form of poolside assistance is available.

Watermanship skills

With the pool divided up into suitable areas, the class may be split into groups, and each group allocated an area in which to carry out some pre-determined watermanship activity. The teacher or assistant may then assess and record the standard of each performance. A list of suggested watermanship skills follows.

(i) The push and glide on both front and back on the surface and submerged, then with variations such as to the bottom and up, standing on hands or somersaulting from the push.

(ii) Treading water, with the without clothes, and also with arms or legs immobilised.

(iii) Directional movement ability, i.e. forwards/ backwards/sideways.

(iv) The surface dives, head first/feet first.

(v) Recovery of a submerged object.

(vi) Swimming through or under submerged objects.

(vii) Floating in various ways, i.e. on the back, the front and a mushroom float.

(viii) Sculling—support and propulsive, head-first and feet-first.

(ix) Stroke transition, i.e. from front to back crawl then rolling over on to breast stroke, smooth and elegant transition being the aim.

(x) Somersaults on the surface and submerged.

An appropriate watermanship, survival or distance award may be taken at this stage.

Competition skills

These are related to the strokes, their starts and turns. For the starts and turns, the teacher will find it advantageous to work across the width of the pool, so that several skills may be assessed during a short swim. The swimming skills may be assessed under two headings: style and efficiency. Body position, leg movement, arm action, rhythm, timing and turning all come under the scrutiny of the assessor of style, who must be knowledgeable. Time/distance or distance/ time systems of measurement are used to assess efficiency.

The time/distance test simple involves timing the swimmers with a stop-watch over a set distance, the distance to be swum varying according to the ability of the pupils. Any of the four competition strokes may be used, and the time taken to swim the stipulated distance will reveal the efficiency of an individual's stroke.

The distance/time assessment, while also testing stroke efficiency, is at the same time a test of fitness and endurance, for the swimmer has to cover as much distance as possible in a given time.

Once more, the teacher will stipulate the stroke or strokes to be performed and also the manner in which they are to be carried out, i.e. one stroke or two different strokes, each for a set time, and whether the swimmers are to be clothed or unclothed. Division of the pool may be made according to the number of group variations. The swimmers may use the 'elongated circuit', moving down one side of a lane and returning the other side.

Life-saving and survival skills

The skills in this category, some of which may have been assessed during the watermanship tests, are as follows:

Life-saving skills

1. Back stroke (life-saving style)
2. Side stroke
3. The two styles of surface dives
4. Towing in the three approved methods
5. Support at the rail
6. Assisted exits from the water
7. In-the-water and bathside resuscitation
8. Questions on water safety in general

Survival skills

1. The two styles of surface dives
2. Treading water (with various limbs immobilised)
3. Swimming while clothed
4. Removing clothing while treading water
5. Using clothing to assist flotation both on and off the body

This, then, is an outline of the grading session content. It must be understood by the teacher that the emphasis during such a session will be on assessment rather than instruction. These sessions should take place at least once a term and it is essential for records relating to each swimmer's ability at each grading to be conscientiously maintained.

5

PRESEASON PLANNING

COACHING OBJECTIVES FOR THE PRE-SEASON

The necessary pre-season coaching tasks include the following:

— Acquiring information pertinent to your coaching situation.

— Developing seasonal goals appropriate for your team.

— Formulating specific goals for each part of your team's season.

— Establishing a policy for awards.

— Determining the authority that should be delegated.

— Selecting the necessary equipment.

SURVEYING THE SITUATION

Organizing your season is the first step to success. In order to plan,. You must have the answers to six questions that will determine the most appropriate training program for your athletes.

1. *What is the background of the potential swimmers?*

   To answer this question, talk to people who have previously been associated with the program. What will be the swimmers' ages? With what programs have they been associated? In what other sports or team situations have they participate? A wide diversity in age and experience may prompt you to divide your work-out time so that swimmers practice with others of similar backgrounds and ability levels.

2. *How much pool time is available?*

   The amount of available determine your team's goals. Expecting to win a state high school championship is unrealistic if your swimmers are only in the pool for 45 minutes a day, 5 day a week. However, you may be able to have a successful season by joining a league with other schools in the same situation. These decisions must be made before the season begins.

3. *How many swimmers will be training per lane?*

   Determine the approximate numbers through a sign up procedure or by checking previous attendance records. Divide the number of swimmers by the number of lanes in your of swimmers per lane. The number of swimmers per lane will influence the types of things you can do, the maximum lengths of continuous swimming, and whether you will need more than one practice session each day to accommodate all swimmers.

4. *What governing body determines the rules and regulations?*

   Does your team belong to a league? If so, are pre-season meetings held for the coaches? Is there a written set of rules? What are your team's responsibilities as a league member, and what are the benefits of league membership?

5. *What are the dates of the biggest meets?*
   Early information about the season's major meets tells you are working toward and the pace you will need to maintain. When you know the date of the biggest meet or championship, you can designate the 2 weeks before this date for meet preparation. This period of preparation is called the taper. Of the remaining time prior to the championship meet, allocate 30 % for early season training, 35% for mid-season work, and 35% for late season begins. Keep the championship meet at the end of your dual meet season with no other meets after this culminating event.

6. *In what events will your swimmers be participating?*
   You must know the events for which your swimmers are training. In some summer leagues, the dominant events are 25-and 50-yard events. In high school, 100-yard and 200-yard events are common. Your training program will be in the dictated by the distances to be swum in competition. For example, if most competition will be in the shorter events, more work should be done on sprinting.

The preceding six questions should be answered before opening your season and, in fact, even you accept a coaching position. If adjustments must be made in the above areas, the pre-season is the time to determine exactly what needs to be done.

DEVELOPING LONG-TERM GOALS

The next step is address the decisions that will establish the team's direction for the season. Goals will vary with each individual coach and situation, but realistic set of team goals that encompasses more than winning meets is an important base for any team and coach. By considering possible goals, potential coaches should be able to decide upon goals that match their coaching situations and swimmer's personalities.

The following general goals should be evident to parents and participants:

— To offer healthy activity.

— To develop mental and physical discipline.

— To provide opportunity for social adjustment and exposure.

— To recognize accomplishment.

— To offer a constructive use of leisure time.

— To develop talent.

— To provide fun.

Shortly after starting the very successful David Douglas Swim Team, Don Jacklin stated his goals in Swimming World as the following:

1. To encourage youngsters of all abilities to compete in the program, allowing each individual to develop to his or her full potential.
2. To encourage individual goal-setting.
3. To spend as much time as possible on a one to one basis with each youngster on goal-setting, values, future plans in life, and anything else they want to discuss emphasizing the whole person.

The above goals are very broad. Nevertheless, they can be developed specifically by teaching children how to race, including race strategy and pace. Through consistent effort to improve their own performance, your swimmers will begin to develop competitiveness and mental toughness-the ability to perform well under stress.

The goal of proper stroke technique must also be considered because this lead to improved times, increased self-discipline, and greater self-esteem.

Take time during the pre-season to develop your personal goals for your team. Well developed goals and priorities enable you to give logical answers to parents' and swimmers questions about your program. Refer to your goals later in the season when you have decisions to make. This policy will develop fairness and consistency within your program.

DEVELOPING SHORT-TERM GOALS

Your next step in planning is to develop short-term goals for each part of the season. You have designated dates on your calendar to mark the beginning and ending of the early season, mid-season, late season, and taper. Now consider what must be accomplished during each designated time period.

Early season

The first third of your swimming season should stress learning the proper mechanics, and developing strength, endurance, and flexibility. These are the essential components needed to improve in swimming. Additionally, you should introduce swimmers to the equipment they will use, to the terminology specific to swimming, and help them to set meaningful goals that they can accomplish.

Teaching proper stroke techniques

When you consider the shortness of each recreational swimming season and recreational practice sessions, conditioning cannot be as major a factor in a recreational program, as it is in a year round program. Therefore, the single factor that will most improve a recreational swimmer's time is improved technique. Only when swimmers can "hold their strokes" should they attempt distance work. Meanwhile, you may use kicking series with boards to improve your swimmers' endurance.

Improving strength, endurance, and flexibility

The results of a dryland exercise program will not be obvious for 6 weeks after you begin the program with your swimmers. It will, however, improve your swimmer's speed and give you something to do on cold, rainy early-season mornings or when the pool is unavailable. It will also establish the fact that practice will always be held and eliminate phone calls on question able days. Because the dryland exercise program is the one time your swimmers are working with their heads out the water, it is also an excellent time for communication. Therefore, besides building strength, endurance, and flexibility, you can use this opportunity to establish swimmers' personal goals, share their interests, and generally enjoy being with them.

Introducing swimmers to training equipment

How to read a pace clock, how to swim in circles, and how to use training aids such as flutter boards and goggles are essential skills to be learned by all team members.

Presenting a swimming vocabulary

For ease of communication and understanding. All of your swimmers should comprehend two new vocabularies. One includes the terms you will use to correct your swimmers' movements and describe certain stroke adjustments; the second includes universally recognized terms such as those in the glossary at the end of this manual. These terms will help your swimmers to understand what is happening at meets and to communicate with other swimming enthusiasts.

Helping your swimmers to set appropriate, meaningful goals

You can best help your swimmers to set appropriate goals by communicating your own goals with statements such as "I saw lots of crawl flip turns in practice today. I hope tomorrow everyone will try them at every opportunity."

Mid-season

The next third of your season, the mid-season, is the time to increase the workload of your swimmers so they develop the capacity to compete vigorously. Included in this process is perfecting the armstroke, breathing, kicking and turning techniques for each racing stroke. Also, because your swimmers will begin competitions you will need foster a team spirit and camaraderie among your swimmers.

Increasing your swimmers' endurance

The distances swum in the early season should be gradually increased by 50%. This goal is not easily accomplished because while you increase the distance you must continue to demand proper stroke techniques and, most importantly, keep the practices fun and interesting.

Perfecting turning techniques

Demand that your swimmers make proper turns at every wall. At this point parents often complain, "You never practice turns anymore, and my child needs this practice." Group endurance will suffer if you stop to have your entire team drill turns. You've just spent the early season, which is 30% of the total season, teaching proper techniques. The answer to this dilemma is obvious when you consider that a team of swimmers over 10 years age is probably swimming 3,000 yards a day. That distance represents 120 lengths of a 25-yard pool, a minimum of 100 turns a day. If you insist that each turn be done well and work individually with swimmers who cannot yet do them correctly, your team will make good turns and develop the reputation of being a "Well- coached" team.

Improving racing techniques

Many of your competitions will be held during the mid-season, so end each practice session with some swims of 25 yards or less, starting with a dive and ending with a turn. Vary this with one length relays or swim widths.

Developing team spirit

Team spirit develops when a coach cares about the team members and the team members care about each other and the coach. This feeling will begin during the early season, but conscious effort and pre-season planning will be needed if the spirit is to continue through the busy mid-season. When you announce your meet schedule, announce a team function to be held during the mid-season. The details can be attended to later by team members, but if the date is not announced well in advance, some members of the team will be unable to attend. Also plan ahead for inexpensive items that will give your team identity. Pins or balloons with team slogans are inexpensive but must be ordered in advance. A company or chamber of commerce that gives away items for their own advertising might be willing to provide items appropriate for your team at little or no cost.

Late season

The next third of your season, the late season, you should help your swimmers develop a sense of pace during races and help them cope with the stress of a long season that ends with championship races.

Helping swimmers gain a sense of pace

Goal-oriented long swims divided into shorter, linked intervals or broken swims and repetition training involving hard efforts at near top speed with long rest intervals are two ways to develop your swimmers' sense of pace and increase their mental toughness.

Encouraging swimmers to handle stress

The increased emphasis in practice on performing certain times puts your swimmers under stress in an environment where you, the coach, can provide guidance on stress management. Self-acceptance by the swimmers when they cannot perform should be emphasized as strongly as the determination to improve.

Taper season

The last 2 weeks of your season, the taper, is when the swimmer's body is allowed to make its final adaptation in preparation for the most important competition of the season. Thus, the taper should be pointed to the biggest or championship meet; usually the last swimming event of the season. The following three goals should be emphasized during the taper season. You should emphasize peaking or swimming as fast as possible by resting, focusing on competition, and enjoying alternate activities.

Helping swimmers to swim their fastest times

During the taper, swimmers in a year-round team would decrease the number of yards they swim. However, your recreational swimmers swim fewer yards in practice than year-round swimmers. Therefore, for recreational swimmers the reduction in work is not as important as the change in activities during the taper. Stop all dryland exercises. Have your swimmers swim pool and give additional practice on starts, turns, and relay starts.

Establishing the proper psychological attitude

Team meetings, gimmicks, and slogans all help to focus the swimmers' attention on their big meets. In preparation, for major competitions urge your swimmers to avoid strenuous activities. Emphasize that your avoid strenuous activities. Emphasize that your swimmers should get enough rest and stay out of the hot sun for 1 or 2 days before the big meet.

Allowing time for enjoyment

Never sacrifice the fun the taper season to the stress that accompanies competition. If the team goals are set pre-season, the extent of the team's accomplishment of these goals will be obvious. The swimmers will know that they are well prepared, and the confidence will be contagious. Thus the final competition will be a positive experience for everyone involved.

AWARDS

Developing definite criteria before the season opens is your first step to establishing significant awards. Swimmers, like other young people, insist upon fairness and will appreciate awards that are presented on the basis of consistent standards. The athletic director or board of directors for your team should receive your standards and review them pre-season. After agreement on the criteria for recognition, swimmers and parents should review and sign a written copy of the standards. Two types of awards are common in recreational swimming: participation awards and achievement awards.

Participation awards

A participation award is for successful participation in a sport. This award may take the form of inexpensive wearing apparel or emblems that can be acquired only by fulfilling the requirements of team membership. This award shows that the swimmer was a member of a team and met certain obligations to achieve membership on that team. The following are the usual criteria for a team participation award:

— *An attendance requirement:* The team members may be required to practice a certain number of sessions per week, except when they are excused. These excused absences should be granted only for good cause and only when they are requested personally by the swimmer from the coach in advanced of the session to be missed. The coach should also grant excused absences on an individual basis if the swimmer appears to be overly tired or ill.

— *A point requirement:* To receive an award, criteria may require each swimmer to accumulate a specific number of points in dual meets. The number of points required is usually determined by the number of meets in which the team participates and the system used for scoring. One fifth-place showing for each meet could be the minimum requirement for a team with a six-lane pool.

— *Conduct standards:* Stipulated conduct and good sportsmanship must be adhered to while the swimmers are representing their school or club. The code would prohibit the use of drugs, alcohol, and tobacco and put forth those standards that are consistent with those within the swimmer's community.

If attendance requirements, points requirements, and conduct standards are presented in writing prior to the beginning of the season, everyone will know what to expect, and post-season complaints will be kept to a minimum.

Achievement awards

The second type of award is one that signifies outstanding achievement in the sport. Some times these awards are made by outside organization. Any organization wishing to honour a team should make all arrangements through the team's athletic director or governing body. As coach, you should monitor awards to ensure that equal awards are given to boys and girls, that recipients are chosen in an equitable manner (preferably by the coach)., and that the value of the award is consistent with the achievement. For example, a 6 inch trophy should not be given to the team's outstanding swimmer while a 10 inch trophy is given to the best 10- year-old because it was donated by a parent.

Presenting outstanding swimmer trophies should be kept to a minimum. A simple certificate given to the most valuable swimmer from each meet is an alternative approach that keeps awards low-key. Certificates can be awarded at a team get-together at the end of the season. As each award is presented, the highlights of the meet can be recalled. Often these certificates will go to your best swimmer, but in some cases you can give the award to a third-place finisher whose improved times inspired other team members or enabled the team to win a crucial point. Plan ahead for these awards and keep notes on meets as you proceed through the season.

If tradition or the organization that you are associated with insists that an outstanding swimmer's trophy be awarded, establish a formal point system. Give points for each practice session attended, for holding a leadership position on the team, for scoring points in dual meets, for having the team's best time in an event, and for holding records. The swimmer accumulating the most points during the season could then be named your outstanding swimmer based on skill, attitude, and leadership.

DELEGATION OF AUTHORITY

The coach's ability to delegate authority can be crucial to a team's successful season. In situations, team managers, secretaries, non-relative volunteers, or assistant coaches are available. In other situations, only parents are available for the many tasks that are so vital to conducting a competitive program. Your first rule should be to work directly with the swimmers personally and delegate to others those tasks that are not swimmer-related. The following tasks can be delegated to trained and supervised parents or others:

— Running meets

— Keeping team records and recording swimmers' best times.

— Organizing team get-togethers and awards banquets.

— Organizing transportation

— Fund raising

— With some guidance, public relations. (Chick all announcements for validity and objectivity.)

The role of assistant coach should not be delegated or assumed by team managers, parents, or other untrained volunteers. In fact, parents should be discouraged from walking onto the deck during work-outs. This portion of the coach's time belongs to the swimmers. A polite pre-season letter on this matter and the phrase, "May I call you about that matter?" To those who ignore your request will solve these problems except with the most persistent parents. Some overly enthusiastic parents will react well if you redirect their energies into other useful projects, but as a resort you must simply refuse to communicate with parents during work-outs.

EQUIPMENT

Most swimming programs operate on a limited budget. Therefore, you must carefully decide upon the equipment that is most necessary for your team. Most experienced coaches choose the following items:

— *A pace clock:* A pace clock gives a coach freedom to

walk around, correct strokes, and get involved in the work-outs instead of standing around reading off times and saying "Ready?!" It also encourages swimmers to be aware of their practice times.

— *Kickboards:* Kickboards allow swimmers to build endurance and improve cardiovascular efficiency even before they can do a stroke for a great distance. Kickboards also allow them to break the stroke into parts so that they can concentrate on and drill the stroke in parts.

— *Backstroke flags:* Backstroke flags are safety items that allow backstrokers to count their strokes to the wall. As soon as swimmers learn to use the flags, they will improve their backstroke times by not looking over their shoulders as they approach the wall.

— *Lane lines:* Swimmers must learn to swim in "circles" during practice. Providing lane lines between each group of swimmers is the only way to achieve this formation safely with large numbers of swimmers in a pool.

— *Materials for running meets:* A starter's gun and ammunition. Stop watch, clip board, and pencil for each lane in your pool and proper scoring sheets and cards for recording times are necessary to conduct meets.

— *Record and bulletin boards:* Record and bulletin boards are important for communication with your team. A record board will help establish goals and provide recognition of accomplishments. A bulletin board will provide information for swimmers and parents.

— *Goggles:* Goggles have revolutionized swimming by eliminating the eye irritation that frequently bothers competitive swimmers. Although goggles sometimes leak, are difficult to get used to, and are easily lost or broken, they are well worth the cost and trouble of using them. In addition, goggles have become an important safety feature because they encourage swimmers to keep their eyes open and thereby avoid collisions. Each swimmer should personally own one or more sets of goggles.

If resources permit, additional equipment such as paddles, pullbuoys, and flippers are desirable at the recreational level. The following literature is also useful for recreational teams. It has a section for parents of swimmers and article written by famous swimmers, coaches, and sports psychologists.

Swimming world and junior swimmer is published monthly and usually offers articles of interest to all water sports enthusiasts. It publishes instructional articles and meet results and explains the training program of national level swimmers. Because the magazine attempts to appeal to a varied audience, some of its articles are of little interest to seasonal swimmers, but most of the articles would be of interest to coaches of seasonal competitive swimmers.

In addition to these periodicals, the books listed in the bibliography at the end of this manual are appropriate for further study by seasonal competitive swimming coaches.

Other equipment that may be acquired by swimmers to enhance the team spirit of the sport includes team caps (an inexpensive way to provide team identification), team swim suits, tee shirts, warm-up suits, banners, sport bags, or jackets. All of these items are helpful in establishing team pride and identification but should be recommended before the season to the parents board be acquired only after their agreement.

6

EARLY SEASON PLANNING

SETTING INDIVIDUAL GOALS

Personal swimming goals are the product of a swimmer's background, commitment to the sport, and emotional maturity and of the coach's input. Goals tell the swimmers where they are going and what they have accomplished on an individual basis early in the season. This may be done by passing out note cards at a team meeting and asking swimmers to write down their goals for the season. The necessity of writing goals forces swimmers to consider why they are participating in the program. The card, which is seen only by the coach, is a starting point for a one-on-one discussion with the swimmer.

With older swimmers, some of their goals should include the performance times the competitor wants to achieve at the end of the season. Meaningful goal times could be the cut-off time that qualifies swimmers to compete in a championship meet or the times that enabled swimmers to score points for their teams in the previous year's championship meet. For a talented swimmer, the club records may provide meaningful goal times. If possible, the swimmer should be the one to decide the goal time with prompting from the coach. A first-year swimmer's goal could be to race in each meet. The coach could associate this goal with the swimmer's perfecting techniques and attending every practice. Novice high school swimmers might state that their goals are to earn varsity letters. Early in the season, the coach could point out the times being achieved by teams the swimmers will soon compete against. The swimmers can then be asked their opinion of the times that will be necessary to gain points against these teams. These times will then become the swimmers' goal times. Next, the coach can refer to these goal times in practice with questions such as, "How close to your goal time was that swim?"

If the same novice swimmers have goal times that would qualify them as high school "All Americans," the coach should accept the unrealistic goals but point out that these are long term goals that will require work over a period of years to be achieved. The coach can then suggest stepping stones to reach these long-term goals. The swimmers could be reminded of their current capabilities and then be asked to determine goal times that will serve as intermediate goals. The coach should also make a few remarks about the commitment necessary to achieve the long-term goals.

Swimmers 10 years of age and younger should not be expected to have the same kinds of goals as high school swimmers. Younger swimmers must place more emphasis on immediate goals because their performance next Saturday is more important to them than their performance in the championships 10 weeks away. Goals such as flipping every turn, holding the breath from the flags to the wall at the end of a swim, or being on time to every work-out are examples of immediate goals that can be related to success at the

next meet. A goal for this age group and for all swimmers should be to memorize their best times in their best events. In a meet, your swimmers should obtain their times from their timers immediately after finishing a race. They will then know immediately if they have improved their performance. Improving a "best time" is a realistic goal for this age group and one that is naturally fulfilled insofar as most swimmers 10 years of age or younger are growing in size and strength. It is possible for swimmers 10 years and under to improve a 50-yard time by 2 or 3 seconds in a season.

In goal setting, the coach's role is to provide the information to allow swimmers to translate their goals into times that they can realistically achieve. The coach should accept all goals but should provide input to stimulate the most talented swimmers to consider difficult goals, whereas swimmers with less talent or commitment must also be made to realize that the goals they are pursuing are worthwhile.

DEVELOPING A DRYLAND EXERCISE PROGRAM

When surveyed, most coaches experiences with seasonal teams considered dryland exercise programs to be very important. Pool time is usually limited at this level, and young people respond best to a varied program. You will obtain the best results when flexibility, strength, and endurance exercises are done in 30-minute sessions three times each week under your direct supervision. This is most easily done before or after swimming practice. Your duties include preparing a list of the exercises before each meeting, checking that the exercises are done correctly, and ensuring that the athletes understand the purpose of the exercises.

The following eight basic concepts should be considered when organizing a dryland exercise program:

1. Dryland exercises should be done every other dry so that muscles can rest and recover between sessions. Running may be substituted on alternate days to provide increased endurance.
2. Each exercise session and swimming session should be started with a warm-up. Flexibility exercises are used to stretch and warm up each section of the body.
3. Exercises should be specific. The specific muscles to be used in swimming should be exercised using the motions and rhythms that most nearly duplicate those used in the water.
4. A muscle should be worked more than normal if it is to become stronger. This is termed the overload principle.
5. To motivate swimmers, the coach should do the exercises with the swimmers whenever possible.
6. Increases in strength require 4 to 6 weeks of regular exercise. Swimmers should be told this and encouraged to be patient.
7. Power is the ability to do strength performances with speed. To develop power, some strength exercises should be performed hard and fast.
8. To be effective, exercises must be done correctly.

A comfortable compromise between variety and familiarity should be reached in your program. Performing exercises that have been done before is reassuring and all exercises should be done until they can easily be done correctly. Some new exercises should be presented at each session to prevent boredom. An excellent resource for further study is Coaching Young Athletes.

FLEXIBILITY EXERCISES

Swimmers can get by with only average flexibility in the hip joint, but their flexibility in the ankles must be well above average for a strong kick. The freestyler and butterflyer need shoulder flexibility in order to recover their arms over the water easily. To improve flexibility, a muscle should be stretched slowly for 20 to 30 seconds. The stretch is then increased slightly just before the muscle is relaxed.

For the calf muscle and heel cord

The swimmer gets into the track starting position with most of the body weight supported by the arms. The left knee is bent under the chest with the foot flat on the floor. Keeping the head up, the swimmer stretches the right leg back as far as possible. The heel should be gently stretched down for 15 seconds while keeping the right leg straight.

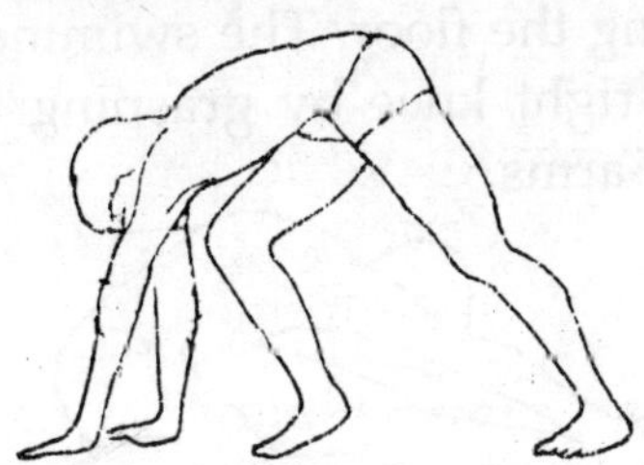

For the calf muscle and heel cord

The swimmer stands 2 to 3 feet from a wall with one foot 6 inches in front of the other. The palms of the hands are placed on the wall with the elbows straight. Keeping the back straight, the head in line with the body, and the feet flat on the floor, the swimmer bends the elbows as far as possible. Hold the position for 20 seconds and then increase the stretch before relaxing. Do this exercise twice, reversing the forward foot.

For ankle stretch

In a straight-leg sitting position, the swimmer flexes the feet toward the legs. Tell your swimmers to hold for 20 seconds and to then extend the entire foot toward the floor, curling the toes downward. The swimmer then holds again for 20 again.

For lower back and back of the legs stretch

Swimmers sit on the floor with their legs straight, knees to the floor, and feet flat on the wall. Tell your swimmers to exhale and reach for the wall, keeping the knees to the floor and the feet in position. The swimmer should eventually touch the wall with a closed fist.

For lower back and inner sides of the thigh

Have your swimmers sit on the floor with the right leg in front and the left leg bent back with the inside of the ankle touching the floor. The swimmer tries to pull the head to the right knee by grasping the ankle and pulling with the arms.

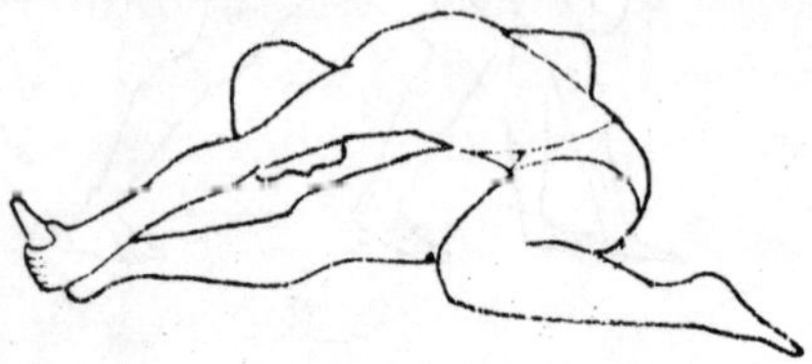

For the shoulder joint

In a sitting position, tell your swimmers to roll both

shoulders up, back, down and around in a continuous movement. Follow this exercise with the same motion with the right shoulder only and then with the left shoulder only.

For the shoulder joint

Have your swimmers hold a towel behind the back. Tell them to lift the arms as high as possible, keeping the head up and the back straight. The swimmers hold this position for 20 seconds. Next the swimmers hold the towel over the head with the arms straight. Bent the elbows so that the towel is lowered behind the head down to the shoulders.

STRENGTH EXERCISES

The types of strengthening exercises used by most recreational swimming coaches can be done without elaborate equipment. One type of strength exercise involves concentric muscle contractions. Concentric contraction occurs when a muscle shortens and contracts sufficiently to overcome a resistance. An example of this is moving from lying on the back to sitting up in the first phase of a sit-up. A second type of exercise involves eccentric contraction, the slow controlled lengthening of a contracting muscle. For instance, when the athlete doing the sit-up returns to the back lying position, the muscles work against gravity in an eccentric contraction to allow a controlled return. In both eccentric and concentric contractions, a part of the body actually moves.

In contrast, isometrics, another type of exercise, are done by contracting the muscle without motion against a stationary resistance. One precaution with using isometrics is that the exercise should be performed at several positions throughout the entire range of motion of the stoke. Since 1957 when Councilman credited isometric exercises with developing strength while encouraging proper stroke mechanics, isometric exercises have been widely used to strengthen swimmers' muscles. Councilman's favourite exercise was to have his swimmers pull over a barrel, thereby practising the high elbow pull of the crawl stroke.

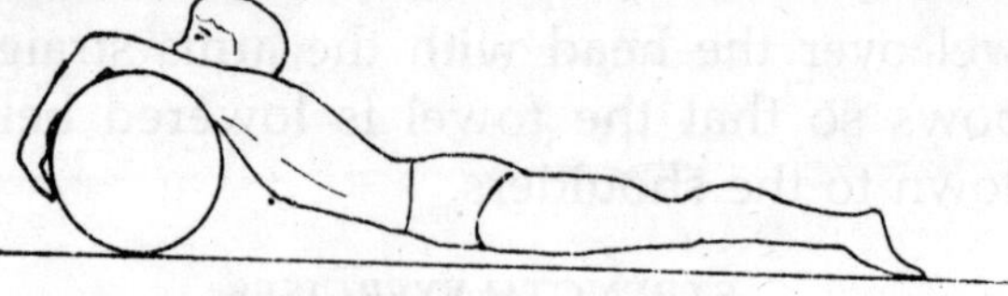

Isometric exercises for arm strength

For butterflyers, freestylers, and backstrokers

The butterfly or freestyle swimmer stands, whereas the backstroke swimmer kneels. The backstroker pushes up while the partner pushes down.

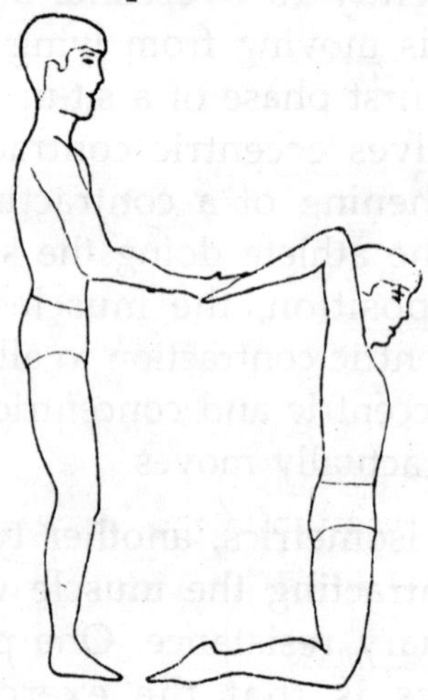

The elbows of both swimmers are kept high in the swimming position. Because recreational swimmers should not yet specialize in one stroke, have partners change positions at the completion of exercise.

For breaststrokers

Two breaststrokers stand facing each other with their palms touching. Tell them to press against each other's hands as they pull backward with the elbows high. The partners change positions after a series of six repetitions and do three sets each.

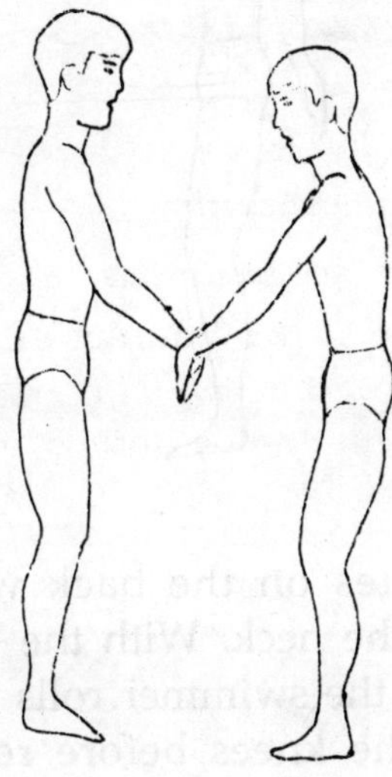

For all racing strokes

Partners stand facing each other with their palms pressing against each other in an up-and-down action. One partner presses while the other resists to practice the press phase of the armstroke.

For butterflyers and freestylers

The swimmer stands with the back 5 inches from the

wall. The palms of both hands push against the wall. This action strengthens the follow-through action of the crawl and butterfly strokes.

Concentric and eccentric exercises

Abdominal strength

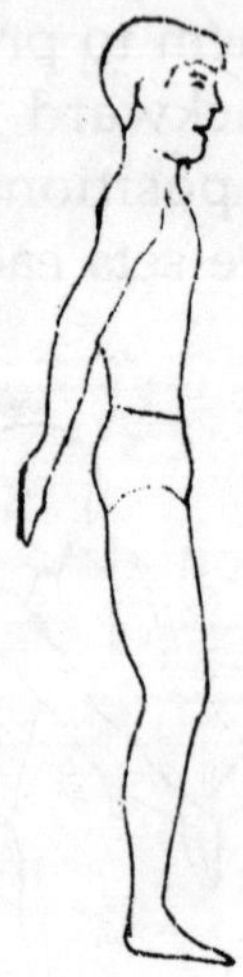

1. The swimmer lies on the back with the hands clasped behind the neck. With the knees bent at a 90-degree angle, the swimmer rolls up and touches the elbows to the knees before returning to the original position.

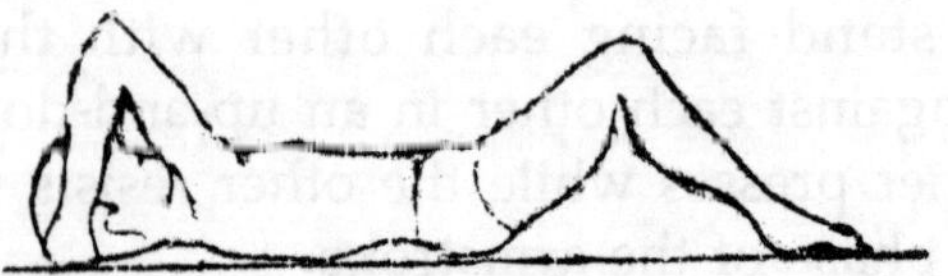

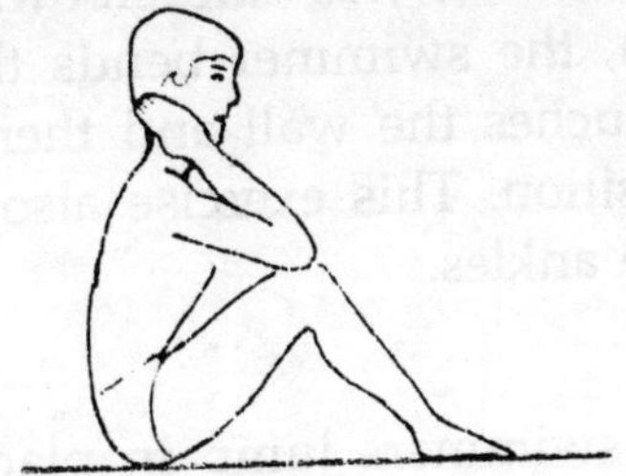

2. Use this exercise on days that you do not use exercise 1. The swimmer starts as in exercise 1 but may have a partner hold down the feet. The swimmer sits halfway up, then twists to the side with the whole trunk (not just the head and arms), and then returns to the starting position.

3. The swimmer again starts with the legs as they were in Exercise 1. But now the arms are at the sides. The swimmer lifts the knees to the chest, raising the hips off the floor. This is followed by a controlled return to the starting position. Be sure that swimmer keeps the knees bent.

Arm strength

1. Have your swimmers do traditional push-ups with the feet pointed and the weight on the tops of the feet. If swimmers cannot do the push-ups, have them hold the support position with the back flat for the time it takes team-mates to do an assigned number.

2. Swimmers stand one and one half arm lengths from the wall. Tell them to lean forward and place the hands on the wall with the elbows straight. With heels down, the swimmer bends the elbows until the nose touches the wall and then returns to the starting position. This exercise also gives a stretch through the ankles.

Leg strength

1. Have your swimmers jump in place, pointing the toes as much as possible and going as high as possible on each jump.
2. Swimmers stand facing a partner, holding right hands. The performer stands on the right foot and squats down, keeping the left leg straight and parallel to the floor. When the leg is 6 inches from the floor, the performer returns to the standing position.

The above concentric and eccentric exercises can be used to increase power. To increase power, the exercises must be done with speed. When working with children under 12 years of age, some coaches repeat the exercises for the time it takes the swimmers to swim their best strokes for 25 yards. With children over 12 years of age, choose a time to correspond to swimming 50 yards of their best stroke. When the swimmer is able to increase the number of performances in the designated time by five repetitions, then the time for the drill is lengthened by 5 seconds. The drill is lengthened until the time span is equal to the best 50-yard time for swimmers under 12 years of age and the best 100-yard time for swimmers 12 or older.

ENDURANCE EXERCISES

Endurance is the relative ability to continue exercising at a given rate of intensity for a specified length of time. Running 3 days each week has been suggested as a way to help improve cardiovascular endurance. Swimming itself is an aerobic activity that builds endurance. In addition, many recreational coaches conduct dryland exercise sessions on Mondays, Wednesdays, and Fridays with a run of about 25 minutes on Tuesdays and Thursdays. Have your swimmers do two of the following endurance exercises for approximately 5 minutes of each dryland exercise session during the mid-season. Omit the endurance work during the late season because 2 days of running and regular swimming work-outs will maintain your athletes' endurance at this time.

Running in place

In this exercise the swimmers point their toes as they run in place to prepare for good push-offs from turns and the pointed toes used in the flutter kick.

Crawl stroking out of water

Crawl stroking while standing in place may be timed by a watch or pace clock. Choose the time that it takes most of your athletes to swim 200 yards and assign the exercise for that length of time. Emphasize to your swimmers the importance of maintaining proper stroke techniques.

Running in place while doing the crawl stroke

Use this exercise on days that you do not use exercise 1 or 2. Count three runs for each stroke.

Crawl kicking

Swimmers lie prone with the arms down by the sides

and under them and the palms of the hands supporting the thighs. They then kick up vigorously with small kicks as in the crawl stroke.

Sitting flutter kicks

Use this exercise on days that you do not use the crawl kicking. Swimmers sit on the back of the hips with their hands on their hips and their legs off floor. They then whip the legs up and down with loose ankles at a rate of 240 per minute exhaling on the first three kicks and inhaling on the next three.

BEFORE THE FIRST WORK-OUT

Swimming work-outs will go smoothly if team members understand (a) how to swim in circles, (b) how to read a pace clock, and (c) how to take a carotid pulse before their first work-out.

Circle swimming

Use a blackboard to diagram circle swimming as shown in Figure Explain that in Lane 1 each

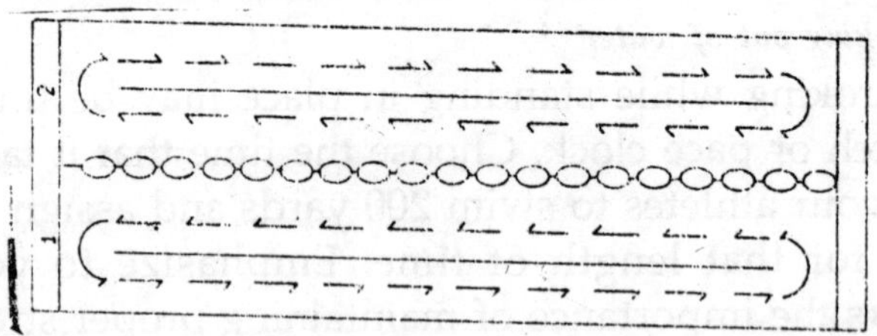

competitor swims down the right side of the lane. A cut to the left is made just before the turn so that thc streamlined push-off from the flip turn is made on the correct side of the lane. The swimmers are then again on their own right side. If one swimmers overtakes another swimmer and wants to pass, the passer taps the foot of the overtaken swimmer. On the next turn, the overtaken swimmer swims to the far corner of the lane and holds the wall for a moment, thus allowing the swimmer who is passing to flip the turn toward the centre of the lane and push off on the right in front of the overtaken swimmer.

The swimmers in Lane 2 of the diagram are swimming in a clockwise circle. This avoids bumping or hitting with the recovery arm because swimmers in adjoining lanes are always going in the same direction. Swimmers in all odd-numbered lanes will circle in the same direction as those in Lane 1. All swimmers in all even-numbered lanes will circle in the same direction as shown in Lane 2 in Figure.

Reading a pace clock

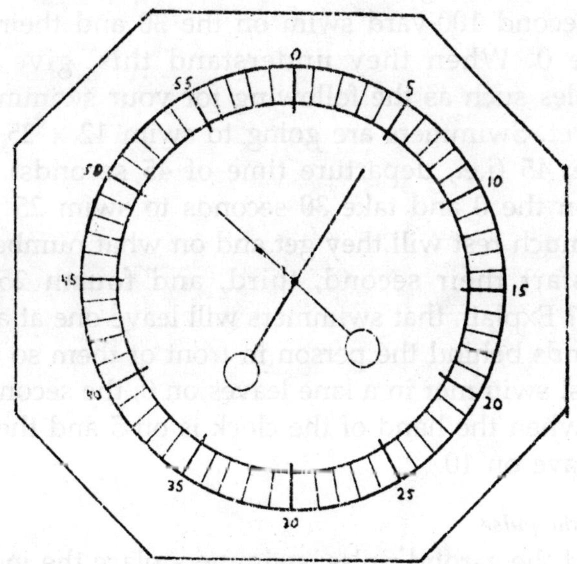

Explain to your swimmers that the pace clock will run continuously during practice. Point out that one hand of the clock goes around every 60 seconds. The other hand moves only one small line each minute.

If a swimmer is swimming a set of ten 50-yard swims (10 x 50) on an assigned swimming time of 1 minute, the swimmer would leave on the same clock number each interval. If that number is 0 and the swimmer takes 40 seconds to swim 50 yards, the swimmer finishes on the 40 m rests for 20 seconds, and starts again on the 0. For example, this is indicated as 4+50 on 1:00 in the practice plans provided.

Ask the swimmers to imagine that they are swimming a set of 5 x 100 yards on a swimming time of 1:30 and that their average time for swimming 100 yards is 1:20. If they start their first 100-yard swim on the 0, they will get 10 seconds of rest before starting their second 100-yard swim on the 30 and their third on the 0. When they understand this, give other examples such as the following for your swimmers to interpret. Swimmers are going to swim 12 x 25 yards on the: 45 (i.e., departure time of 45 seconds). They start on the 0 and take 30 seconds to swim 25 yards. How much rest will they get and on what number will they start their second, third, and fourth 25-yard swims? Explain that swimmers will leave one at a time, 5 seconds behind the person in front of them so that if the first swimmer in a lane leaves on 0, the second will leave when the hand of the clock is on 5 and the third will leave on 10.

Taking the pulse

To find the carotid pulse, swimmers place the index or middle finger on the carotid artery beside the windpipe and under the jaw.

Have your swimmers take the pulse for 6 seconds and multiply the result by 10 to determine the pulse rate per minute. Resting pulse rates (the rate when the body is at rest) in children vary but can be expected to be slightly faster than the 72 normal pulse rate in adults and persons in their late teens. Following an all-out 2-minute swim, the pulse rate will be 180 to 200 beats per minute regardless of the resting pulse rate. A very easy 2-minute swim should bring the pulse rate to around 110. As the swimmer's cardiovascular condition improves, the pulse rate on the easy swim should become lower. Thus the pulse can be used as a diagnostic tool to determine how hard a swimmer is working on a particular phase of the work-out.

ELEMENTS OF EARLY SEASON WORK-OUTS

Early season work-outs for swimmers over 10 years of age should contain the following elements:

— *Stretching period:* Approximately 10 minutes should be designated for stretching on dry land before each work-out and before meet warm-ups. Use flexibility exercises listed earlier in this manual.

— *Warm-up:* A distance swim without concern for the time, usually 200 to 400 yards of the crawl stroke, should be included. Other racing strokes may be done, but the butterfly is never done until the swimmer has warmed up.

— *Stroke work:* During the early season, each work-out should include group work on a specific stroke or skill. Later in the season, stroke work is done on an individual basis.

— *Interval training:* In interval training, a certain distance is swum and followed by a rest. Swimmers repeat this cycle a specified number of times within a given time frame. This may be given to the swimmers as "5 +50 on 1 minute," if you know the swimmers take approximately 40 seconds to swim 50 yards and will have 20 seconds to rest. If you are unsure of times, the interval training could be given as 5+50 with 20-second rests. The stroke to be used is specified to the swim they are to perform. The following phrases describe the quality of the swim:

Medium speed
Second length harder than the first
Every other 50 hard
Every other 50 within 10 seconds of your best time
Keep every 50 under 40 seconds
Try to raise your pulse above 150

Keep in mind that longer rests are used when quality swims are required and shorter rests are used for swims of less expected quality. However, when using interval training, allow the swimmer to rest only partially rather than completely.

— *Repetition training:* Repetition training includes sprinting and may include hypoxic work. It is done with enough rest to allow the pulse rate to return to under 100 beats per minute between each effort. Repetition training includes work in all the strokes.

As listed, the stretching and warm-up elements of a work-out are always given first; the interval swimming and kicking may be given in either order in the meddle; and the repetition training is usually given at the end. A period of stroke work should also be included in each early season work-out. This is easily incorporated into the interval training portion of the work-out. Work-outs for swimmers 10 years of age and under should contain the previously listed elements but with shorter distances and more time spent on the kicking sets and stroke work. A game, race, or rely should be included at the end of each work-out for swimmers 10 and under.

7

THE BACK CRAWL

The back crawl, as its name suggests, is performed with the swimmer lying in a supine position. The arms alternate continuously with each other, by recovering clear of the water then re-entering to carry out the propulsive stage of the stroke. The legs kick with an alternating rhythm, which is biased towards the vertical plane and is synchronised with the arm movement. The swimmer does not encounter any breathing problems as a rule while the stroke is being carried out, owing to the fact that his face is clear of the water, although, as will be suggested later, some form of respiratory discipline is advised.

The stroke performance of back crawl is governed by ASA laws which state that... the swimmers shall swim upon their backs throughout a race.... Any competitor leaving his normal position on the back before the head, foremost hand, or arm has touched the end of the course for purpose of turning or finishing shall be disqualified.

Stroke technique

Body position

The side view of a back crawler's attitude in the water should reveal that the chest is lying flat and horizontal and just level with the water surface. Due to the mechanics of the leg kick, the swimmer's hips must ride slightly lower than those of the front crawler. However, the tendency to 'sit' in the water allowing the hips to sink lower than required must be avoided. The effect of the 'sitting' position on the swimmer's forward progress is to bring about an increase in both profile and eddy drag forces, thus down-grading the performance.

The head should be approximately in line with the body and the eyes should be looking up very slightly towards the feet. The created bow wave should pillow the swimmer's head and may wash over her forehead and on her face. With excessive tilting of the head the swimmer will assume the chin-forward, 'sitting' position.

When viewed from ahead, the swimmer's shoulders should be seen to be rolling towards the direction of the pulling arm; they should reach a maximum deviation from the horizontal, as the hand and arm pass through the shoulder plane.

The law states that the swimmer should remain on the back during the actual swim. This may be interpreted as limiting the body-roll angle to a maximum of forty-five degrees, which is compatible with the mechanics of the arm action. Unlike front-crawl technique, in which the swimmer's head rolls in similar respect to that of the body, the back crawler's head tends to remain relatively still, while the shoulders carry out the rolling motion which is brought about by the arm movements.

The shoulders should not be laterally displaced as result of the arm action, but should be always co-axial with an imaginary straight line stretching from one end of the pool to the other. As the swimmer moves away from the observer, her toes may be seen to be *just* breaking the water surface. Her hips should move with a slight rolling reaction, which in turn is associated with leg action.

Taking an overhead look at the swimmer, her 'long axis' should be in line with the intended direction of movement. There should also be no bending of the body due to incorrect limb movements, which will tend to increase the profile and eddy-drag characteristics of the stroke.

As with any stroke, the swimmer's body position in the water is closely related to the efficiency of her arm and leg movements and their co-ordination with each other.

Leg action

The legs move alternately in a plane which is biased towards the vertical. (The movement does not take place in the true vertical plane owing to the transmission to the hips of the swimmer's shoulder roll.) Part of their function is to stabilise and balance the stroke. The downbeat movements also contribute quite substantially towards elevating the hips and maintaining the desired body position. Basically, the back-crawl leg action is similar to that of the front crawl, the main difference being, of course, that the movement is inverted or upside down.

Considerable propulsion can be developed during the upbeat, while the downbeat contributes very little towards moving the swimmer forwards. During the downbeats, the ankles are semi-relaxed while, during the upward sweep of the feet, the extension of the ankles (plantar flexion), is effected by calf muscle (triceps surae) tension. This 'bending back' of the feet during the upbeat is assisted by the generated water pressure on the insteps.

During the stroke-learning period, this variation in muscular tension cannot really be taught: if the swimmers are required to maintain the extended-toe (ballet-toe) position, attacks of cramp are very likely. Therefore, although eventually not desirable, 'floppy feet' are probably more advisable in the initial stages of instruction, allowing the technique to develop naturally with further practice.

The leg movement is generated from the hip joint and the upbeat is initiated by rotation of the thigh. The lower-leg extensor muscles (quadriceps femoris) are semi-relaxed during this early stage of the upward movement. Then, as the knee nears the surface, the extensors swiftly contract to accelerate the lower leg in a vigorous and propulsive upward arc.

The inward-pointing toes do not necessarily break the water surface although they can rise above the water level owing to the speed and inertia of the leg. The upward motion of the foot causes a turbulent reaction and the 'local water' is lifted. It is below this water mound that the foot should remain. The foot only splashes as it passes excessively through the water surface. The knees should at all times remain below the water surface and, if they do appear during the performance, the swimmer is probably using a 'cycling' motion, which reduces the effectiveness of the movement.

Owing to the downward-pointing lower leg, the

generated propulsive forces at the start of the upbeat are almost in the horizontal plane and being directed backwards in the most advantageous manner.

As the upward movement progresses, however, the backward forces are transferred into vertical downward-acting reactions and propulsion diminishes. When teaching this upward-kicking movement, it may be described to the pupils as 'letting the water bend the knees rather than the swimmer deliberately bending them'.

The flicking movement of the foot, which results from a semi-relaxed ankle joint, is not unlike that of a footballer's action as he kicks the ball with his instep (minus the follow-through). This is a good demonstration point.

Ankle flexibility together with the ability to hold the feet in a plantar-flexed position, is of great importance in achieving a worthwhile leg kick. Learner swimmers sometimes tend to keep their ankles stiff and held at right angles to the shin, a foot position which cannot possibly produce any worthwhile propulsion.

The downbeat provides stabilisation and body elevation, but no measurable propulsion. The depth of kick should be from 450 mm (18 in.) To 600 mm (24 in.) and will vary with the physical characteristics of the swimmer. The tall, strong and rangy individual will probably drive his or her legs deeper into the water than a swimmer with short legs or less flexibility.

The big toes should pass very close to each other as they alternate. This excludes any unnecessary contraction of the thigh abductor muscles and retains the feet in the most advantageous position for propulsion.

All other circumstances being equal, the back and front-crawl leg kicking movements are capable of producing comparable degrees of propulsion, although the arm movements contribute the greater share of the propulsion in both strokes. In fact, the front crawl is the faster of the two strokes: assuming that this higher speed is attributable to the more powerful arm action, it may be said that the possible percentage of leg-to-arm participation in the front crawl is less than that of the back crawl.

Therefore it may be argued that, in relation to the overall stroke, the back-crawl leg action may be more efficient than that of the front crawl.

Arm action

As in the front crawl stroke, the motion of the arms is alternating and it is from this movement that the major propelling forces are developed. The arm cycle may be divided into two main phases, the underwater or propulsive movement and the recovery, which is carried out over the water surface. In order to analyse the complete movement, these two phases will be sub-divided in the following manner.

Propulsive phase	*Recovery phase*
catch	release
pull	recovery over the water
push	entry

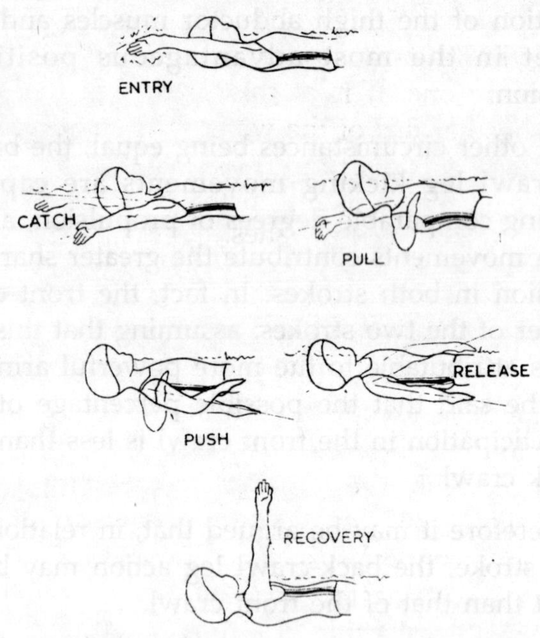

Propulsive phase: catch

To reiterate an earlier statement: the catch may be justifiably described as the foundation of the propulsive phase of the stroke. The movement commences immediately the hand has entered the water directly in line with and ahead of the shoulder joint. The hand, with fingers flat and together. sinks to a depth of between 150 mm (6 in.) and 300 mm maintains a slightly flexed attitude in the direction of the little finger (initiated at the entry stage) and also in the natural direction of the palm. The path of the hand is downward and beginning to move outwards away from the line of the swimmer's shoulder.

The catch movement is a flowing continuation of the entry but, in order to establish propulsive pressure on the hand and lower arm, it is a rapid and accelerating one. It is at this point that the swimmer establishes her feel of the water. The shoulders should, at this early stage of propulsion, have commenced their lateral roll, thus assisting in the correct positioning of the arm for the start of the pull.

Propulsive phase: pull

The back-crawl pull (and push) has been the subject of much controversy for many years. Should the movement be executed with a bent or straight arm? The straight-arm supporters cite the famous Adloph Kiefer, probably the father of the modern back-crawl style. Kiefer's underwater action showed that his pull/push movement was executed with his arms absolutely straight, and using this style he won the 1936 Olympic 100 m back stroke title in a time of 1.05.9.

Contemporary exponents of the stroke, almost without exception, use the bent-arm pull/push. This type of action is used by Roland Matthes, probably an even more famous back stroker than Kiefer, who won the 100 m back stroke at the 1972 Olympic Games with a time may be attributed solely to the differing movements will never be known.

With young children, it may be advantageous for them to begin learning the stroke by sweeping their arms in a semi-circle from the point of entry to the position of release. For some obscure physiological reason, many children, when asked to bend their arms during the pull, find it necessary to bend the recovery arm as well.

It must be stated, however, that the bent-arm pull/push has been scientifically proved to be the more mechanically sound movement, with the swimmer's arm flexed at elbow and wrist for the underwater sweep.

For teaching purposes, to obtain maximum propulsion for the maximum time, the swimmer's hand and lower arm should be facing towards her feet for as long as possible during the propulsive sweep. Coupled to this is the simple feature of maintaining the hand below the water surface and elevation above the level of the elbow for the major part of the time. Observing these simple rules, the correct limb tracks tend to sort themselves out reasonably well in the initial stages of learning.

After the catch has been completed, the swimmer's hand starts to move downwards, outwards and in the direction of the feet. The elbow starts to bend and drop below the level of the hand. The wrist is flexed so that the palm of the hand faces towards the feet as early as possible during the underwater journey.

The finger-tips are submerged to an approximate depth of 230 mm (9 in.) at this stage and the hand continues to move below the water surface in a horizontal elongated 's' pattern.

The angle between the forearm and the upper arm decreases to almost a right-angle as it reaches the shoulder plane. Shoulder strength tends to dictate the magnitude of this angle, with stronger swimmers able to cope with the increased leverage resulting from greater angles up to, say, 120 degrees. The shoulders continue to roll to the pulling side. This lateral movement assists in maintaining the propelling hand below the water surface and also serves to keep the shoulder of the recovering arm clear of the water. The pull continues until the hand and arm simultaneously reach the lateral shoulder plane. It is at this point that the hand is laterally furthest away from the body and at its shallowest depth.

Propulsive phase: push

Throughout the pulling phase the elbow leads the hand, but now, as the hand itself passes the shoulder into the push, it takes up the leading position with the palm still facing towards the feet and the finger tips still approximately 230 mm (9 in.) below the water surface. The palm faces backwards for a short distance, and the elbow and hand start to move in towards the body once more.

At about the level of the swimmer's waist, the forearm moves in a vertical arc about the elbow joint, and the hand, with palm now facing downwards, passes close to the hips, thus creating a final thrusting action towards the bottom of the pool.

The arm, in completing the propulsive stage of the cycle, assumes a straight mode with the hand eventually facing palm-downwards some 230 mm below the swimmer's hips.

Recovery phase: release

This is rather a long movement.

From the completion of the push, the arm, remaining straight, moves vertically upwards, close to the body. The hand may either be retained in the palm-downwards mode, or, by axial rotation of the arm, it may be turned to face inwards thus ensuring a thumbs-out-first release from the water. The back-of-the-hand-first release from water both form part of the accepted stroke technique, and the phrases should be used during the teaching of the stroke. It does not matter which method is used as long as the wrist is reasonably relaxed as the hand leaves the water. There is a further school of thought which advocates a little-finger-out-first technique. This movement tends to place the medial rotator muscles of the arm into unnecessary tension and seems to have no advantage over the more natural and relaxed methods.

Recovery phase: recovery over the water

This takes place in the true vertical plane. The elbow is maintained straight and the wrist is held in a semi-relaxed position.

During this semi-circular movement, the arm is medially rotated so that, at the end of the recovery, the hand faces outwards, thus facilitating a little-finger-first entry.

The speed of recovery should be controlled to synchronise with the slower propulsive movement of the other arm. The arms should remain at approximately 180 degrees out of phase with each other throughout the whole cycle. Controlling the speed of the recovery, and entry, ensures that the arm does not crash heavily into the water, creating water turbulence and consequent drag.

A 'high' recovery of the arm in the true vertical plane avoids bending the body which occurs if the arm is swung sideways during recovery. This distortion of the body about its long axis often occurs if the backward swing of the arm is low and wide. The low and wide recovery also has a tendency to tip the swimmer to that side owing to the weight of the arm acting downwards.

Shoulder flexibility is an important factor during the recovery movement, with the loosely-muscled swimmers able to achieve the high swinging action more readily than the weight-lifters and gymnasts.

Recovery phase: entry

During the recovery over the water, the swimmer's arm should have been medially rotated so that, at re-entry, her arm is straight and facing outwards with fingers together and straight.

Just prior to her little finger entering the water, her wrist should be flexed to the side of the little finger. The lateral point of entry should be directly in line with the shoulder plane and the distance ahead of the swimmer is automatic, providing the straight-arm mode is maintained. At the point of entry the shoulders should be laterally horizontal with the water surface. Once more shoulder flexibility is important in achieving the shoulder-in-line entry. The 'less flexibles' may probably have to be content with a wider (say' ten to two') entry.

It is important that the entry of the hand into the water is controlled and that its speed is unchanged from that of the recovery over the water, thus preventing it from crashing into the water and setting up unnecessary turbulence for the body to pass through. In turbulent conditions, local eddy patterns and air bubbles form pockets of 'negative' pressure which, when the hand moves into the catch, make it difficult for the swimmer to build up 'positive' pressure or get the feel of the water on the palm and lower arm as propulsion commences. A continual 'flowing' movement during the transition from the recovery into entry is also necessary in order to prevent the transmission of unnecessary mechanical forces that would be developed by the sudden acceleration or deceleration of the arm on entering the water. These forces, reacting at the back crawler's tend to make her bob up and down as she swims.

Breathing

Respiration should present no major problems to back crawlers because their faces are clear of the water most of the time. An aquatic breathing pattern should be as natural and as closely allied to that of a comparable lend exertion as possible.

In practice, it is found that back crawlers use a normal 'we need a breath' reflex action and think no more about it. Indeed, many back-crawl specialists at all levels of competition, when questioned about their breathing habits while swimming, all found it difficult to say, without first experimenting, exactly how and where they breathe during the stroke cycle. However, it seems that most swimmers breathe regularly and inhale as one arm recovers over the water. The breath is expelled either gently through pursed lips, or through the mouth and nose in a semi-explosive fashion during the recovery of the opposite arm.

Co-ordination

As in front crawl, the timing of the leg beat usually follows a natural pattern based on the formula of six leg beats to one complete arm cycle. This rhythm results in a smooth and flowing movement.

The mechanical actions of the legs balance out the

reactions that are developed during the arm cycle. For instance, for most of the time that the right arm is recovering, the acceleration of the arm after release and the fact that the arm is out of the water tend to make the swimmer roll to the right. If we now examine the leg kick during the same short period, we should see that the right leg is moving down, thus lifting the right hip and countering the tendency to roll to that side. Contra-rotating forces tend to cancel each other out and stabilise the swimmer in a flat and horizontal attitude in the water. It is, in fact, unusual to see the back crawl being performed with anything other than a six-beat stabilising rhythm.

Preparatory standards for teaching the stroke

Swimming unaided and unassisted on the back can sometimes be alarming for the beginners. Therefore, before the teacher commences to teach the back crawl (proper) strike progressions, there are a few watermanship skill which the pupils should be able to perform with some degree of confidence and alarcity. These are as follows :

1. *Confidence exercises:* face wetting, blowing bubbles and submersion. (Although on their backs, the swimmers are bound to get their faces wet and water up the nose.)
2. Regaining the feet from a supine position.
3. Pushing and gliding from the poolside.
4. Back paddling at least 20 m (22 yards): this is an ideal introduction to back crawl swimming.
5. Treading water
6. General water mobility exercises: in back crawl the

performs are swimming 'blind' and collisions in deep water are likely. Stopping, starting, rolling over, reserving and moving sideways in deep water are therefore necessary skills.

Teaching the back crawl

The back crawl is a natural progression from the paddle, a stroke which should have been attempted by the pupils at some time in their swimming careers.

Back crawl is a popular stroke with younger because it can be performed without them having to put their faces in the water. The fact that some members of the class may not yet have relinquished their armbands does not exclude them from taking part in the practice.

Probably the greatest initial difficulty to be overcome by learners is that of remaining afloat while they recover their arms over the water. The change in buoyancy experienced as each arm leaves the water and its full weight is transferred to the swimmer's body tends to make him sink.

The usual reaction to this 'sinking feeling' is for the prospective back crawler to 'sit' in the water or simply panic and struggle to regain the feet after one brief attempt at the arm stroke. It is therefore necessary, before starting this new set of exercise, that every one of the pupils is able to regain his feet from a supine position without too much difficulty.

Activity: demonstration swim with commentary

As an introduction to the first back-crawl lesson, the pupils should be treated to a visual demonstration of the stroke. This may be carried out by one of the more adept swimmers in the class or preferably by a back crawler of some distinction, if one is available. This visual demonstration is a really important feature of the lesson and a little forethought and planning is well worthwhile, to enable the class to witness the stroke being performed in a substantially correct manner.

The teacher will now have the chance to point out all the major features of the stroke and describe where, how and shy should take place

It is worth repeating that the teacher should position himself strategically on the poolside and arrange the pupils so that they can see and hear clearly.

The main teaching points of the stroke may be categories and applied as previously described.

The swimmer's flat and horizontal body position should be emphasised, showing how his head is pillowed against the water and that his eyes are gazing upwards and slightly towards his feet.

The fact that the toes rise to the surface and do not create too much water disturbance should also be underlined, as should the fact that the swimmer's knees submerged throughout the kick.

The arms are recovered high over the water in an arc and, throughout this movement, they are held straight but not stiff. Another point worth highlighting is the fact that, during the arm recovery, the thumb (or the back of the hand) leaves the water first, and the little finger is always leading as the re-entry takes place.

The long underwater phase can be described,

showing how the palm of the hand faces the feet for as long as possible during the pull and that the hand stays below the water surface aided by a slight shoulder roll.

The teacher should point out how easy and rhythmical the stroke looks when it is performed correctly, with the leg beat blending in smoothly with the arm movement.

The swimmer is seen to be breathing quite easily and naturally and this fact s also worth a mention.

Activity: initial full-stroke swims

This short demonstration now sets the scene for the first exercise whereby the class show just how good they are at performing the back crawl. It may take the form of width swims, in which the pupils attempt the complete stroke before going on to, concentrate on individual aspects of the stroke action.

Teaching points

1. The body position in the water nay be affected by the positioning of the swimmer's head or by the effectiveness of the leg kick. A back crawler who lies back in the water, with his ears just below the water surface, stands a good chance of maintaining himself in the flat and horizontal mode. The swimmers should be encouraged to look up at the roof of the pool, rather than in the direction from which they are swimming. Excessive backwards head tilt sometimes tends to 'over-correct' a swimmer's sinking hips. The effect of this is to raise the legs too high in the water, thus causing unnecessary splash which reduces the effectiveness of the leg kick.

Another feature of an excessive backwards head tilt is that the water tends to wash over the face and enter the nose, causing, at this early stage of learning, some distress. 'Sitting' in the water has already been mentioned and, where this occurs, the 'bottom-up' instruction, or something similar, should be given.

The swimmer's leg should be terminating their whip-like upward beats with the extended feet lying just below the water surface. The downbeat should be with straight legs which will assist in raising the hips and maintaining them in this elevated position.

Body roll should be limited to approximately forty-five degrees with any increase in this probably being due to the swimmer's hand pulling too deeply in the water.

2. The leg-beat rhythm should be regular and the depth of kick should be limited to 600 mm (24 in.). With pupils of short stature, the depth of kick should be limited to, say, 300-450 mm (12-18 in.) Kicking depth may be changed by varying the rates of beats.

   The kick should always originate from the hip joint with the knee joint extending rapidly during the upbeat. Flexibility of the ankles is necessary for effective propulsion and the term 'floppy feet' adequately describes the required condition.

3. During the arm movement the thumb-out-first and little-finger-in-first features should be emphasised. Elbow should be straight but not necessary stiff during the high over-the-water recovery.

The propulsive phase should take place from the position where the hand enters the water, behind and in line with the shoulder, then continue on to where it brushes the thigh before commencing the recovery movement once more.

It is unnecessary to emphasised the bent-arm put at this particular stage: merely sweeping the hand around to the side should be adequate.

The swimmer's hands should remain relatively flat with fingers together throughout the movement.

Each arm should remain approximately opposite the other (windmill-fashion) during the cycle.

4. The breathing cycle needs no mention at this stage, as the face should remain clear of the water at all times during the stroke performance.

5. A six-beat rhythm should be the aim of each pupil, but during this early attempt at the stroke such refinements may well be absent.

   In order to assist in establishing and maintaining a stroke rhythm, a one-two-three/one-two-three count may be made silently by the swimmers as they reverse the width of the pool.

6. Premature glancing back over one shoulder, in order to avoid a collision with poolside, may be prevalent during these early practices. The movement usually produces a longer-than-usual roll towards the head-turning side. This peculiarity may be avoided by the pupils identifying a part of the overhead structure which appears in their sight, just before they touch the side.

   Another method of gauging the proximity of the

poolside is by counting the number of arm strokes across the pool prior to the touch.

Activity: leg action

The following set of practices are designed to develop the back-crawl leg kick, the movement being essential in establishing the flat and horizontal body position together with propulsion and stability.

The first exercise is identical to that which was performed at the start of the front-crawl leg practices; however, the description and related teaching points are repeated here so that the reader may follow the suggested sequence without having to refer back.

Practice 1: sitting on the poolside kicking the legs

Teaching points

1. The kick is an alternative leg action.,
2. The leg movement originates from the hip. Leg propulsion is based on the technique described in chapter 19 and it is essential that this hip-generated kick is emphasised right from the start of the practices.
3. The legs should be close together in the lateral plane. This is more for physical comfort rather than for hydrodynamic reasons. Spreading the legs unnecessarily brings into action the abducting leg muscles not normally used in this action.
4. The kicking depth should nor be more than 450 mm (18 in.). The length of a child's legs has a direct bearing on the rate of the leg beat and the depth of kick. If the kick is deep, the rate of movement will be slower that of a shallower flutter-like action.

5. An initially semi-relaxed knee joint enables the whip-like movement, which creates propulsion, to take place on the upbeat.
6. Relaxed ankles ('floppy feet') and 'toeing-in' are essential for back crawl; some pupils are able to shake their feet about quite loosely, while others show less flexibility. The 'toeing-in' or inward rotation of the feet, is a natural function for some people, but as it is most unlikely that the whole class will be 'pigeon-toed', this point is worth stressing. The reason for medical rotation of the foot is that it increases the effective propulsive area.
7. The whole leg action should flow smoothly and not be jerky in any way. Stiffening the joints requires muscular energy, therefore such action not only produces incorrect movements, it also tends to hasten the onset of fatigue.
8. The rhythm of the leg kick should be regular, with the teacher setting the pace by counting out a six-beat pattern, one-two-three/one-two-three, and so on, which will probably be the best and most natural one to use during the teaching of the stroke.

Practice 2: leg kicking in the water-holding the rail

This second exercise is also a static one with the limited usefulness which this always implies. The main purpose of the practice is for the pupils again to observe the action of their legs but this time to be more or less in the supine swimming position.

It is useful too in that the teacher is able to stand immediately above the pupils in order to observe and give advice where needed. The best teaching position, however is where the pupils are able to see as well as hear the teacher. This may be at the end of, as in this particular instance, on the opposite side of the pool.

The main disadvantage of this exercise, and that which limits its use, is the uncomfortable position which the pupils may be required to adopt while the rail. This should be borne in mind when carrying out the practice.

Teaching points

All the teaching points mentioned in the first exercise will be relevant to this practice. In addition to these, the following may be included:

9. While holding the rail or channel correctly, the pupils should be encouraged to extend their arms in order to bring the head away from the pool wall. This extension of the arms should make the exercise a little more comfortable should the pupils find that their necks cramped or hunched up.

10. The leg movement should be an accentuated upward flick of the feet (similar to kicking a football), generated from the hip. The toes should just rise to water level but not break the local, slightly turbulent water surface.

    If the hip-originated movement is being performed fairly correctly, there may be no need to emphasised the submerged knee position at the peak of the upbeat. However, if any members of the class are 'cycling', some over-correction may be necessary in the form of an instruction to maintain straight legs throughout the kick.

11. When the head is in contact with the rail and the

pupil is pulling himself close to the wall, he may tend to sir in the water. If this should happen, the 'bottoms-up' or 'tummies-up' instruction must be given.

In this anchored position, a slight increase in kicking speed and a conscious effort on the part of the pupils to straighten our is usually sufficient to attain the desired flat and horizontal attitude. The previously mentioned extension of the arms also assists in maintaining the correct mode.

By this check on regaining the feet from a supine position should be made before the new exercise commence. If any members of the class are unsure about the procedure, a brief session of standing-down practices should be carried out both with and without floats, until the teacher is satisfied with the standard of proficiency.

Practice 3: leg kicking with two floats

Teaching points

The following teaching points may be added to those given for the previous practices:

12. The correct and secure method of holding the two floats whole swimming on the back is essential because, when held in this vertical mode, the upward water buoyancy forces tend to snatch them from the swimmer's grasp. A firm hand grip, combined with tucking the elbows in to press the floats against the body, must be emphasised.
13. Positioning the head is important, and the desired horizontal and flat mode can be enhances by the pupils pillowing their heads back in the water so that their ears are just in line with the surface.

Looking up at the overhead structure while swimming on the back should now be an established part of the teacher's instruction. Excessive backward tilting of the head may cause choppy water tow ash over the swimmer's face. If this occurs, a *slight* forward tilting of the head towards the feet should remedy the problem.

14. The being the first mobile exercise, it is worth reiterating yet again that the leg movement should originate from the hips, and the ankles should be relaxed with the feet extended and 'toed-in'.

Practice 4: leg kicking with one float

We may now progress to the next standard of practice, which is that of using less buoyancy support during the kicking exercise.

A single float may be held across the chest on the tummy. Once more, the exercise should commence with instruction on how to hold the float. In the case of the cross-chest grip, the float is hugged or cuddled to the chest by placing the arms over the upper surface and gripping it securely on opposite (long) sides with both hands.

The tummy-grip exercise, should it be used, may be upgraded slightly by allowing the pupils to kick across the pool to the half-way stage in the supported mode, then releasing the float for the second half of the swim and use the hands to carry out a paddle or sculling action.

These float-supported exercises may enable the children who are still wearing armbands to divest themselves of their aids or allow them to be partially deflected. The final exercise of support-to-unsupport may require some armbands to be worn once more and the teacher should be alert to make any adjustments that may be needed. It is important that these children carry out the practices in a water depth which is shallow enough for them to regain their feet without much difficulty.

Teaching points

All the teaching points relating to the leg-kick technique are applicable during these practices.

Practice 5: leg kicking with scull

During the previous exercise, the pupils were introduced to leg kicking with no assistance from the floats. If, during some earlier lesson, they have carried out the back-paddle practices, this swimming exercise should present no problems to them. If, on the other hands while paddling on the back.

The kicking exercise is now performed utilising the sculling movements to swim across the pool.

Teaching.points

Teaching points relating to the actual stroke technique are applicable here with the following addition:

15. The method of sculling, although necessary to the exercise, should not become a major part of the teaching. The amount of instruction relating to this particular movements should be minimal, bearing in mind that the paramount feature of the exercise is the back-crawl leg action.

Practice 6: leg kicking with hands resting on the upper thighs

Teaching points

All the previously mentioned teaching points are

relevant, with perhaps most emphasis being placed on the flat and horizontal swimming mode with head well back in the water.

Practice 7: leg kicking in a fully (athletically) stretched position

For this final exercise in the leg action practices, the swimmer takes up a fully stretched attitude with arms stretching back behind the head.

The arm-stretched mode is closely allied to that of actually swimming. It is also similar to the submerged position that a swimmer adopts after a start, or push-off following a turn, during a back-crawl race.

Teasing points

All the teaching points previously mentioned are applicable here, with the following addition:

16. The arms must be fully stretched to maintain streamlining. They should also be fully supported at all times by the water. Clasping the hands together gives the appearance of the converging bows of a boat, and has a slight effect in reducing the swimmer's frontal resistance.

Activity: arm action

Useful back-crawl arms-only practices are very limited in number. This is due to the fact that, when actually performing the stroke, the swimmer utilises the stabilising forces that are developed by the leg kick to counterbalance the turning forces created during the width-of-the-body arm pull which tend to make her zig-zag.

In general, mobile arms-only exercises are used only as a training aid with both legs being supported by some floating device. Even here, however, the exercise has its limitations, in as much as neither body-roll nor leg-movement reactions are present. With these facts in mind, we will restrict our practices to three static forms of exercise aimed solely at establishing the correct limb tracks.

Practice 1: Standing in the shallow end of the pool and rotating the arms in the back-crawl manner, the teacher demonstrating the action from the poolside

Teaching points

1. The arms must be kept straight but not stiff throughout this exercise.
2. The hands should remain flat and the fingers together. A slight flexion of the wrist may take place at the start of the pulling action.
3. Each arm should remain approximately 180 degrees out of phase with the other at all times, windmill-style.
4. The pulling movement should commence just after the little finger has entered the water. The position of the hand at entry must be directly in line with the shoulder joint. Shoulder flexibility is an important factor in the correct placing of the hand and arm directly behind the shoulders. Should a swimmer's shoulder girth be tightly muscled (boys are generally less flexible about the shoulders than girls), he may find it rather difficult to achieve the desired arm-entry position.

   Where this physical limitation occurs, the teacher must make allowances and accept whatever the pupil or pupils can achieve. Indeed, the teacher may himself find difficulty in demonstrating the correct action because of this flexibility problem. If this is so, the problem should be worked on and improved by exercises and, in the meantime, one of the pupils should be used as a demonstration model.

Termination of the pull should be with the hand facing the outer thigh and adjacent to it. The hand should be approximately 230 mm (9 in.) behind the lateral shoulder plane when the outstretched arm is horizontal. This would be equivalent to a water depth of 230 mm (9 in.) if the swimmer were lying in the horizontal mode.

Practice 2: feet hooked under the rail

Teaching points

The previously mentioned teaching points may be adjusted to apply during this exercise, the main difference being, of course, that the movement is being performed in the correct horizontal swimming mode rather than in the standing position. In addition,

5. The depth of pulling movement is the most important feature during this practice and care be taken that the hands do not sink too deeply. The depth of 230 mm (9 in.) is just about right for good results.

Practices 3: Full-stroke movement, preferably across the width of the pool

The pupils may now become mobile once more by carrying out the full-stroke movement but using the legs in the form of a shallow flutter-kick.

The emphasis will be on the arm action with the leg movement assisting to maintain a good swimming position. This full-stroke practice is recommended rather than one whereby the legs are supported by some artificial means. The reasoning behind this suggestion is that:

1. The sideways arm pull tends to distort the natural alignment of the swimmer (snaking), owing to the absence of any leg-balancing forces at this stage:
2. Using the float while swimming in this supinated position, by holding it between the legs, demands a little more skill than the swimmers may possess at this stage in the practices. Consequently, time may be wasted in retrieving rather than actually utilising the floats.
3. Using the float tucked under one arm while swimming with the other tends to make the pupils 'sit' in the water. The practices outlined here, however, are not by any means mandatory and, if the teacher finds that selective use of the floats produces the results he desires, such activities should be included in the programme.

The teacher should ensure that the weaker swimmers are nearer the shallow end of the pool. Starting with their feet hooked under the handrail, and lying back in the water, the pupils perform the arms-only movement.

After a couple of warm-up cycles, the pupils with their arms continuing the motion, gently push away from the rail. They perform a shallow flutter-kick in an attempt to swim across the width of the pool.

Teaching points

The main teaching points have been referred to in the preceding arm-action practices. It will probably be necessary, however, to stress some of the points, such as the correct body and head position. The hips should be riding high ('bottoms up') in the water and the pupils should look up at the roof. The emphasis should be placed on a thumb-out-first/little finger-in-first arm movement incorporating a vertical or near-vertical semi-relaxed straight-arm recovery. The arm cycle should be without pause. Arm entry should be directly in line with the relative shoulder, the upper arm brushing the ear. The pull/push movement should still be carried out at this stage using a semi-circular arm sweep. The depth of pull should be maintained at a maximum of 230 mm (9 in.) and body roll should be minimised.

It is not usually necessary to mention the breathing during the early performances of the stroke, due to the fact that the face is held clear of the water most, of not all, of the time. It might be worth recalling, however, the fact that the swimming should be breathing in through the mouth and out mainly through the nose and not holding their breath.

The full-stroke exercise, with limited leg movement, leads naturally on to the next activity.

Activity: stroke co-ordination

The leg kick was largely ignored in the previous in the previous exercise, but now the complete movement as well as the rhythm and timing will be fostered.

It will be found that it is necessary to link the leg timing to the arm movement rather than vice versa and it is best to teach a six-beat movement (six leg beats to one complete arm cycle). In practice, if the pupils are instructed to aim for a one-two-three/one-two-three leg rhythm as the arms carry out the complete movement, the stroke timing will evolve as a natural process.

Stroke variation

The whole stroke is now ready for analysis and, before the straight-arm action becomes too deeply integrated. A slight variation in the pulling movement should be introduced. The teacher will be aware of the fact that better propulsion characteristics are attained by facing the palms of the hands directly backwards for as long as possible during the arm stroke.

With this fact in mind, and with the pupils at a stage where they are able to absorb a slight variation in the initially taught technique, the straight-arm pull may be modified to the technically superior bent-arm pull/push movement.

The swimmers are now shown, by a practical swimming demonstration if possible, the technique of the bent-arm, action. A short explanation of the advantage of the movement should also be given, underlining the fact that the palms are facing towards the feet for a longer time during the underwater cycles, thus providing more propulsion.

Teaching practices

The pupils now revert to a previous static exercise, namely that of hooking the feet under the rail and carrying out the arm movement while lying in a supine mode. This time, however, instead of the straight-arm pull, the bent-arm action substituted.

When this new movement is more or less established, the pupils may once more carry out full-stroke practices incorporating the modified arm stroke.

Teaching points

1. Immediately the hand and arm enter the water, the catch is made, with the arm initially remaining straight. The elbow then bends and, with wrist held firm, the pull/push movement is carried out with the palm facing towards the feet for as long as possible during this underwater arm sweep.

2. The finger tips must remain sufficiently deep so as not to cause bubbles or any water-surface disturbance.

3. At the conclusion of the push phase, the hand should be just wide of the thigh with palm facing down.

4. The release may be carried out by either the thumb or the back of the hand leaving the water first.

5. Arm recovery is as previously described with the arm held straight.

Further full-stroke work may be carried out, introducing the correct underwater push-glide-stretch into swim sequence. This turn may lead to back-crawl straight and turning practices.

Coaching objectives for the backstroke

You should understand how to effectively teach the backstroke to beginning swimmers.

a. Helpful terms referring to the backstroke.

b. Body position, armstroke, kick, and breathing for the backstroke.

c. Coaching points to be emphasized in the backstroke.

d. Drills for learning and developing the backstroke.
e. Start and turn appropriate for the backstroke.
f. Coaching points to be emphasized in the backstroke start and turn.

Coaching points for the armstroke

1. Arms should move continuously and in opposition.
2. Little finger should lead in the entry.
3. Hands should enter at 11:00 and 1:00 o'clock positions on the face of a clock.
4. Elbows should be at a 90-degree angle on the pull.

Backstroke kick and breathing pattern

Your swimmers should use a six-beat flutter kick with each backstroke arm cycle. This demonstrated on land in a sitting position. The legs and feet should be relaxed. On the downbeat, the legs are straight; on the upbeat, the knees bend slightly. When done in the water, only the big toe of each foot should be seen causing the water to churn at feet. The depth of the up-and-down movement of the kick is approximately the same as the width of the swimmer's shoulders. Explain that breathing is continuous and should be synchronized to the arm movement by inhaling on the recovery of the alternate arm.

Coaching points for the backstroke

1. Six kicks should be made with each arm cycle.
2. Legs should be almost straight.
3. Only the big toe should break the water.
4. Synchronize breathing to the recovery of the alternate arm.

Drills for practising the backstroke

One swimmer lies on the back on a bench on dry land. Move the swimmer's arm through the "S" pattern to give the swimmer the feel of the movement and allow team-mates to visualize the process. If a swimmer in the water is pulling incorrectly, do not hesitate to have the swimmer leave the pool and practice the stroke in this manner.

Shallow water drill

Have your swimmers stand in armpit-depth water. One arm reaches back, entering the water with the little finger leading. This arm makes the "S" pattern with the hand, emphasizing the press down at the end of the stroke. The swimmer then tries the drill with the other hand. The first time the drill is done, allow the swimmer to turn the head and watch the hand. When the motion is grooved, the head is held stationary during the drill. Finally, the swimmer does the drill with alternate arms.

Double arm backstroke drill

A regular kick is as both arms are brought over the top of the water simultaneously. This drill is easier than trying to move the arms in opposition. The drill also develops shoulder joint flexibility.

One arm is in the water over the head. It acts as a rudder while the other arm performs the pull. Arms are reversed at the end of each length. A variation of the drill places the arm not in use by the hip. More body roll is allowed when the drill is performed in this position.

Head stand on a block or diving board at the end of the pool. From this position, you hold up diving score cards or lap counters. The backstrokers keep their eyes on the numbers in order to know the ones have been flashed. To ensure that your swimmers keep their heads at a 45-degree angle, raise the numbers as they get farther away. At the end of the length, ask demands a stationary head position with the eyes 45 degrees off the water.

Backstroke turn

Swimmers approaching the wall for the backstroke turn must remain on their backs. Swimming rules state that the backstroker's shoulders must not turn over beyond the vertical plane until the foremost hand touches the wall. A competitor who continuously looks at the wall when approaching a turn loses time, breaks the streamlined position of the body, and risks a disqualification. However, the distance from the flags to the turning wall may vary from pool to pool. Although you want your backstrokers to keep their heads in a stationary position allow them to take one look when approaching a turn. This can be done if swimmers are trained to count their strokes from the flags to the turning wall during practice, so have your flags in place at all times.

The pivot position

Teach the pivot position first. The portion of the turn can be taught on dry land againist at wall. Demonstrate that the extended hand touches low with the elbow bent and the finger pointing toward the opposite shoulder. The swimmers turn and roll onto the upper back a the legs are brought upward toward hand that hit while the head moves to the open side. Have feet touch the wall where the hand was have your swimmers practice this movement to land and be sure that they wear a sweatshirt for protection. Next, try this in the water. Ensure that the swimmer's forward hand touches the turning wall 8 to 12 inches below the surface of the water. Again the fingers of the touching hand point toward the opposite shoulder.

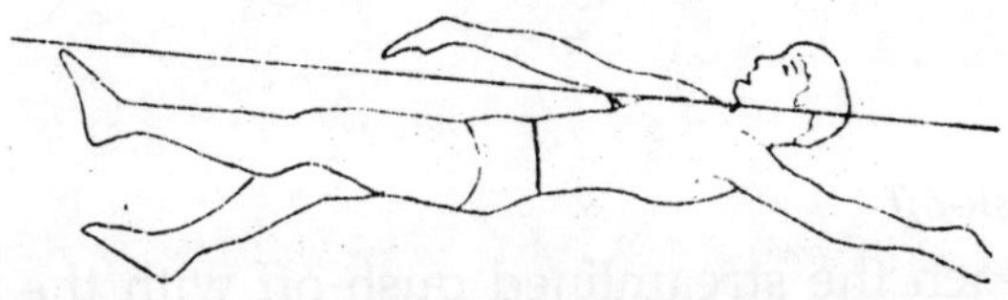

The kick continue until the elbow of the touching hand is bent. Then the knees a squeezed together, and the head and shoulder are submerged as they move away from the hand that hit.

With the aid of the free hand, moving in reverse sculling motion toward the head, to knees are thrown over the surface of the water toward the hand that hit the wall. Swimming that have done the freestyle flip turn should able to grasp the concept of a half back

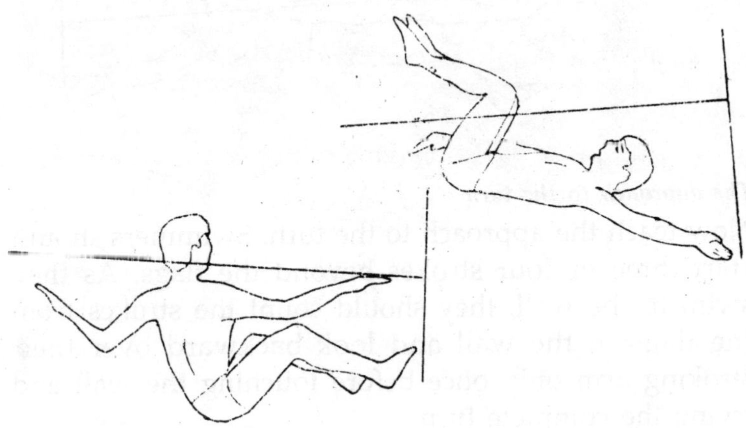

son result. As they do this, they should end up playing the feet on the wall where the hand touched.

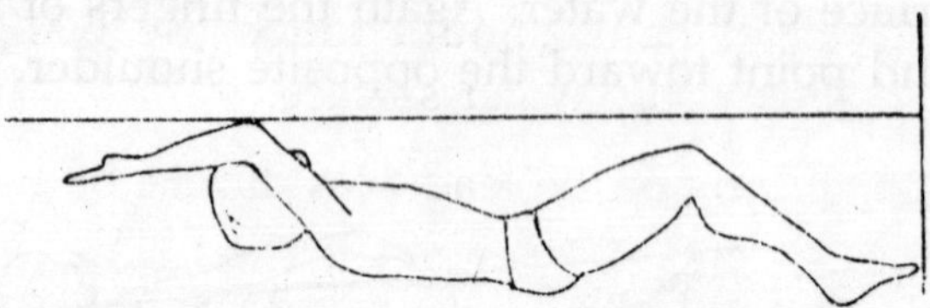

The push-off

The teach the streamlined push-off with the swimmers on their backs in the water. Swimmers should experiment to find a spot 8 to 12 inches below the water surface for their feet. They should be able to push off efficiently from this spot. The hands are placed one on top of the other as in a face-down streamlined position. Be sure to emphasize stretching out with the arms and positioning the head between them as the swimmer leaves the wall.

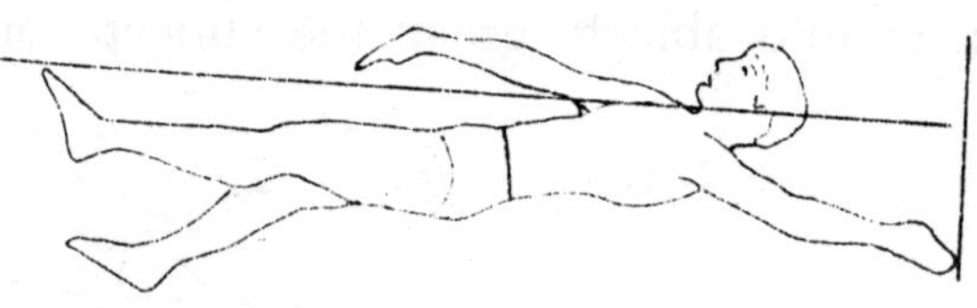

The approach to the turn

Now teach the approach to the turn. Swimmers should start three or four strokes beyond thc flags. As they swim to the wall, they should count the strokes from the flags to the wall and look backward over their stroking arm only once before touching the wall and trying the complete turn.

Coaching points for the backstroke turn

1. Head should be in a stationary position when approaching the turn.
2. Lead hand should touch the wall 8 to 12 inches below the water surface.
3. Elbow of the lead arm should be bent.
4. Head should move away from the hand that hit.
5. Feet should hit the wall where the hand touched.
6. Body should be streamlined, one hand on top of the other, for the push-off.

8

THE FRONT CRAWL

STROKE TECHNIQUE

Body position

In order to obtain a true picture of a swimmer's body position during his stroke performance, he must be viewed from the side, from above, from in front and from behind. It must also be remembered that in all styles, the body position relates to the individual physical characteristics of the swimmer.

When viewed from the side, the front crawler should be seen to be swimming in a flat and horizontal attitude, shoulders, back and legs no more than a few centimetres below the surface. Any deviation from this basic horizontal position will increase the profile area, amplifying the drag forces already created by the movements.

Increase in profile area is most commonly caused by the legs sinking too deeply in the water as a result of lifting the head too high or not kicking hard enough to elevate them towards the surface. Poor inherent buoyancy characteristics may also contribute towards the swimmer moving with his legs in a depressed attitude. In endeavouring to rectify the 'see-saw' effect of lifting his head, the swimmer may try kicking his legs harder. This action will probably in turn cause his back to arch with the final result looking very similar to the crawl stroke used in waterpolo. This is a very exhausting stroke with bad streamlining characteristics. So, as far as speed swimming is concerned, the elevated-head-and-shoulders shoulders type of stroke must be avoided. The position of the swimmer's head should be viewed from directly in front: the still water line should be approximately at the natural hair line. Raising the head higher increases the drag forces: raising his head approximately 70 m above the water-line/hair-line position and moving at a speed of 1.5 m per second, a swimmer under observation increased his body drag forces by as much as fifty per cent.

It must be understood, however, that the head tends to be higher when swimming fast: when travelling slowly only the crown of the head may be in view. If can therefore be seen that lifting rather than turning the head to take a breath can have a considerable effect on body drag as well as disturbing stroke rhythm.

Drag and its effects on propulsion, it was mentioned that the front crawler increases his efficiency with a body roll. The roll also assists in directing the leg movements towards establishing the arm-recovery reaction. Roll should be equal from side to side. As the swimmer moves away, the view from the rear should show that his heels are just breaking the surface. His hips should be rolling slightly less than his shoulders, and his buttocks should be just below water level.

The hip roll will be transmitted to the leg kick so that the beat does not take place in the true vertical plane. As swimming speed increases, the kick tends to be more biased towards the vertical plane, owing to the smaller angle of body roll associated with the increase in stroke rate. Viewed from above, it is essential that the swimmer's long body axis is in line with the general direction of motion. Any deviation from this course can probably be traced to incorrect breathing-in technique or faulty arm-stroking. If the swimmer's long body axis swings out of the true directional alignment, there will be an increase in profile as well as wave drag.

It may be seen that, in general, faulty body positioning is related to stroking or breathing technique. Therefore, in assessing a swimmer's attitude, all stroke movements should be taken into account, together with any physical characteristics and, possibly, fear of putting the face in the water. Only when this analysis has been made can corrective practices be put into operation.

Leg action

The leg movement is an alternate and continuous action in the vertical rather than the horizontal plane. The action maintains the body in a horizontal position, creates propulsion, and balances the stroke by reacting against the action of the arms.

Owing to physiological limitations, the leg kick is nowhere bear as mechanically sound an action as the arm movement.

Throughout the kicking cycle, the feet are extended, like a ballet dancer's on tip-toe. Failure to achieve this extended position results in a loss in propulsive foot area and less thrust. During the upbeat, the feet are held in this plantar-flexed attitude by contraction of the soleus and gastrocnemius (calf) muscles. On the downbeat, the ankle-joint extension is assisted by the hydrodynamic pressure forces developed during this high-speed movement. The toes are also slightly pointed inwards in order to present a larger propelling surface to the water. This, to most swimmers becomes a natural movement after practice, if indeed it is not already in evidence at the start.

The kicking movement originates from the hips with no conscious flexing at the knee joint. The depth of movement should be no more than 450 mm (18 in), but depends on the swimmer's height, the shorter-legged swimmers usually kicking shallower than the taller ones.

On the downbeat the knee tends to lead with the lower leg and extended ankle *initially* rotating in an *opposite* direction of the quadriceps group of muscles which moves the leg swiftly downwards, the extended foot acting rather like a flipper, the generated water pressure acting on the instep tending to knees: this instruction helps produce the *initially* controlled but relaxed rotation of the lower leg on the downbeat.

It can easily be seen why a swimmer's legs should not be kept rigid during this vertical type of kick. Knee extension or leg stiffness during the initial downbeat would prevent any propulsive forces being generated at all; indeed they would tend to be directed downwards, elevating the hips and maintaining the swimmer's body in the horizontal and flat mode.

A high rate of leg kicking demands a considerable amount of muscular energy. Consequently, the circulatory system is required to channel more blood into the massive leg muscles than it normally would, because of the greater oxygen usage. This use of blood and oxygen is detrimental to the muscles which move the more efficient arms. The legs themselves are heavy in relation to the arms, and the rapid accelerating and decelerating movement of such large masses against the generated water pressure is exhausting for even the fittest of swimmers. The frequency of leg kick usually varies between two and six beats per complete arm cycle, depending on the swimmer's technique and the distance being swum. Generally, the leg kicks are more frequent and deeper over shorter distances. There may also be a decrease in the depth of kick, which in turn gives the appearance of a leg 'flutter'. The middle-and longer-distances. Techniques tend to economise in energy by maintaining a shallow leg movement, say to 300 mm (12 in.), and at the same time decrease the rate to perhaps a tow-beat action. There is, however, no reason why the two beat kick should not be used in the sprints and the higher-rate kick used in the longer distances, provided that in each case they perform their designated tasks efficiently and correctly.

It is generally accepted that a swimmer who produces a 100-m time of about sixty-seven seconds uses his leg kick with reasonable effectiveness. However, at faster speeds, the legs tend to play less part in the propulsion and tend to create drag. This is like hanging on to a fast-moving motor boat and kicking the legs to make it go faster: no matter how quickly are legs were moved they would not increase the boat speed but could well reduce it by creating more drag.

Stroke balance may be partially achieved by the application of the Newtonian action/reaction law previously described. For instance, a downward action of the right arm has a lifting reaction tending to raise the swimmer's front end and sink his legs. However, if at the same time as this arm movement the left leg is acting downwards, the reaction is to lift the left hip, thus counterbalancing the depression of the legs. Generally, the effect of the leg action in maintaining balance can be seen more readily when the legs are not being used and supported by some suitable training aid. The movement of the arms will tend to contort a swimmer's body in many ways, as they perform their stroke cycle with no accompanying leg reaction to balance out the propulsive forces that are set up.

Thus, when body streamlining and stoke balance has been achieved, if there is enough propulsion to overcome the inherent drag characteristics of the legs themselves, the leg action may be termed effective. If further propulsion can be gained without undue exhaustion, the action may be termed efficient and economic.

Arm action

The arm action is predominant and produces by far the most propulsion in the front crawl.

The arm cycle may be divided into two phases: the underwater propulsive part of the stroke, and the recovery which takes place over the water surface. The action is continuous and alternating, with one arm moving under the swimmer to create propulsion while the other recovers over the water to the start or entry position. In order to analyse each individual part of the propulsion and recovery actions, the whole movement has been broken down as follows:

Propulsive phase	Recovery phase
Catch	Release
Pull	Recovery every over the water
Push	Entry

Propulsive phase: catch

The catch may be justifiably described as the foundation of the propulsive phase of the stroke. As soon as the hand has entered the water and moved below the surface, the catch commences. By a constant speed or an accelerating downward and backward arm and the swimmer begins to 'feel' the water. For maximum effect, the fingers should be together (or almost together), the hand flat and the wrist very slightly flexed). The depth of movement required to create the desired pressure is usually about 300 mm (12 in.) The fingertips should be directly in line with the vertical central plane of the swimmer's body. At the entry stage, the elbow should be slightly higher than hand and it should remain so during the each. The propulsive pressure on the palm of the hand and lower arm may be established by the speed of movement at entry. However, it is not desirable that the entering hand crashes into the water, thus creating excessive turbulence and drag.

The catch movement is therefore an *accelerating* movement following a *controlled* entry.

Propulsive phase: pull

The arm pull follows on from the catch and continues until the pulling hand and arm lie in the same lateral plane as the shoulder.

Arm propulsion, in the true sense of the word, can

only take place when there is sufficient pressure created on the propelling surfaces of the hand and lower arm to sustain swimming speed. This propulsive pressure is dependent on the speed of the arm movement in relation to that of the water. This means that if the swimmer is travelling at V metres/second in the opposite direction in order that the propulsive pressure is maintained.

If the swimmer is not accelerating (i.e. he is moving at a constant speed), the pressure build-up on his hand and arm must be sufficient to overcome all the various forms of drag created by the water. If he increase his speed, he must overcome these drag forces and also the inertia of his body. The increase of propulsive power must be developed by an even faster stroking rate.

There is one other point worth mentioning here: if the arms move too quickly through the water, excessive eddies are set up in the wake of the limb movement, thus reducing the effective power. This may be termed *over-pulling* or slipping. So the optimum speed of the arm throughout the pull must be found by good and knowledgeable teaching and by the swimmers themselves appreciating the 'feel' of the water. (Feet' of the water is very difficult lo definc and it is only by personally 'stroking and caressing' the water that the teacher can begin to experience this phenomenon.)

During the pull, the palm of the hand should be facing, as near is possible, immediately backward, thus directing the propulsive forces in the most advantageous manner. The fingers must be together, or almost together, and the hand itself should be flat. To establish this backward-facing palm, the wrist will initially need to be slightly flexed and, in order to achieve a good purchase on the water, the elbow should also be flexed and remain elevated above the hand. Excessive bending of the elbow brings the hand nearer to the swimmer's body and, while the pull is mechanically easier owing to the shorter lever arm (over-pulling can take place easily here), it is less effective. A weak-shouldered swimmer may make things easier (but less effective) for himself by, amongst other things, pulling close to the chest.

The fingers are positioned so that they move in the vertical and central plane of the body. Excessive movement of the hand across this central plane in either direction tends to introduce longitudinal body rotation and increase profile drag.

Lateral body roll begins towards the start of the pull and reaches its maximum as the hand and arm pass through the shoulder plane.

Propulsive phase: push

Transition between the pull and the push should be smooth and unnoticeable; it takes place at the shoulder plane. At this phase change-over, the fingers lie approximately in the central body plane and the arm is flexed at the elbow. The hand faces directly back and lies in line with the forearm. As the arm moves, for the first time in the underwater part of the stroke, the hand leads the elbow. Extension of the wrist ensures that the palm continues to face towards the feet. As the hand approaches the waist line, it starts to track outwards and upwards until, at almost full rearward extension, the hand lies very close to the hip and in line with the forearm.

The body will now be rolling to the opposite side to facilitate lifting of the hand from the water in preparation for the recovery phase of the arm cycle.

Recovery phase: release

Arm recovery takes place as soon as the catch/pull/push phases are complete. In order to commence the movement, the hand and arm need to be lifted or 'released' from the water. This action takes place while the body is rolled to the opposite side, and the elbow precedes the hand on leaving the water.

If the push phase has been carried out correctly, the hand will be close to the hip or the top of the thigh when release takes place. If a shortened version of the push has taken place, the hand will probably leave the and indeed in more adroit swimmers when they begin to tire.

As the release takes place, the hand should be should be close to the body and relatively relaxed, the little finger is usually the first to emerge and the hand lies in line with the forearm. As soon as it is free from the water, the arm has to be recovered over the water to the entry position in preparation for the next underwater part of the cycle.

Recovery phase: recovery over the water

A recovery action, by its very nature, does not contribute towards propulsion. If it is carried out incorrectly, the movement can be detrimental to the swimmer's overall performance. It is therefore essential that recovery technique is not neglected, and that an smooth, efficient and comfortable movement is established at an early stage of the stroke development.

The swimmer's shoulder flexibility will probably

be the paramount factor affecting his arm recovery. Should the 'rotational freedom' of the shoulder joint be great, the swimmer will be able to achieve the desired elbow-high and hand-low swinging trajectory, with little body roll. A 'tight-shouldered' individual, however, will need to roll further, but not necessarily excessively, in order to maintain a high elbow action while at the same time just clearing the water with his hand. The hand trajectory will more than likely be a wide sweeping one.

Muscular energy is needed to left the arm from the water and set it in motion then, once sufficient speed is achieved, the anterior shoulder muscles may be partially relaxed and allow the limb to swing, under its own momentum and a little guidance, into the re-entry position. This partial, muscle activity thus allows a controlled but relaxed arm recovery movement to take place.

The hand traces a path just above the water surface, moving in an are about the shoulder joint. The wrist and finger joints are relaxed. At the points of release and (re-) entry, the elbow is slightly flexed. This angle of flexion varies during the arm movement and reaches a maximum (approximately ninety degrees) as the arm and hand pass simultaneously through the plane of the shoulder.

It is not uncommon to see a competition swimmer recovering his or her arms with no elbow flexion what so ever. In method, the hand, being further from the source of rotation, i.e. shoulder joint, has to travel further than it would if the elbow were bent: the path of the hand is often elevated above that of the elbow. This usually means that the speed of the hand is faster than it would be in the conventional bent-arm type of recovery, and that consequently there is less control over the movement; the hand thus crashes into the water creating unnecessary commotion, and sometimes enter the water on the wrong side of the central body plane. The effect of this crossed-over entry action is to bend the swimmer into a banana shape as he swims: this of course increases the drag and interferes with the definite and smooth rhythm which the swimmer is attempting to establish.

The higher rotational speed of the arm also generates a greater centrifugal force, which is proportional to the rotational arm speed (squared). This force acts directly along the axis of the arm and away from the swimmer, tending to pull his shoulders in the direction of the hand. Excessive rotational speeds also necessitate high acceleration which in turn introduces unwanted inertia forces which tend to contort and retard the swimmer.

Recovery phase: entry

The hand enters the water finger tips first and forward of the shoulders in a controlled mode. The lateral* point of entry lies between the central body plane and a parallel plane passing through the shoulder joint. The fingers should be together, or almost together, and the hand flat; there should also be also be slight flexion of the wrist. The elbow should also be flexed and elevated a little higher than the hand, in order to achieve this finger tips-first entry.

The high-elbow/low-hand entry has several important advantages. Firstly, an elbow-first entry would create excessive wave drag. Secondly, it establishes the hand and arm position in preparation for the subsequent catch phase. Thirdly, the flexed elbow helps to reduce the tendency for the swimmer to over-reach. This fault has an averse effect on the deltoid-dominated muscular action, by increasing the effective radius from the shoulder joint to the centre of (propulsive) pressure. The swimmer may out not be strong enough to cope with this extra leverage and may tire quickly.

Entering the hand laterally outside or across the desired entry point (or area) can have the effect that the subsequent catch and pull movements rotate the swimmer across the line of progress.

This conclude the description of a single arm cycle. The opposite arm moves in a similar fashion to that described above, but as one arm propels the other recovers. The whole action may be described as alternating and continuous.

Hand trajectory

When viewed from directly below, the complete pattern of arm movement may be similar to that shown in fig. 16.6. The trajectory of the hand during the propulsive phase usually takes the shape of an elongated S or ogee. However, its path of movement may be affected by the degree of lateral roll of the swimmer's body beyond or away from the central plane.

Breathing

Breathing movements should be carried out in such a way that they blend rather than interfere with the general stroke pattern. It is better to let the stroke technique dictate the breathing pattern rather than vice versa.

A breath is taken on the arm-recovery side as the swimmer's head is rotated in the same direction as the body roll, thus enabling him or her to inhale as the mouth clears the water.

Assisting the inhalation sequence is the fact that, due to the water speed, the swimmer sets up a bow wave around his head. This in turn creates a 'breathing trough' around the face and reduces the amount of head rotation that is necessary in order to snatch a quick breath.

As soon as air has been inhaled, the face returns to the water and, at the same time, the recovery arm swings around towards the entry point. The head now resumes its approximate hair-line/water-line relationship in preparation for the breathing-out process. As the swimmer's body rotates in the opposite direction to that of the breathing side, the head may roll smoothly with it or remain facing forward and downward.

Methods of breathing out into the water and the associated timings are many and varied. Probably that which has least effect on the stroke for a short period before exhalation takes place explosively into the water in preparation for the next breath.

This particular method is often used during short swims up to, say, 100 m, but is not advised for the untrained swimmer for longer distance as it becomes rather exhausting after a while. Constant training in breath holding is reputed to increase the blood-capillary network and enable competition swimmers to hold their breath for long periods during racing swims, without apparent ill effects.

Exhalation into the water may be of the trickle or explosive pattern, taking place through the nose and/ or mouth. *Trickle* exhalation through the nose only is probably the best method during a slow or medium-paced swim. During a sprint or rapid-arm-cycling swim the *explosive* method of exhalation will most likely be the favourite. Here, breathing out should take place just prior to the face leaving the water in order to snatch the next intake of air.

Whichever method is adopted, it always good practice when learning to allow a slight trickle of air to escape from the nose as it passes through the water surface. This prevents water droplets finding their way to the back of the throat, causing coughing and spluttering.

A breathing technique may be used where by the swimmer takes a breath at every stroke or every other stroke, etc., *on the same side* (unilateral). Alternatively, the swimmer can take a breath on *alternate sides* (bilateral technique) every one and a half arm cycles. The trickle or explosive technique may be used with either of these methods.

It is advisable for the learner swimmer to adopted regular breathing patterns during his initial swims. These patterns should fit in unobtrusively with the overall technique to produce a natural and even rhythm.

Air must always be taken into the lungs whenever it is needed; the not advisable for the untrained as it tends to starve the lungs of oxygen and leads very quickly to fatigue. Also, if the breath is held, the breathing muscles themselves are tensed, thus requiring more oxygen than usual. The nearer the swimmer can come to the track athlete in his breathing technique, the better. The runner is able to take a breath at the rate that needs it. The swimmer should endeavour, as far as possible, as far as possible, to do the same.

Co-ordination

Co-ordination and stroke rhythm should develop naturally with practice. Early teaching faults are usually associated with the breathing technique. To create a balanced and even stroke, the swimmer's legs must move in such a way as to react against any out-of-balance forces created by the arms during propulsion and recovery.

A rhythmic leg beat of six kicks per complete arm cycle produces good stroke-balancing characteristics. Using this timing, the swimmer is able to co-ordinate his limb movements to produce counter-balancing forces which maintain his body in a reasonable state of equilibrium.

The four-beat rhythm also provides reasonable stroke stabilisation, but, with the decrease in frequency, the amplitude of the kick may need to be increased. The two-beat or cross-over rhythm is a pure stabiliser, being used mainly in distance swimming. Here, each complete arm cycle is accompanied by synchronised body roll and this results in the kick being biased towards the horizontal rather than the vertical plane.

The results of good stroke co-ordination are immediately apparent to the onlooker, but the smoothness of a swimmer's performance may be affected by speed. For instance, he may display jerky stroke movements at the lower end of his speed range but, as he increases his stroke rate, the whole movement evens out into a flowing rhythm. Early teaching are best directed toward the six-beat rhythm with any special adjustments in technique and timing being left until later, should the swimmer decide to take up the sport in a competitive way.

Teaching the competition strokes

Each feature of the competition strokes has been analysed and systematically broken down into what is considered a logical sequence of teaching progressions or part-practices. The teacher may not wish to use the sequences of activities exactly as they are presented. However, it is not advisable to omit too many of the progressions, otherwise the continuity of learning may be lost. On the other hand, the teacher may find his own favourite activities have been omitted from the series: if their inclusion is justified by their usefulness, by all means add such activities to the overall programme.

Each set of stroke-related practices has been presented in a continuous form, but in fact, with only a certain amount of lesson time available, the individual activities will need to be sub-divided and integrated into a sequence of lesson plans.

An important feature in teaching the activities is *repetition.* In the majority of instances it is only after returning to the part-practices many time that a particular movement or combination of movements establishes itself among the swimmers. As a teacher, never be reluctant to step backwards; it is not necessarily a backward step.

Preparatory standards for teaching front crawl

Before commencing the following programme of front-crawl practices, it is advisable that pupils are able to perform the following activities with a degree of skill:

1. Confidence exercises-face-wetting, blowing bubbles and submersion.
2. Regaining the feet from a prone position (should the shallow-end swimmers wish to stand up part-way across)
3. Push and glide from the poolside (for starting off)
4. Front paddle for at least twenty meters (as an introduction to elementary prone swimming)
5. Treading water (should the deep-end swimmers need to stop for any reason at any time)
6. General water-mobility exercises (swimmers may have to move sideways to avoid others; also they may have to stop and then start swimming once more)

TEACHING THE FRONT CRAWL

There will be few pupils in the average class who have not watched some variation of the front crawl stroke being performed. They may, of course, know it by some other name, such as the 'overarm' stroke, or describe it, sometimes quite picturesquely, by gesticulating their arms wildly. However, probably *none* of the pupils will have had the stroke technique actually demonstrated to them.

If an able performer can be found for the occasion, an excellent way to start the first front-crawl lesson is by staging such a demonstration.

Activity: demonstration swim with commentary

This visual approach has already been mentioned and it will found to be invaluable in the teaching of any stroke. A return to such demonstration of full-or part-stroke techniques is well worth consideration at any time. The demonstration swim need only be of short duration, with the pupils gathered around the poolside so that they have a good view and can at the same time see and hear the teacher without averting their eyes too far from the swimmer.

A simple descriptive next should be used without too many long words and technicalities, bearing in mind the ages of the pupils involved and also how much they are able to absorb at any one time.

Explanation may take the form of a description of the swimmer's body position in the water, followed by the main features of the leg action. The arm movement may be divided into two stages, namely the pull (underwater phase) and the recovery (over-water phase, including the entry).

A brief mention of the breathing technique may be made, pointing out that the swimmer is breathing out into the water. It is worth noting at this stage that probably the greatest hurdle that the pupils will have to overcome in learning the stroke is the breathing technique. The breathing-in phase of the sequence is precise and exhaling into the water is unnatural, so in order to get full concentration on style, it is advisable that initial full-stroke practices are carried out with the breath being held for short duration. These early practices may take the form of short swims across the pool with the swimmer's head held in such a way that the face is immersed and the water line is approximately at the natural hair line. The head position may be described as looking forward and slightly downwards. The early swims in this attitude will help to establish the desired horizontal position and at the same time provide a good foundation for future stroke work.

At the end of the demonstration, question time should be kept to a minimum. This is not usually difficult because the pupils are usually eager to have a go. Having shown the pupils the stroke being performed and explained something about its technique, full-lesson participation may now commence.

Activity: initial full-stroke swims

Without any further instruction, the class now have the chance to demonstrate their skills, such as they are, by swimming a short, pre-determined distance under the watchful, and not too critical, eye of the teacher. A short dash back and forth across the pool will enable the teacher to assess the task in hand and give the class an opportunity for a warm-up.

Teaching points

1. Achievement of the correct head posture is a very important feature of the stroke practices. The water line should be approximately at the swimmer's natural hair line, taking account of individual physical characteristics. Excessive lifting of the head in fear, or for any other reason, tends to elevate the chest and sink the legs, thus making it difficult for the swimmer to maintain the desired horizontal mode. In their depressed attitude, the legs tend to lose their rhythm and a regular kick becomes more

difficult to achieve. A pedalling action is a common result, and this in turn of course does not lift the legs or propel the swimmer forward.

Countering the effect of the 'head-up' attitude may be carried out by a vigorous leg movement. This is very exhausting, and for novices and weak swimmers almost impossible. Waterpolo players swim in this position in order to observe the field of play. It takes, however, many hours of exhaustive practice to achieve a successful performance of this special head-up technique.

2. The legs must be elevated to provide lateral body stabilisation. An even rhythm in the leg beat provides the reactive balancing effect to the arm action. Uneven rhythm results, for instance, in excessive body roll to one side. If the swimmer's leg action gives propulsion at this stage, this is a bonus.
3. High elbow recovery and entry.
4. Continuity of the stroke movement is very important and is dependent on many inter-related factors within the stroke technique. At this early stage of learning it is advisable not to spend too much time endeavouring to correct faults in the overall technique, but rather to proceed to part-stroke practices and concentrate on obtaining good results there before returning to the full stroke.

Activity: leg action

When performing prone leg practices, pupils will often turn their heads and try to look behind them in rode to see how their legs are shaping up.

If they can actually see how their arms or legs are performing it invariably assists in achieving the required result.

Practice 1 : sitting on the poolside and kicking the leg (fig. 16.9)

Teaching points

1. The kick is an alternating leg action.
2. The leg movement originates from the hip. Leg propulsion is based on the techniques described earlier in this chapter and it is essential that this hip-generated kick is emphasised right from the start of the practices.
3. The legs should be close together (in the lateral plane). This is more of a physical advantage than a hydrodynamic one. Spreading the legs unnecessarily brings into action the lateral leg-muscle groups not normally used in this action.
4. The kicking depth should be not more than 450 mm (18 in.). The depth of kick has a direct bearing on the rate of the leg beat. If the kick is deep, the mechanics of the action dictate that the rate of movement is slower.
5. Relaxation of the knee joint enables the whip-like movement, which produces the major part of the leg propulsion, to take place on the downbeat.
6. Relaxed ankles ('floppy feet') with 'toeing-in' is important. By relaxing the ankles, some people are able to shake their feet about quite loosely. The 'toeing-in' of the feet is, for some people, a natural physical attribute; for others this foot position has to be cultivated. The reason for 'toeing-in' is that it increases the effective propulsive area of each foot.

7. A smooth action. The whole leg action should flow smoothly, although without the resistive effects of the water to moderate the movements slightly, this land-based exercise may be jerky. Tensing the joints will also tend to produce incorrect movements and hasten the onset of fatigue. Cramp may even set in at this stage.
8. Good rhythm and timing. The timing should be regular with the teacher setting the pace by counting, say, a six-beat pattern: one-two-three one-two-three, and so on. The six-beat rhythm will probably be the best one to use during the teaching of the stroke.

Practice 2: poolside rail-supported leg kicking

The pupils are in the water holding the handrail or channel to continue the kicking practices. This exercise may be a revisionary one from the earlier front-paddle teachings but, as this is not always so, the lesson is presented here as being for the first time. Perhaps a little more finesse will be accomplished on this occasion.

The method of holding on to the rail or channel will probably need a short explanation. Some learners find difficulty in raising their legs to the surface while holding the rail or channel; others use their natural buoyancy and kicking ability to elevate themselves quite easily. If they are using a handrail the pupils can undergrasp it and press their elbows to the wall' the lever action raises their outstretched bodies and legs to the surface. A certain amount of control is needed in order to keep the legs in the water when the kicking exercise commences. A slight relaxation at the elbow joint will lower the legs if they rise too high.

Where only a channel exists around the pool, there is another holding method which may be employed. Holding the channel with one hand, the child places the palm of the other hand, with fingers pointing downwards, pushing with the lower hand, the outstretched body and legs will rise to the surface. The position on the wall of the pushing hand is and places the left hand flat on the wall and too far to the left, his body will swing round to the right. Conversely, if the left hand is too far to the right the pupil's outstretched body will veer round to the left. By carefully positioning the hand under water, however, a happy medium can be found that aligns the swimmer correctly. The exercise has a limited value because without the freedom of forward movement it is difficult to judge the efficiency of the leg action. It does however enable the teacher to talk to the pupils and attempt to make adjustments to their various techniques, while they are static and can see and hear him easily.

Teaching points

All the teaching points given for the first exercise are relevant here, together with the following:

9. The feet must be kept in the water at all times, with the heel in the uppermost part of the kick just breaking the surface.

Practice 3: leg kicking using floats

The exercise enables the pupils to become mobile in the water by using floats. A pair of these are tucked one under each arm, or, where a single float is used, it is held in the hands with the fully outstretched in front. The movement shows immediately whether the pupils possess anything resembling a propulsive technique.

Teaching points

The afore-mentioned teaching points are all applicable to this exercise, and the following should now be added:

10. The pupils should once more be shown how to use to floats, by tucking them under the arms and grasping them firmly on the long sides, or one float which is grasped in the centre with thumbs on the top and fingers underneath. Alternatively, they may rest their forearms over the top of the float and curl their fingers over the end, the water lifting the float up against the forearms. When swimming with one float, arms must be kept fully stretched in front, with the float riding flat on the water surface. If a float is brought in close to the body by bending the arms, the swimmer tends to learn on it and force it below the surface, rendering it less effective.

Practice 4: fully stretched kicking

This is a leg-kicking exercise carried out in the fully stretched position with the face in the water. The water line should be at the hair line and the breath is held while width practices are carried out. With this exercise we have now reached the true flat and horizontal swimming attitude which should be emphasised strongly.

Teaching points

The teaching points have all previously been mentioned, except that of maintaining a fully stretched an streamlined position, and also the following:

11. The swimmers should be shown the method of head lifting and breathing, should they not be able to hold their breath for a full width.

Activity: breathing

Practice 1 : standing in the shallow end of the pool near the side and holding the rail

The main aim of this first breathing exercise is to give the swimmers enough confidence to put their faces in the water-then breathe out. Some of the pupils may have performed this exercise at an earlier stage and for them this is a recapitulation, but, for others, the practices may be completely new.

The most troublesome and off-putting part of this early exercise is when water is allowed to enter the nasal passages during exhalation. The results can be distressing and sometimes painful. Let us, therefore by careful choice of practices, attempt to minimise the coughing and spluttering which can take place. Working on the theory that, if air is flowing down the nose, water and gently trickle the air out through their noses. The important feature to emphasis here is that nasal breathing must continue as the face leaves the water. If the children all adhere to this simple instruction there will be minimal distress.

Rubbing the water from the eyes will probably be common practice during these early breathing exercises. The teacher should attempt to discourage this as the lesson progresses.

The exercise should be continued until the pupils are able to repeat this face-ducking movement several times. The teacher should look for complete face submersion and the tell-tale sign of bubbles surfacing around the ears. Variations in the methods of breathing out into the water may now be introduced. A straightforward nodding action rather than turning the head can still be used.

The pupils may experiment with a nose-and-mouth and a mouth-only trickle exhalation with the accent on breath control. If trouble with water ingress into the nasal passages during the latter exercise is experienced, the pupils should return to nose-only or nose-and-mouth breathing until they have learned to control their respiration.

Sprint swimming necessitates an explosive delivery of air into the water, so the pupils may now try this method of breathing out. Thy should take a breath, then place their faces into the water and quickly exhale through mouth and nose. A short pause between the submersion and explosion relates the movement to actually swimming the sprint front crawl stroke. As soon as the air is expired, or at the 'tail end' of the blow, faces are lifted clear of the water in preparation for the next intake.

After a short while, the pupils will probably have acquired some skill in submersive breathing, and may now proceed to the next series of exercises. These relate not only to the methods of breathing out into the water, but also to the technique of inhalation.

During the performance of the front crawl stroke, the swimmer's face is turned to one side to enable a breath to be taken, and this is brought about rather than head lifting, into the breathing cycle.

The pupils hold the rail and stand in the same way as in the previous exercises; they then place their faces into the water and breathe out by a method that may be stipulated by the teacher or be left to each individual pupil's discretion. In order to take the next breath, the pupils rotate their heads until their mouths are just clear of the water for a gasp of air to be taken. As soon as inhalation has taken place, they return their faces into the water and then breathe out. A breathing rhythm may now be established as the exercise is repeated. Turning the head to breathe while static is slightly different form inhaling while move through the water with reasonable speed. The forward motion tends to create a bow wave around the head, and it is in the trough formed by the wave that the swimmer inhales. The is therefore no need for the head to be rotated quite so far when swimming.

Emphasis on the head position should, at this stage, be brought into the teaching. The water line should be approximately at the hair line and if, the eyes were open, they would be looking forward and downward at about thirty degrees.

A development in the practices is for the pupil to withdraw the arm which is on the 'breathing side' away from the hand rail and place it down by his side. This allows more freedom for the head roll to take place and may accommodate a slight shoulder roll, thus bringing the movement nearer to that of actually swimming. Care must be taken, however, to ensure that the head still rotates in relation to the shoulders and not, in a stiff-necked fashion, with them. A further practice may be employed, whereby the pupils are encouraged to breathe in on the opposite side to their first choice. This introduces a bi-lateral quality into the sequence and may be related to competition swimming.

Teaching points

1. The breath must be taken in through the mouth and exhaled through the nose and/or the mouth.
2. The water line should be at the natural hair line during the exhalation phase of the cycle.
3. The head must be rotated and not lifted.
4. If trouble with the ingress of water into the nasal passages is experienced, the technique of breathing out through the nose as the face breaks the surface should be emphasised.
5. Rubbing the eyes after submersion must be discouraged as this is impractical when actually swimming.

Fear of putting one's face in the water is quite common and, should the teacher encounter such inhibitions among members of the class, due consideration must be shown and the teaching, adjust accordingly. It takes considerable courage for anyone with this type of phobia to submerge his face in the water and even more to breathe out while still there. It must be further understood that some individuals never overcome this fear, and it is therefore advisable not to enforce these practices on a pupil who is genuinely frightened of immersing the whole of his face. Instead, treat the whole matter lightly; encourage him, for instance, to take a warm shower and look up at the stream of water as it cascades down, or tell him to try blowing bubbles in the sink at home; the security of a warm bath at home could also be a good place to attempt the exercise.

One final point: as the practices develop, suggest opening the eyes in the water. Encourage this, but again do not enforce it. Some pupils find not difficulty in looking around under the surface, while others may be affected by the water additives and end up with sore eyes.

As time progresses and games are played, most young people will learn to put their faces in the water in order to see something or other and will probably breathe out during the process, and difficulties which may have arisen earlier will gradually disappear.

The previous set of exercises has been carried out in a static manner; we now attempt to integrate the breathing pattern with the leg action and, in doing so, re-introduce some mobility into the programme.

Practice 2: float-assisted leg kicking

Teaching points

All the teaching points emphasised during the static practices are relevant, and the following may be added:

6. The flat horizontal swimming position should be maintained at all times. The exercise will probably display how lifting the head rather than turning it tends to sink the legs. A class demonstration of this fault, and its remedy, might be useful at this stage.
7. A regular breathing rhythm, synchronised with the leg beat, should be established. This may take the form of one breath for every four or six kicks.

If the practices have been carried out with reasonable success, the class should now be traversing the pool with confidence and be ready to proceed to the arm practices. However, should the teacher feel that a little more practice is required, he or she should persevere a little while longer.

Activity: arm action

Practice 1: standing

The first exercise relating to the arm movement may take place while the pupils are standing in the shallow end of pool and facing the teacher as her or she demonstrates the actions from the poolside.

Teaching points

1. Entry of the hand into the water must be finger tips first. The elbow should be flexed and slightly higher than the hand, which in turn must be flat with palm facing downwards.

   The flexed and elevated elbow should allow the hand to enter the water at approximately thirty degrees to the horizontal. Laterally, the fingertips must enter at a point somewhere between the central plane of the body and the outside of the shoulder. This places the arm in a mechanically sound position in order to commence the pull. Over-reaching must be avoided at all costs as the fault tends to distort the swimmer's shoulders and the long axis of the body. It also places the pulling muscles at a mechanical disadvantage prior to the pull.

   The excessive stretching forward of the arm also causes the elbow to drop, which in turn can result in an incorrect elbow-first entry.

2. After entry, the hand must initially move fairly rapidly so that pressure may be built upon the palm and lower arm. The technical term for this part of the stroke is the catch, and if the teacher feels he must single it out for mention, it may be described as being the point where the swimmers

'catch and feel' the water on the palms of their flat hands before pushing it back behind them.

3. Throughout the pull-and-push phases, the hand must not move beyond the body's central plane or wander excessively outside the width of the shoulders or hips (whichever is the wider). Moving too far away in a lateral direction from the central plane tends to introduce 'snaking' into the stroke and this causes all sorts of problems.
4. The hands should be flat and the fingers together, or almost together, at all times during the propulsive phase of the stroke.
5. The palm of the hand must face directly back towards the feet for as long as possible during the underwater phase of the cycle. This is necessary in order to ensure maximum forward propulsion throughout the full arm sweep.
6. The elbow should leave the water before the hand, and it should also be forward of the hand when this release takes place. If the reverse situation occurs, it usually means that the push phase is non-existent or that excessive body rolling is taking place.
7. The recovery hand must follow an outward-swinging arc, just clearing the waves. The elbow must be higher than the hand throughout. Straight arm recoveries have the effect of distorting the long body axis. Relaxation is the key word during recovery, which should be accompanied by a slight body roll.
8. The co-ordination between the arms seems to come

automatically to young swimmers. If any description is needed, it could be something to the effect that the arms are almost opposite each other as they move. (If the teacher's demonstration has been correct and clear, there should be no doubt about this point.) Some teachers call it a windmill style but this tends to conjure up a straight arm-recovery movement in the minds of young swimmers.

9. The whole arm movement should be continuous and alternating and the shoulders must remain submerged throughout.

Practice 2: walking in shallow water

Teaching points

All the previous teaching points are relevant here, together with the point are lifted. Therefore to add some breathing technique to these practices is the next step.

Practice 3: standing or walking with breathing, with or without a float

Practice 4: float-assisted single-arm practice

This practice is carried out with a float held by one hand in front of the swimmer, while he or she performs single-arm strike cycles accompanied by the leg action. The movement may be performed with or without breathing and can be used both as a progression or as a corrective exercise.

Teaching points

All teaching points previously mentioned are relevant, together with the method of holding the float.

Activity: stroke co-ordination

Dog paddle

Most of the pupils will probably have started their swimming careers by learning front or dog paddle. So, having improved the leg action and body position and introduced stroke-related breathing, we may return to this simple stroke. We can also introduce into it some of the new techniques that have now been learned, thus bringing the swimmers one step nearer to the ultimate goal of front crawl.

The arm pull should be slightly modified for this new dog-paddle exercise so that it becomes longer and consequently slower than the minimum of profile resistance. The action should also include a slight body roll in the direction of the pulling arm.

Teaching points

1. A horizontal body position must be maintained at all times, with water-line/hair-line relationship being of paramount importance.

   The less able swimmers in the class will initially try to breathe in by lifting the head as one hand presses down into the catch. This lifting action will have the effect on the legs of making them sink deeper than required and upsetting their rhythm. Continual emphasis must therefore be made on rotating rather than lifting the head in order to inhale.

   A slight body roll should be integrated into the stroke; this is one of the essential features of a good front crawl and assists with the breathing technique.

2. The leg movement must be continuous, with all the previously mentioned teaching points being observed. The beat should be a shallow flutter or a six-beat pattern. This kicking rate is ideal for the long arm pull and the subsequent slow recovery.

3. The arm stroke should be a long one rather than the shortened version that was used in the earlier front-paddle practices, in order to accommodate the timing of the leg beat.

   The hands should pull alternately under the swimmer's body with each palm facing directly backward for as long as possible throughout the movement.

   Arm recovery is carried out under the water surface and, in order to minimise resistance during this part of the stroke, each elbow should be brought close to the body as it moves forward. Also, during this forward movement, the hands must be flat, with the finger tips pointing ahead. (The swimmer's elbow may tend to break the surface at the end of the pull: this does not really matter.)

4. Breathing methods should conform to those that were practised earlier. It is most important associated with respiration.

   Breathing in should be accompanied by a lateral head roll and breathing out should be into the water.

   The teacher must be careful not to venture into the realms of coaching. As long as the pupils have tried to carry out the various methods of breathing, it is probably best left, for the time being, to each individual to adopt his or her own technique, as long as it is reasonably correct.

5. The head should be swivelled independently of the shoulders to prevent excessive rolling to the breathing side.

Activity: full front crawl stroke

The exercises may be carried out initially as a fully integrated style, then with the pupils concentrating on a single skill at a time within the overall technique while still *performing the full stroke movement.*

This method of full-stroke teaching has the advantage that each swimmer is devoting full attention to an individual practice, but at the same time performing it in relation to all the other unique stroke factors which affect it.

Individual limb practices tend to be carried out in isolation and, as overall technique improvers, they leave much to be desired. As body exercises and muscle developers they are, of course, ideal, and are used constantly during a training programme.

They form a vital part of learning the strokes from the beginning, and are also invaluable during fault correction. However, only when the complete stroke is practised can a single stroke feature be assessed. One example of these shortcomings has already been given: the front-crawl which is, of course, an integral part of the overall stroke technique. The legs therefore do not work in the variable plane that they experience during full stroking. However, for leg and tummy muscle development, float-assisted leg practices are ideal. Similarly, with the various breathing practices carried out at the rail, the static mode does not produce the bow wave or body roll which are present during complete stroke performance, hence the head needs to be rotated further in order to inhale. Full stoke practices may commence with short swims to the rail with the breath being held. The distance can then be gradually increased until a full width is being completed.

Breathing action may then be introduced using an infrequent pattern, i.e. one or two breaths per width, taken at will. The frequency may then be increased until the pupils are able to manage one breath per arm cycle. The width exercise may take place in 'waves' whereby one set of swimmers takes off at the teacher's signal to follow the first set of swimmers.

If it is convenient, longer distance should be attempted by the more adroit members of the class. This gives a chance for each individual stroke to develop, although the teacher must be constantly looking for technique faults. Remember, the longer a fault is practised, the deeper it becomes integrated into the stroke, and the more difficult it is a to remove.

It may be advantageous now for the class to be split yet again into ability groups, in order that more specialised instruction may be given to the less able pupils and more demanding practices performed by the more adept swimmers.

If an attending class teacher is willing and able to assist, he or she could watch over an activity that does not need specialist knowledge.

Teaching points

All the previously mentioned teaching points apply during full-stroke practices. General stroke co-ordination should be encouraged with emphasis on a smooth rhythm and regular breathing habits. The teacher must always be prepared to return to part-stroke practices in order to concentrate on one specific teaching point. Remember the earlier statement regarding individual exercises and their necessary integration into the whole stoke.

The series of exercises are meant to form the foundation for a set of lesson plans. Alteration and addition to the sequence may be necessary, according to the standard of the pupils, the time available and the environmental conditions.

Diving in and pushing off from the side are also important and can be related to general stroke technique.

9
THE BREASTSTROKE

The formal performance of the breast stroke is rigidly, controlled by Amateur Swimming Association laws. These laws appertain to the competition style only, but it is considered to be good general teaching practice to adhere to them. The main reason for this, is that many children at some time or other enter a race at school or at a club gala. Disqualification from the breast-stroke event because of incorrect stroke technique could be a bitter and unnecessary disappointment.

The breast-stroke laws state that:

> The swimmer's body shall be kept perfectly on the breast and both shoulders shall be in line with the water surface. All movements of the legs and arms shall be simultaneous and in the same horizontal plane without alternating movements.
>
> The hands shall be pushed forward together from the breast and shall be brought back on or under the surface of the water.
>
> In the leg kick, the feet shall be turned outwards in the backward movement. A 'dolphin' kick is not permitted.
>
> A part of the head shall always be above the

general water level, except that at the start and at each turn the swimmer may take one arm stroke and one leg kick while wholly submerged.

As can be seen, the two main restrictions are that the stroke movements must be carried out in a simultaneous fashion, and that the corresponding parts of each limb must be in the same horizontal plane at all times. In other words the movements of the limbs on the left-hand side of the swimmer's body must be a mirror image of those on the right-hand side and, at the same time, each part of the limbs on the left-hand side must be the same distance from the general water level as the corresponding parts of the limbs on the right-hand side.

The breast stroke is the slowest of the competition strokes and, with the restricted limb movements and underwater recoveries, it is likely to remain so.

There is another form of breast which may be termed the 'leisure style'. Here, while the basic mechanics of movements are similar to that of the competition stroke, the rate at which the limbs articulate, as the name suggests, is much slower.

Informal swimmers usually perform in a continually head-up, easy-breathing mode and, where the leg kick is reasonably strong, the stroke cycle often terminates in a prolonged glide. Learners are often taught in this 'glide-emphasis' fashion in order to demonstrate and develop the efficiency of their leg kicks.

Another version of the leisure style is with slow but continually 'revving' arms and legs, providing the swimmer with a steady but not too rapid rate of progress.

The basic mechanics of propulsion are similar in all the styles, but the movements of the formal or competition stroke demand more discipline and fitness. Consequently, it is this precise pattern of movement that we teach.

STROKE TECHNIQUE

Body position

Viewed from the side, the swimmer's body should be as streamlined and horizontal as the technique of the leg kick will permit.

If the hips should be too elevated, there is a possibility that the feet, when they are in the fully recovered position, will break the surface of the water, thus decreasing their effectiveness during the propulsive stage of the movement.

The position of the swimmer's head, as the reader no doubt remembers from earlier chapters, can have a profound effect on body position. This is especially so in the beast stroke where the hair line should be in the region of the water line except during a breathing intake. Lifting the head too high tends to elevate the upper part of the chest, and in turn the swimmer's body is rotated to that the legs sink lower in the water. This upright swimming position can often be seen among learners and people who do not like getting their faces wet.

The fault whereby the swimmers's heels break the surface if the hips are riding too high in the water may be counteracted by slightly lifting the head. It is worth mentioning that a 'leg' swimmer's hips usually ride lower in the water than those of an 'arm' swimmer.

The angle of the upper legs in relation to the long body axis is important to overall body streamlining. Should the hip joint be flexed excessively during the recovery of the legs in preparation for the kick, a considerable amount of resistance is set up by the resulting profile of the thighs.

Accompanying this over-flexing of the hip, there is a tendency also for the swimmer's bottom to bob up and down with each leg cycle.

From the front, the swimmer's shoulders should lie in line with the water surface: in other words, the lateral shoulder plane must be horizontal. The head should not bob up and down excessively in order to accommodate the breathing pattern. The movement of the arms, as will be seen later, has the effect of raising the swimmer's head above the water levels as well as propelling him forward. This elevating effect should itself bring the mouth almost if nor completely clear of the water, whereby an inward breath may be taken. In some instances, a slight lift may be needed to augment the natural shoulder rise.

As the arms perform their cycle there should be no water-surface disturbance created by the recovery or catch movements. Neither should the feet ever break the water surface.

From above, the swimmer should be seen to be proceeding in a straight line with his long body axis parallel with the direction of movement, with no tendency to side stroke.

The whole symmetrical and simultaneous patter of movement can easily be seen from this angle and any deviation from the correct technique readily identified.

Leg action

For many years people have devoted two alternative theories about the propulsion in the breast-stroke leg action. The first is the 'wedge' action theory concerning the vigorous inward movement of the legs from the astride position. Experts were convinced that water was squeezed backwards as the legs closed, the reaction of which propelled the swimmer forward. The second theory is that the swimmer is driven forward by the pressure of the soles of the feet on the water, similar to the action of a frog's kick.

Consider first the 'wedge' action theory. The initial fact to remember when dealing with a 'low viscous' fluid such as water is that when pressure forces it to escape from a confined space it will always find the easy way out or, in other words, it will seek the path of least resistance. A swimmer completing the final movement of wedge kick.

Comparing the legs with two similarly shaped sections, we can see that by making the two near-cylinders coverage the majority of the trapped water is displaced in directions which are at right-angles to the long axes of the sections, this being the line of least resistance. Some water escapes from the extreme ends of the sections, but the amount is minimal.

It can now be seen that for any considered section of the swimmer's legs, the larger amount of water will always be displaced from between them in an upward and downward direction (away from the long axis) rather than along the length of the legs as they are closed together. Consequently the water pressure which is developed in the direction of the leg axis is minimal and has no propulsive effect.

The second theory, relating to a frog like kick whereby propulsion is gained by the sole of the swimmer's foot pushing directly backwards, would seem to be rather unlikely. The limited amount of propulsive power that can be generated by the sole of the human foot, compared with the mass of the body to be moved through the water and the drag to be overcome, is insignificant.

The frog is able to swim quite successfully by pushing directly back on the water. However, if a brief study is made of the frog's anatomy and the relationship between the size of its body, the strength of its legs (used for jumping quite long distances) and the sole area of its feet, it can easily be seen how the animal is able to move so quickly and efficiently through the water using a straight-back kick. With our relatively tiny feet we cannot compare ourselves with the frog.

So, if the kick is not developed by either of these actions, how do breast strokes generates the thrust from their legs which is sometimes quite considerable ?

The answer to this question is that, during the propulsive phase of the kick, the soles of the feet are positioned in such a way (by dorsi-flexion and opening) that they perform what may loosely be described as a unidirectional sculling motion as they sweep together-unidirectional because the movement is on one direction always towards the inside of the foot, as compared with a true sculling motion which is oscillatory. Let us examine the foot carefully in order that we may see how its anatomical shape assists in developing this thrust to propel the swimmer forward.

A normally shaped human foot viewed from the front, together with picture of the sole area. Also shown in the view of the sole is that approximate area that is normally in contact with the floor, when a person is standing.

An imaginary cutting plane X—X is passed through the foot and the shape of the resulting section is shown in the top right-hand picture.

It may be seen that the under shape of the foot is slightly inclined inwards and produces an aerodynamic from similar in shape to the true one as illustrated. If the aerodynamic shape moved in the direction of the arrow, pressure is built up on the under surface to create 'lift'. Similarly, by moving the foot (in the water) in the same fashion, propulsion may also be created. Also, as the angle of the sole of the foot and its speed through the water increases (up to a point), the propulsive effect increases. Hence the necessity of the whip-like movement of the feet. This is the theory of the scull applied to the feet.

If the feet are moved inwards simultaneously, as in the breast-stroke leg kick, twice the amount of propulsion is developed. The propulsion increases approximately as the square of the speed that the feet move together (i.e. at twice the speed, the feet produce four times the amount of propulsion).

It may also be noted at the beginning of the kick the feet point outwards and at the end of the movement they point backwards. They therefore rotate through approximately ninety degree, rather like the action of a propeller blade. The feet, throughout the 'whip' part of the kick, moves so that the soles of the feet are inclined towards their direction of movement, thus augmenting the 'sculling angle' already existing in the anatomical form of a normal foot. (A flat-footed person does not possess this natural foot arch, but this does not mean he cannot make good breast-stroke swimmer.)

So, it may be seen that if the breast stroker is able to perform this foot scull in an efficient manner, good propulsion may be gained from the leg kick.

Howard Firby in his fine book on competitive swimming mentions an experiment in which he fashioned a pair of 'back-to-back feet in the form of a propeller. When fitted to a simple boat the 'feet' rotated and propelled the boat through the water.

A few years ago we too carried out a similar investigation, in order to demonstrate the unilateral sculling action at the feet during the breast-stroke whip-kick. For the purpose of this text, the simple (and not too scientific) experiment was repeated and a description now follows.

We sculptured a pair of quarter-scale right feet from a solid piece of timber. The feet were modelled in a heel-to-heel fashion and when completed the profile resembled that of a boat's propeller, the contour of the instep combining with the natural arch of the sole to produce a hydrodynamic shape. The propeller was then fitted to a simple; elastic-powered boat.

When first tested in the bath at home, the foot-propelled boat demonstrated rather unladylike qualities by turning over on her back, showering her constructor with water in the process. However, by the deft use of a polystyrene float, the stability problems were quickly rectified.

The wooden feet were fashioned as though they were in contact with the floor. Consequently for the first water test, it was the natural arch-dominated characteristics of the feet which were to be responsible for propelling the boat forward.

When wound up and placed in the water, the boat moved steadily but slowly forward, The test was repeated several times at various propeller speeds but the forward speed seemed to be limited.

In order to pursue the investigation further, the feet were remodelled in order to produce a more definite angle between the soles of the feet and the floor (when standing). This angle of inversion was set at approximately fifteen degrees.

Replacing the reshaped and 're-charged' boat into the water, it now moved at a considerably increased speed with the propeller churning away at about the same rotational speed as during the previous tests. When related to the breast stroke, the demonstration seemed to indicate that, although dorsi-flexion of the feet is vital throughout the kicking movement, propulsion is enhanced by inverting both feet as they close together.

The additional medial flexing of the ankle joint seems to add considerably to the unilateral sculling effect of the natural foot arches. Under-water observations of good breast-stroke swimmers seem to confirm this.

Recovery

Due to the position that the legs are required to assume in preparation for the propulsive part of the kicking cycle, the profile drag effect related to leg recovery is greater in the breast stroke than in any of the other three competitive stroke. However, by good technique and teaching this may be minimised.

The kicking cycle commences with both legs in a fully stretched and streamlined attitude, the feet being together, or almost together. This is the position the legs should have assumed at the end of the last kick.

The body attitude ensures that the swimmer's heels are approximately 200mm (8 in.) below the water surface.

At the appropriate moment in the complete stroke cycle, the hips and knees are flexed and the heels are drawn up towards the swimmer's seat. During this movement the knees are spread apart to approximately the width of the swimmer's shoulders, and the heels, as they near the seat, may also move apart a short distance.

During this drawing-up movement, the toes should maintain a backward-pointing mode in order to assist in the general streamlining characteristics, although in reality they lie within the forward profile of the swimmer, i.e. looking from the front, the feet cannot be seen and therefore do not add to the swimmer's profile.

Care must be taken in order that the forward movement of the thighs is not excessive, thus increasing the profile drag more than is necessary.

The following figure shows how the effective forward thigh profile varies with the angle of leg recovery, and also how the streamlining characteristics of the legs are affected. It can be seen that in illustration A the swimmer's hips are elevated rather high in the water causing the feet to break the surface and reduce their effectiveness. Illustration B shows the swimmer's legs recovered so that they form the same approximate angular relationship with the surface but this time the hips are riding lower in the water and the feet are submerged.

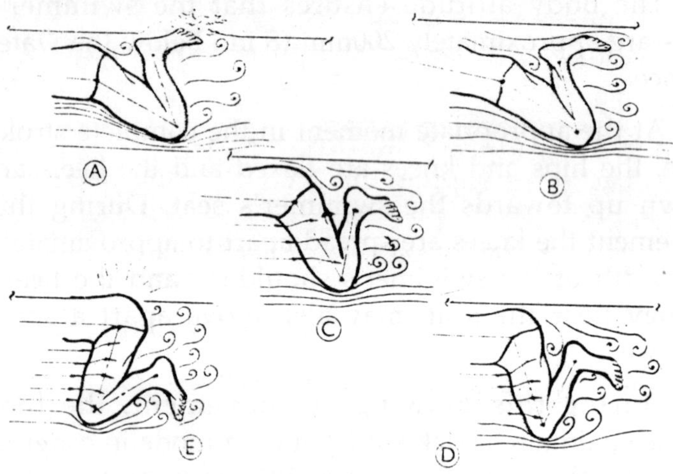

Basically both these examples exhibit good streamlining characteristics due to the shallow angle of the thighs with the water surface. The hips form an angle of approximately 150 degrees with the body axis and the seat is about 200 mm (8 in.) below the water surface. Streamlining is quite good at this angle with the area of turbulent eddies reduced as far as possible for the recovery position.

This limb attitude is very near to the ideal position required to accelerate the feet into the propelling part of the cycle.

Mechanically, the lower-leg extensor muscles (the quadriceps) are at a disadvantage at this recovery angle, but the forces required to overcome the inertia of the lower leg and created water pressure are well within the capabilities of these very strong activators.

Illustrations C and D show that, by progressively drawing the knees up under the hips, the streamlining characteristics tend to deteriorate.

At position E not only are the drag effects very severe, but also the seat is above the water surface. The effect here is that the swimmer progresses through the water with a 'bobbing bottom'.

Now let us suppose that our swimmer has taken up a leg-recovery position as illustrated in B, and is ready to perform the propulsive part of the kick.

The propulsive part of the cycle

The competitive stroke law states that 'the feet shall be turned outwards in the backwards movements.

This compulsory 'toeing-out', as we have seen, assists in developing an efficient leg thrust. Combined with this outward turn, both feet are moved into the dorsi-flexed position. It is important that this' flat-foot' mode is maintained throughout the kick in order to generate the uni-directional foot scull described earlier.

The propulsive part of the leg movement commences with a vigorous extension of both the thighs and the lower legs. The feet, still in the dorsi-flexed and 'toeing-out' mode, accelerate outwards and backwards. At almost full-limb extension, the feet start to sweep inwards and together. During the final part of the movement and as the legs decelerate and close together, the feet are stretched into the plantar-flexed attitude for a streamlined glide, if one is to be incorporated into the stroke, or subsequent leg recovery.

The path of the feet during the propulsive movement together with an approximation of the way in which they accelerate into the whipping phase.

It is also important that the soles of the feet are inclined or angled towards each other (foot inversion) for full propulsive effect.

It should also be noted how the feet act as 'partial propellers' by rotating through almost a right-angle during the kick.

Arm action

Too many breast strokers rely solely on their leg kick for propulsion, with their arms performing only a short, sideways, almost symbolic pull in keeping with the general rhythm and timing of the stroke, but contributing nothing towards moving the swimmer forward.

If any stroke is to be reasonably efficient, limb movement must provide propulsion for as long as possible within the overall cycle.

Breast-stroke arm movement is the shortest one of the competitive group of strokes It is also the least efficient mainly because of this limited travel and also its underwater recovery.

Many breast strokers terminate their arm

propulsion at the end of the backward movement, then thrust their hands forward to the start position once more.

There is, however, some extra propulsion to be gained by the swimmer carrying out a sculling movement with the hands as they travel inward towards the central body plane, prior to the forward thrust. Figure 18.6 shows a typical limb track of the arm cycle, illustrating this sculling feature.

The underwater recovery of the arms is detrimental to the overall stroke efficiency. Bearing this point in mind, as soon as the propulsive movement is completed the elbows should be drawn close to the swimmer's body in order to minimise their profile drag area. To reduce drag, as soon as the hands have completed their task they should be positioned flat and streamlined and should remain in this position as they are pushed forward.

At the commencement of the movement, both arms should be fully stretched ahead of the swimmer with the palms of the hands approximately 100 mm (4 in.) below the water surface. As with all propulsive limb wards, fingers together and thumbs touching. As with all propulsive limb movements, the initial phase of the cycle is a catching action whereby pressure is built up on the hands and lower arms and the swimmer' feels' the water.

To accomplish the catch, the hands should be rotated to face outwards and downwards at a 'palm angle' of approximately forty-five degrees. At the same time the wrists are slightly flexed in order that the palm may face sure to the intended direction of movement.

The hands are now moved in an accelerating mode-outwards, backwards and downwards. The extent of the catch movement depends mainly on the rate of acceleration of the hands which, in turn, should not be too rapid, otherwise cavitation and eddies will develop behind the hands and lower arms, leading to 'overpull'. Another feature of the initial hand movement is that, if there is any surface turbulence, the hands are too high in the water. The propulsive hand trajectory must be out, back and downwards, with no noticeable water-surface disturbance occurring at any time.

Pull

Normally, the catch will take place during the first 300 mm (12 in.) of hand movement, to be followed immediately by the pull.

During the pull, the elbows may become slightly flexed and remain elevated above the hands, the palms directed so that they face backwards.

At a position slightly ahead of the shoulder plane, the hands should be at their widest distance apart and, when viewed from head-on, theoretical lines drawn between the palm centres and the front of the swimmer's head should form at least a right-angle.

It is at this point forward of the shoulders that the are of movement of the hand changes direction to move inwards and, at the same time, a lateral rotation of the forearm takes place to incline the downward-pointing hand inwards, in preparation for the scull. This is the termination of the pull, and the swimmer's hands should be slightly forward of and below his elbows.

Scull

This forearms, being now medially rotated, ensure that the palms are inclined inwards in order to perform the uni-directional sculling movement.

The scull takes place just below the shoulders and continues until the hands pass under the shoulder joints on their way into the recovery.

During the performance of the less formal styles and also during the initial stroke-learning period, the scull will be non-existent. It is only later as techniques are improved that this characteristic becomes a feature of the arm stroke.

Recovery

Recovery of the hands takes place with them being pushed forward in a flat and streamlined mode below the surface of the water. The direction in which the palms face during the forward push is unimportant, just as varies from swimmer to swimmer.

During the recovery movement the elbows should be tucked in close to the body in order to minimise the profile drag effects, although this feature tends to vary with the speed of the arm cycle.

At the termination of the movement, the swimmer's arms should be stretched ahead, the hands should be flat with fingers together. The palms should face downwards and be at an approximate depth of 100 mm (4 in.)

A rather common fault which takes place during the push forward is that the hands are not held flat, consequently the swimmer tends to push himself backwards. Recovery, is an 'evil necessity' in swimming and therefore must take place with the minimum of interference to forward movement.

If glide is to be included in the technique, it should be performed with the arms in this fully stretched position and held until the start of the next arm cycle.

Breathing

Most breast strokers breathe during every stroke because it is convenient and simple to do so. The downward-moving arms tend to elevate the shoulders so that, with a slight backward tilt of the head, the face emerges clear of the water at approximately the end of the pulling movement. It is at this point in the stroke cycle that a breath is taken through the mouth.

Immediately following the intake of air, the swimmer's shoulders tend to sink as the arms are pushed forward. The head is now tilted forward into the 'normal' swimming position whereby the hair line is approximately at the water line.

Exhalation should take place through the mouth or mouth and nose. The latter technique is probably the more practical, the ensuring that the nasal passages are maintained clear and preventing the ingress of water to the 'uncontrollable' region at the back of the throat.

A slower 'revving' stroke will enable the swimmer either to hold the breath for a very short while, then exhale in an explosive manner prior to the next intake, or to exhale by a controlled trickle through mouth and nose or mouth only, so that complete exhaustion of air occurs just before the head is raised for the next intake.

The latter method is probably a more natural system of respiration. A simple method of teaching the exhalation part of the breathing cycle is to persuade the learner to 'blow his hands away' as he pushes them forward during the recovery.

The leisure forms of breast stroke display an elevated head position and breathing out usually takes place above the surface in a less disciplined manner than that of the competition style. Beginners carrying out early breast-stroke practices also tend to maintain a head-high posture, breathing in and out at will. It is advisable, with competition in mind, for the teacher to introduce some breathing discipline at an early stage of the stroke teaching, thus ensuring that there will be less likelihood of faulty breathing habits developing at a later stage.

Finally, some success may be gained in the teaching of the breathing technique by concentrating on the exhalation part of the cycle rather than the inhalation phase. A swimmer may breathe in and hold his breath for some considerable time, but, if exhalation has occurred, the subsequent intake of air must take place almost immediately. Bearing this fact in mind, the breathing practices may focus on 'blowing the hands away' rather than breathing in at the end of the arm pull.

Co-ordination

Synchronisation of the arm, leg and head movements is an important feature of the breast stroke and should the timing of the individual action be even slightly out of phase with each other, a jerky and inefficient action will result.

Probably the major feature of the relationship between the leg and arm movements is that the arms should be fully extended in front of the swimmer before the peak of the kicking thrust is reached. In order to achieve the correct sequence of movements, the arms should begin their pulling action while the legs are in the stretched position. Then, at the end of the pull and the beginning of the inward hand scull, the legs begin their recovery cycle. If this initial timing is achieved, the arm will be fully stretched in front of the swimmer when the propulsion peak of the leg kick occurs. If a breath has been taken at the correct stage, it enables the head to be lowered into the normal swimming position as the arms are thrust forward, thus enhancing body streamlining during the leg kick.

At the end of the leg kick, there may be glide introduced into the stroke. The length of this glide is dependent on the power of the swimmer's leg kick and the rate at which he is stroking. If a leisurely style is being performed, the glide can be quite a long one. Another factor affecting the glide length is the swimmer's natural buoyancy. Should the legs have a tendency to sink readily, his ability to glide will consequently be less.

Competition swimmers tend to swim with a constantly 'revving' action and no apparent glide, because, of course, the glide is a slowing-down process.

When teaching the stroke, we tend to think of the arms, legs and breath all 'shooting out' at the same time, and encourage the swimmers to 'let it all hang out' at once.

Preparatory standards for teaching the stroke

The preparations for teaching breast stroke are identical with those required for teaching the front crawl: before commencing the following programme of breast-stroke practices, therefore, it is advisable that the pupils are able to perform the following activities with some semblance of skill.

1. Confidence exercises-face wetting, blowing bubbles and submersion
2. Regaining the feet from a prone position
3. Pushing and gliding from the poolside
4. Front paddling at least 20 m
5. Treading water
6. General water mobility exercises

TEACHING THE BREAST STROKE

The breast stroke is a popular first teaching stroke, especially where adults are concerned. The main reasons for this are that the stroke is performed in the 'natural' prone position and also that, during its performance, the exponent may keep his or her face clear of the water. It is also a leisure stroke and, swimming being so universally popular, the stroke will probably be seen in this guise more often than in any other.

The arm cycle is not a complicated action, but the leg movement is rather alien in its nature, compared with that of the other three strokes whose swinging motion is closely allied with walking or running.

Breast-stroke leg kick is essentially a movement of co-ordination, flexibility and control, with the ability to perform the action being almost inherent, rather than one which is acquired. I firmly believe that true breast strokers are born rather than made, and as far as the leisure swimmers are concerned, it is not essential that perfection is achieved.

Breathing during the performance of the stroke does not usually present any problems. As mentioned earlier, the swimmer is able by design to keep his or her face clear of the water quite easily throughout the whole movement. It should be noted, however, that some kind of breathing discipline must be introduced during the early practices, in order that young swimmers are able to progress naturally into the competitive style. The demands a lower position of the head of the water.

Most of the class will probably have tried swimming a version of the breast stroke in their paddling days. Many hybrids may be evolved at this early stage, such as a wide-sweeping arm pull with a front-paddle leg kick, or a downward simultaneous pull combined with the infamous 'screw kick'. The true breast strokes will be seen displaying not necessarily an absolutely correct movement but a *sense of symmetry* which is one of the main ingredients of a correctly executed style.

It has been mentioned before that children are expert mimics. With this fact i mind, therefore, it is sensible to given them something to copy. So, if at all possible, before letting them loose on the exercise treat them to a visual demonstration of the stroke accompanied by a clear and concise explanation of all the main features of the style. Needless to say, the demonstration must be carried out by someone who is able to swim the breast stroke using correctly timed and skillfully executed movements.

When the teacher has made sure that all the class are well positioned to see and hear the demonstration, the show may begin.

Activity: demonstration swim with commentary

The demonstration is best performed lengthways down the pool because one of the stroke features that needs highlighting is the powerful leg kick and the resulting glide. Swimming widths does not exhibit this feature to advantage.

The stroke may be performed in a leisure fashion initially, then as a racing style. Here the teacher will be able to point out the main difference between the two techniques, such as the lower head position and the stroke continuity which produces a shorter, almost non-existent glide in the racing stroke.

Adhering to the previously established sequence of explanations, the swimmer's body position may be singled out as the initial feature, showing how the hips are slightly lower in the water than when the other strokes are performed. It should be quite obvious how this lower swimming position enables the feet to be submerged during the latter part of the leg recovery and early propulsive phase.

It will be seen also how dominant is the swimmer's leg kick and how noticeable is the sudden surge forward, which is caused by the rapid 'whipping' movement of the feet. This whip-like leg movement should be highlighted as one of the most important features of the stroke.

The pattern of the downward and backward arm pull will need to be viewed from the side and from ahead of the swimmer, and the class should be encouraged to change their positions in order to make these observations.

The demonstrating swimmer should show how the breathing movements are carried out in both the leisure and racing strokes. The pattern of breathing in through the mouth, as the shoulders are elevated by the downward arm movement, then the breathing-out motion through the mouth and nose as the hands are thrust away into the recovery, should easily be seen by the class.

A further one on the 'flat hand-low resistance' recovery may also be made by the teacher when referring to the push forward. Timing the stroke may be memorable described as 'letting it all hang out' at the same time. In other words, pushing the hand out, kicking the feet out and breathing out, all at the same instant in the stroke cycle. This combination of movements will easily be seen to be happening each time the swimmer kicks into the glide. It should be suggested to the class that if they concentrate on these simultaneous actions, the timing of the stroke is inclined to look after itself.

As the breast stroke is very law-restricted, the teacher should briefly explain the ASA laws, pointing out how the performer is adhering to them.

After witnessing the demonstration, the class may be invited to perform their version of what they have just seen.

Activity: full stroke
Practice: initial full-stroke swims
Teaching points: Right from the outset, the ASA laws which govern the performance of stroke should be introduced into the teachings. There is no need for these stroke laws as such to be mentioned to the class; the children probably will not absorb such technicalities during the early stages of learning. The teacher, however, should be thoroughly aware of the peculiarities associated with the various limb movements and, consequently, be able to include these features in the instructions which are given.

1. The points relating to the symmetrical and simultaneous aspects of the stroke performance must be the major teaching features. Each arm or leg movement must be a mirror image of its corresponding limb and the swimmer's shoulders and hips should be square and laterally parallel with the water surface.

2. The feet should remain below the surface at all times and, during the propulsive part of the kick, they must be retained in the cocked and 'toed-out' position. (The term 'cocked' must be carefully explained as 'the toes are brought up towards the shins'.)

3. The arm actions should be directed towards attaining the backward and downward patterns of movement, with no water-surface disturbance being in evidence at any time.

   The shoulder line should be the limit of backward arm movement and any tendency to over-pull should be highlighted.

4. The swimmer's head may be kept high during this exercise, and consequently there should be no breathing problems in evidence.

   These few teaching points would seem to be adequate at this early stage, more precise instruction being given during the part-stroke and later full-stroke practices.

Activity: leg action

Practice 1: land exercise—sitting on the pool surround and carrying out an 'inverted' leg movement.

In order to demonstrate the leg movements to the class, there is a choice of several positions that the teacher may take up. For instance, by sitting on the edge of some convenient elevated poolside seat and raising his or her legs above the floor, the teacher should be able to carry out this land exercise quite satisfactorily for all to see. If there is a 1-m diving-board, this makes an ideal base for the demonstration.

Alternatively, the pool surround may be used if it is dry or if there is something suitable to sit on. Here, the teacher is able to assume a position similar to that which the pupils will take up during the exercise.

A further method of demonstration is for the teacher to stand on one leg (suitably supported, of course) and demonstrate the kicking motion with the other leg. The movement itself, however, may not be quite so clear to the pupils, and is not really recommended as an initial choice for class display purpose.

A method of demonstration that has been used successfully is to select a suitable member of the class and, with the others gathered around so that they may all see, the pupil sits on the floor in the correct position. By grasping one of the pupil's feet in each hand, the teacher manipulates them in such a way that they perform the correct pattern of movement. The advantage of this system is that the teacher is able to interrupt the movement at any stage in order to point out precisely why the legs or feet are working in some particular fashion.

In the initial stage of the practice, the pupils should perform the pattern of movement in a sequence of separate phases as follows.

The first movement Starting in the sitting position with feet outstretched and together, the heels are now drawn up towards the seat. As the knees bend in order to accomplish the movement, they also move away from each other until they reach a distance of approximately shoulder-width apart.

Perhaps the paramount feature of this recovery part of the movement is that the feet should have taken up a cocked or dorsi-flexed attitude by the time they have reached the end of the drawing-up movement, the heels being some 150-200 mm (6-8 in.) from the seat.

The second movement The legs are now straightened and the feet are moved outwards, so that the pupils, so that the pupils are all sitting with their legs astride and in contact with the floor. The cooked-foot position should be maintained with toes pointing outwards.

The third movement The legs, still straight, should now be closed together.

The pupils may initially carry out several individual cycles of the movements to numbers, in an attempt to master the pattern. Once the action has been established in their minds, it may be performed without a pause, in a similar manner to that of actually swimming.

Teaching points

1. Emphasis should be placed on a slow recovery (knee bend) followed by a vigorous straightening and closing of the legs. Continuity of movement should be a feature of the final versions of the exercise.
2. Outward pointed feet flat and at right-angles to the shins (cocked) must be in evidence throughout the exercise.

The duration of the exercise should be short and, in order to retain its value, it should be followed immediately by repetition of the pattern of movement in the water.

Practice 2: leg-kicking practice at the rail

Teaching points

1. The pupils should display a definite whip-kick, an accelerated out-round-and-together propulsive movement compared with the slower recovery.
2. The teacher must be persistent regarding the 'flat-foot' or 'Charlie Chaplin' stance being maintained throughout the propulsive phase, but culminating now in both feet taking up an athletically stretched mode at the end of the kick.
3. The heels should be together or almost together as they are drawn up to the buttocks.
4. The observance should be made throughout the

whole motion of the ASA law whereby 'The feet shall be turned outwards in the backward movement. A "dolphin" kick is not permitted.

5. The slower recovery movement should be limited to a position whereby the angle between the thighs and the trunk does not exceed 150 degrees. The effect of excessive leg recovery, i.e. when the knees retract below the swimmer's hips, is for the bottom to bob up and down and, because of this distinct feature, the fault is easily identified.

6. The mirror-image effect of one leg compared to the other must be maintained, with the hips, knees and ankles of each leg being retained in the laterally horizontal and symmetrical image is not attained, the movement results in producing some version or other of the dreaded screw-kick.

Screw-kick The ASA law relating to the breast-stroke leg kick states that: 'All movements of the legs shall be simultaneous and in the same horizontal plane without alternating movements. ' The screw-kick occurs when there is non-observance of these rules. Movements of the legs are out of phase with each other, with one foot usually lower in the water and travelling in a different direction from its companion.

Invariably one of the swimmer's feet is pointed throughout the kick, and propulsion-if there is any-is developed by the instep and shin rather than the sole of the foot. The 'screw' may be caused by the lowering of one shoulder, but it is not always accompanied by this fault.

7. From the stretched position and back again, the leg movement should remain continuous.
8. The swimmer's hips should be low enough in the water to prevent the feet from breaking the water surface as they are drawn up to the seat, or again, at the start of the backward kick.
9. The heels should be drawn up to within approximately 150-200 mm (6-8 in.) of the swimmer's seat during the recovery.
10. Holding the rail or scum channel in such a way that the swimmer is elevated to a suitable depth for practice is a fairly simple operation and the teacher should therefore make sure that the pupils are able to perform this feature of the exercise satisfactorily, rather than adopt the partner support system.

Practice 3: leg movement with partner (carrier) support

Teaching points

All the teaching points previously mentioned relating to the leg kick are applicable to this exercise, together with the extended-arm method of holding each other, as described.

The pupils should by now be displaying a movement allied to the correct breast-stroke kick. In order to get some idea of how effective the movement is, the next exercise is a mobile one.

It has been said earlier that if the pupils are able actually to witness their limb movements, correction of any faults that may be present is made easier. In the following practice, the swimmer is able to observe his leg movements while at the same time being supported by one or two floats.

Practice 4: leg movements in a supine float-supported position

Teaching points

The general pattern of the kick is the same as when it is performed in the prone swimming position. All the appropriate features of the kick will therefore be relevant.

A repeat of the exercise may now be performed with the swimmers lying on their fronts.

Practice 5: prone swimming legs-only movement, first with two then with a single float

Teaching points

Probably one of the most common faults will be too much reliability on the floats. The pupils should therefore be encouraged to stretch their arms in front of them and not lean on the floats for support. The correct methods of holding the floats should be continuously stressed during the exercises.

The rest of the related teaching points are all as previously mentioned. The establishment of a glide is the only new point to arise in the exercise and this must be carried out with the swimmers assuming a fully stretched position.

Practice 6: unsupported push and glide to the rail with one or more kicks

Teaching points

All the leg-movement teaching points are as previously described.

If the swimmers are able to maintain a fully stretched face-in-the-water mode, this will assist them in establishing a good body position for the exercises.

Practice 7: unsupported leg kicking across the pool width

Teaching points

All the teaching points relating to the leg movement are now recalled once more, and are as follow:

1. The appreciation of the whip-kick whereby the pupils display a definite accelerate out-round-and-together propulsive movement compared with the slower recovery.

2. The teacher must be persistent about the 'flat-foot' or 'Charlie chaplin' stance being maintained throughout the propulsive phase but culminating now in both feet taking up an athletically stretched mode at the end of the kick.

3. The heels may be together or a short distance apart when they are drawn up to within 150-200 mm (6-8 in.) of the buttocks.

4. The ASA law should be observed throughout the motion: "The feet shall be turned outwards in the backward movement. A "dolphin" kick is not permitted.

5. The slower recovery movement should be limited to a position whereby the angle between the thighs and the trunk does not exceed 150 degrees. The effect of excessive leg recovery is for the swimmer's bottom to bob up and down and, because of this distinct feature, the fault is easily identified.

6. The mirror-image effect of the movement must be maintained, with the hips in the laterally horizontal mode. Where this simultaneous and symmetrical action is not attained, the movement results in a version of the screw-kick.

7. From the stretched position and back again, the leg movement should remain continuous.

8. The swimmer's hips should be low enough in the water to prevent the feet from breaking the water surface as they are drawn up to the seat, or again at the start of the thrust.

Having now completed a full set of breast-stroke leg practices, the pupils should be ready to absorb some new activities concerning the arm stroke.

Activity"arm action

Practice 1: standing in shallow water the teacher demonstrating the action from the poolside

Teaching points

1. The starting (static) position for the arms should be:
   - (a) Hands—with fingers together, straight and flat
   - (b) Thumbs—touching
   - (c) Palms—facing directly downwards
   - (d) Wrists—unflexed with the flat hands in line with forearms
   - (e) Elbows—straight but not stiff
   - (f) Shoulders-upper part just below the water surface. (It is advisable for the teacher to tell the pupils to keep their shoulders in the water throughout the movement.
   - (g) arms—generally stretched forward parallel with water surface.
2. The hands must be kept flat throughout with fingers together.

3. In order to face the palms directly backwards for as long as possible during the actual pull, the wrists should be flexed for most of the movement.
4. The elbows should be maintained relatively straight during the pull.
5. The movement should be downwards, outwards and back: if there is any surface disturbance, the path of the arms is incorrect.
6. The hands should not travel back beyond the plane of the shoulders. It is advisable for the teacher to insist that they definitely, terminate their backward movement, say, 150 mm (6 in.) forward of the shoulders.
7. As the pulling movement commences, the hands still maintained in a flat mode are faced diagonally downwards and outwards accompanied by a slight flexion of the wrist.

Practice 2: Pulling and sliding or walking

Teaching points

All the teaching points mentioned in the precious static arms-only exercise are relevant.

Some, if not most of the pupils, will tend to move with their shoulders raised well above the water surface. Pointing out that this is 'flying rather than swimming' and that they should 'be fish, not birds' usually helps. Also, they will probably tend to push their arms back further than the plane of the shoulders in order to assist themselves along, their main objective being to produce forward movement rather than the correct breast-stroke arm action. With this in mind, it is best to avoid any reference to speed, otherwise the whole purpose of the exercise will be lost. Initially, the leisure style of breast stroke should be performed so that the swimmer's head is held high enough above the surface to avoid any breathing problems. However, with competition and rough water conditions in mind, it is advisable to introduce some breathing discipline during these part-practices. Also, as the breathing sequence is more closely allied to the arm movement than to the leg movement, it is considered to be advantageous to include some breathing instruction at this particular stage.

Practice 3: pulling and breathing while standing, then while walking or sliding

Teaching points

1. Inhalation must be through the mouth and exhalation is best carried out through the mouth and nose in a trickle fashion. It is worth reminding the class that breathing out through the nose is advisable because, if air is coming down the nose, water cannot go up it.

2. Inhalation, when coupled with 'blowing the hands away' takes place towards the end of the arm pull.

3. During the exhalation, the swimmer's mouth and nose should be lowered into the water while he continues to look forward. Exhalation may continue into the early phase of the arm pull.

We should by now be in a position to bring all the breast-stroke movements together. Concentration may therefore be centred on co-ordination and timing of the individual actions in order to produce a synchronised and aesthetic performance.

COACHING OBJECTIVES FOR THE BREASTSTROKE

You should understand how to effectively teach the breast stroke to beginning swimmers.

a. Helpful terms referring to the breaststroke.

b. Body position, armstroke, kick, and breathing or the breaststroke.

c. Coaching points to be emphasized in the breaststroke.

d. Drills for learning and developing the breaststroke.

e. Starts and turns appropriate for the breaststroke.

f. Coaching points to be emphasized in breaststroke starts and turns.

BODY POSITION

The breaststroke body position is in transition from one in which the swimmer is flat in the water to one in which the swimmer moves up and down with a dolphin-like movement.

The traditional breaststroke was swum by Chet Jastremski, American Record holder in the 1960s. It is the stroke taught in American Red Cross swimming classes. Because most novice competitors progress from beginner swimming lessons, they will know the traditional breaststroke. Coaches will therefore find it easier to teach the elements of the traditional stroke. The natural breaststroke as swum by David Wilkie and Tracy Caulkins, record holders in the 1970s, is very successful with year-round swimmers. Occasionally, novices will do this strokes. If a young swimmer is successfully performing it, do not change the technique.

According to swimming rules for the breaststroke, the body must remain on the breast with both shoulders in the horizontal plane.

	Traditional	*Natural*
Body Position	Body remains flat in the water.	Body is angled as the hips move up and down.

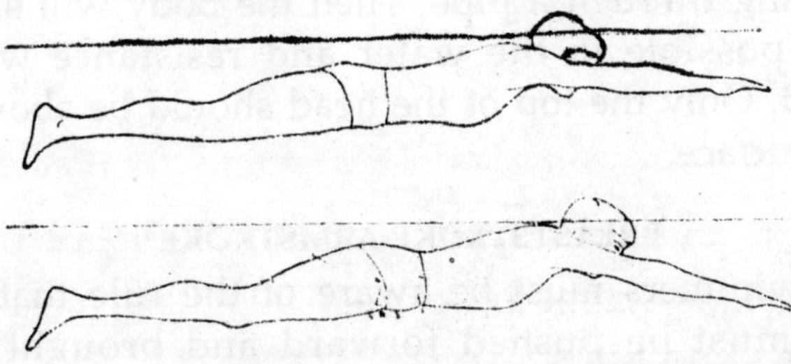

	Traditional	*Natural*
Breathing	The chin is lifted; only the head pivots on the neck.	The head remains stationary, the hips drop, and the head and neck come above the water for a high breath.

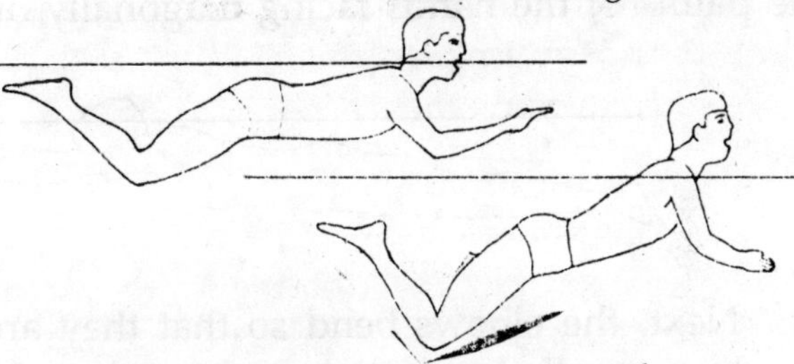

	Traditional	*Natural*
Timing	The breath is taken as the arms come to a point under the shoulders.	The breath is taken as the arms begin to recover to the front

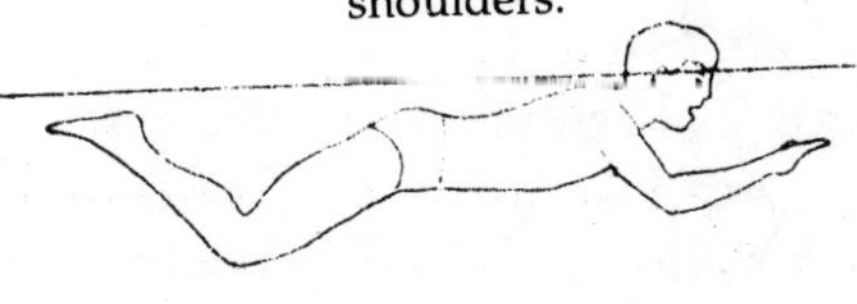

These rules also specify that some portion of the head must be higher than the normal flat surface of the water except on the start and on strokes before and after the turns.

Tell your swimmers to imagine that they are swimming through a pipe. Then the body will stay as flat as possible in the water and resistance will be reduced. Only the top of the head should be above the water surface.

BREASTSTROKE ARMSTROKE

Your swimmers must be aware of the rule that both hands must be pushed forward and brought back simultaneously on or under the surface of the water. When instructing your swimmers in the armstroke, have them begin the pull with the elbows straight and the palms of the hands facing diagonally outward.

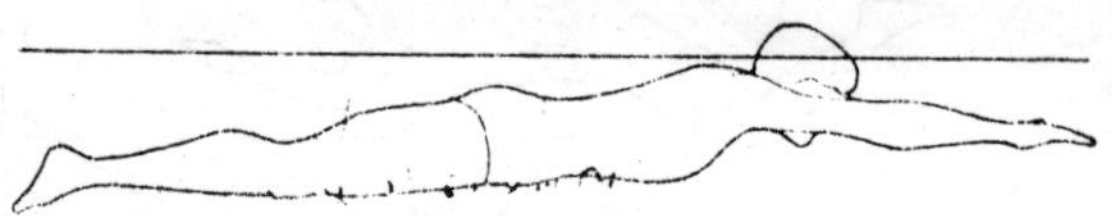

Next, the elbows bend so that they are up as the hands are pulled outward, backward, and downward to just below the shoulders.

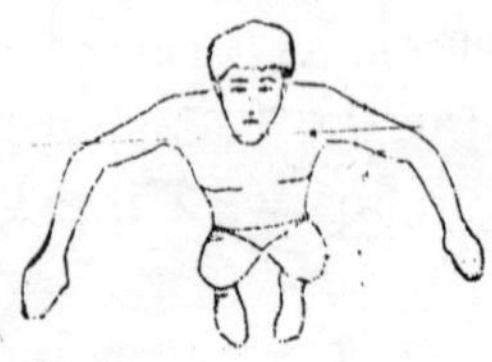

Tell your swimmers to move the hands diagonally inward as the head is lifted for a breath. Then the hands meet and start forward to a fully extended position.

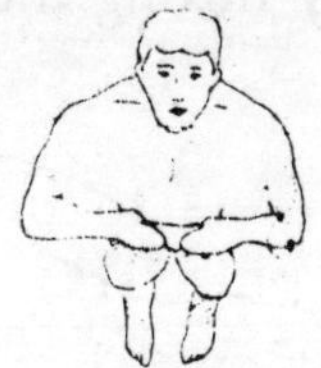

As they swim the breaststroke, swimmers should feel they are drawing a heart or eyeglass shape with their hands.

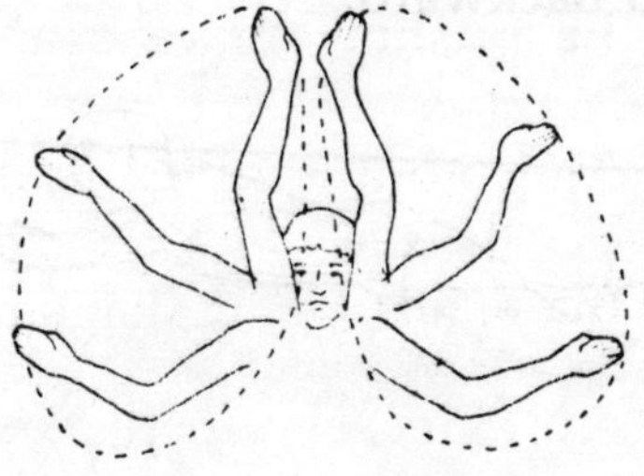

COACHING POINTS FOR THE ARMSTROKE

1. Start the pull from a streamlined position.
2. Elbows should be up as you pull.
3. The path of the hands should form a heart shape.

THE BREASTSTROKE KICK

Swimming rules for the breaststroke specify that the feet must be drawn up with the knees bent and that the movement of the legs and feet must be simultaneous and in the same horizontal plane. No butterfly kick or front of the leg is permitted.

First have your swimmers practice the kick

supporting themselves against a wall. From an extended position, tell them to bring the heels up towards the buttocks by flexing the hips and knees.

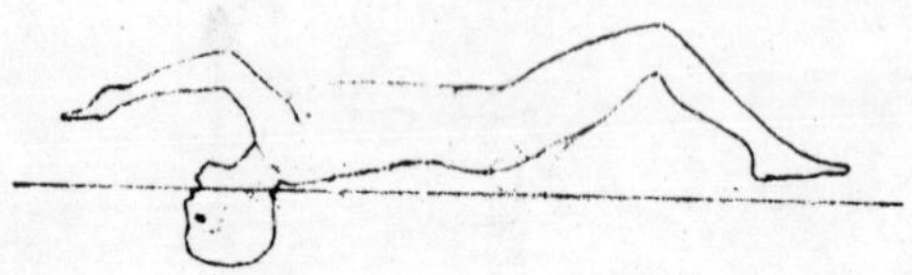

Next, the ankles are flexed with the feet set outward. The feet return to extension by pushing downward and backward.

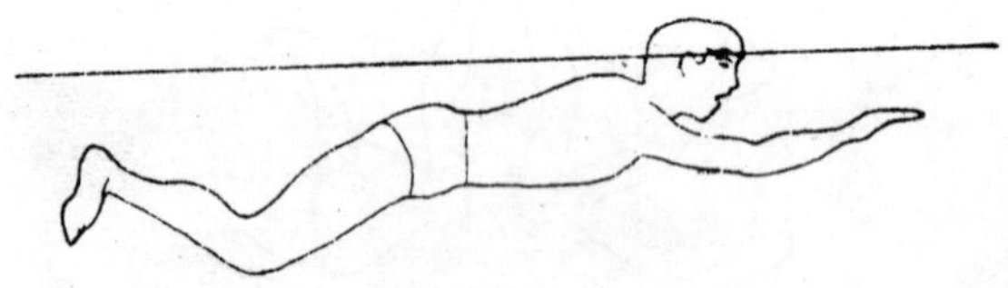

After your swimmer can perform the kick easily, coordinate the kick to the telling your swimmers that the arms start first and the kick starts when the hands start the rounded portion of the heart-shaped path. The arms start to pull again just as the legs finish the kick. This kick provides the main propulsive in the traditional breaststroke.

COACHING POINTS FOR THE BREASTSTROKE KICK

1. The feet should be set out as the heels are brought up.
2. Bend legs at the hips as well as knees.
3. Push feet downward as well as backward.

BREASTSTROKE BREATHING PATTERN

In the breaststroke breathing pattern, the head is lifted, for the breath as the hands come to a point under the breast and the shoulders are at their highest point in the water. The chin remains in the water while the neck is hyper extended to lift only the mouth above the water level.

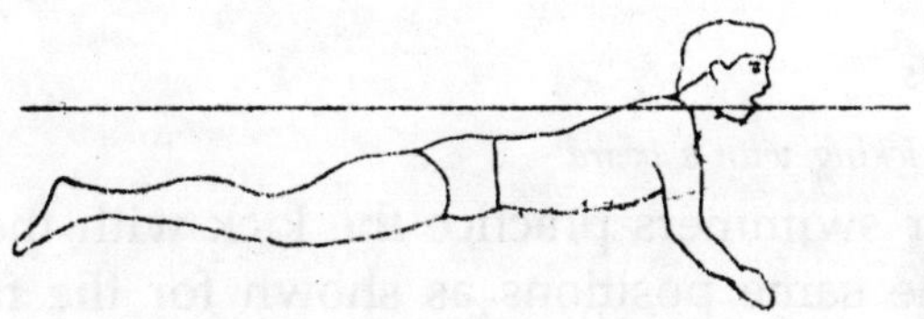

Tell your swimmers to return the face to the water and begin exhaling as the arms begin to return extension. The chin is tucked, but the top the head breaks the water line.

DRILLS FOR PRACTISING THE BREASTSTROKE

Armstroke and breathing drills

Armstroke land drill

Swimmers stand on the deck and are given a count for each part of the arm pull. On the count of one, the swimmers extend both arms fully at shoulder height in front of the chin with the thumbs touching. On two, the hands separate and pull outward, downward, and backward to the shoulders. The elbows should be bent and up, with the hands apart slightly more than shoulder width. On three, the thumbs come together, and on four the arms extend to the position they were in at the count of one.

Armstroke with kick board

Have your swimmers try the armstroke with a kick

board between their legs. Crossing the ankles will keep the board in place. When they can do this correctly, add the swimmers lift the head to the drill by having the swimmers lift the head after the hands finish the outward phase of the stroke. Stress to your swimmers that their elbows should be up and that their hands should follow a heart-shaped path.

Kicking drills

Breaststroke kicking with a board

Have your swimmers practice the kick with the board held in the same positions as shown for the freestyle kick.

Breaststroke kicking on the back

Your swimmers will enjoy doing this drill as a warm-up, or it may be used as a teaching drill. After your swimmers understand the kick, tell them to try it on the back with their hands by their sides, bringing the heels to the buttocks on each kick.

Breaststroke kicking without a board

Have your swimmers lie in a prone position with their hands at their sides. The feet are then pulled up or set in the dorsi-flexed position. Tell your swimmers to touch the feet with the hands before they are thrust back. The head may be in the water or above it. If the head is in the water, the breath is taken after the hands touch the feet and before the thrust of the kick.

reaststroke for power

Use this drill when working on stroke mechanics and body position. First emphasize to your swimmers that they should get as much power as possible from the kick. Next, ask them to count their strokes while trying to swim the pool using as few strokes as possible (10-

12 strokes in a 25-yard pool is better than average for swimmers 10 years of age; 7-9 strokes for older recreational swimmers.

Breaststroke start

Swimming rules allow one arm pull and one leg kick underwater following the start and the turn. However, a portion of the contestant's head must break the surface of the water before another strokes is started. The same grab start used in the freestyle is also used in the breaststroke. For the breaststroke start, instruct your swimmers to drop the head earlier and to dive deeper than for the freestyle but with the same streamlined position.

Tell your swimmers to hold the position following the dive for at least three counts. Then, when they feel their momentum decrease, the arms should begin to pull, with the elbows bending to 60 degrees to bring the hands toward the hips.

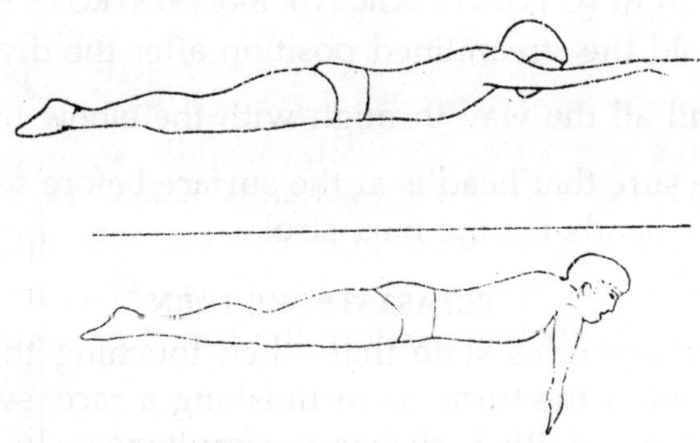

Now the hands accelerate in a fast, whip-like action as the arms are extended. Your swimmers will know the pull is complete when the palms of the hands are directly alongside the body. They should then hold this position for about two counts.

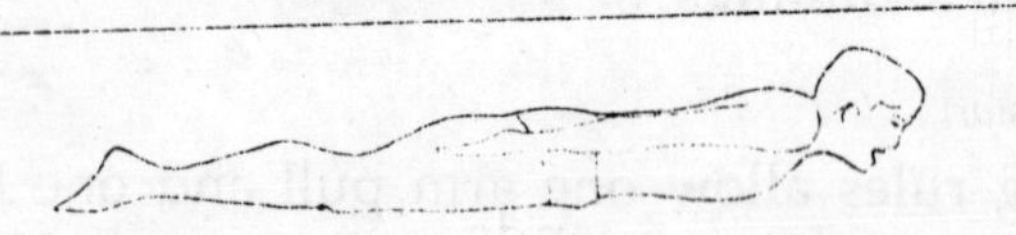

Swimmers recover the arms and legs at the same time. The hands and elbows are kept close to the body to minimize drag, and the head is lifted as the knees are flexed to begin the kick. The arms are extended overhead with the hands below the surface as the legs thrust backwards. Tell your swimmers to check that the head is at the surface to be legally ready for the next stroke.

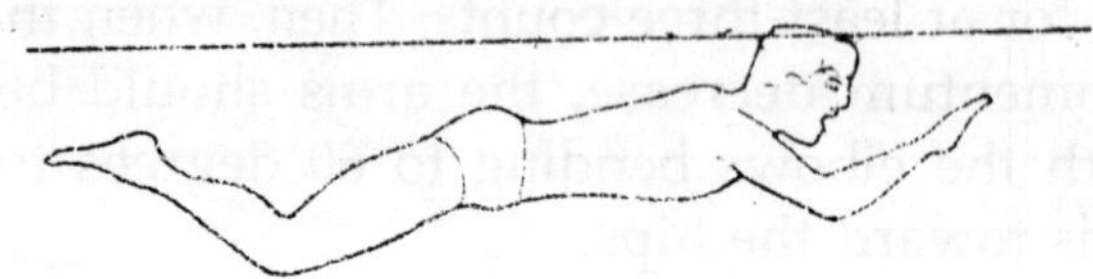

COACHING POINTS FOR THE BREASTSTROKE START

1. Hold the streamlined position after the dive.
2. Pull all the way through with the elbow high.
3. Be sure that head is at the surface before separating the hands for the next stroke.

BREASTSTROKE TURN

Swimming rules state that when touching the end of the pool at the turns or in finishing a race, swimming must touch with both hands simultaneously either at or above the water level. As the swimmer touches the wall or grabs the gutter with both hands, the knees are drawn up to the abdomen. The feet move toward the hips in a straight line just under the body, and swimmer pivots the hips towards the wall. The hands come off the gutter as the feet are placed on the wall 18 to 24 inches below the surface. Swimmers should be told to leave the wall on their side but to return to the abdomen while extending in the streamlined position with both arms over head, as discussed in the guidelines for freestyle and backstroke turns. Explain that in contrast to the crawl, in the breaststroke push-off the head is held down, and the swimmer is 2 to 3 feet below the water surface.

10

RULES AND REGULATIONS

GENERAL RULES

General Rules are basic regulations for FINA competitions in all kinds of Swimming, Diving and Water Polo events as well as for uniform regulations for the development of competition facilities. In these Rules, competitors shall include swimmers, divers, water polo players, or synchronized swimmers, either male or female.

FINA recognized that these Rules may be adjusted for competitions within a given federation but recommends that all Members adhere to those Rules as closely as possible.

ELIGIBILITY

A competitor is eligible to compete in competitions unless he has competiting Swimming as his sole occupation or business on which he is financially dependent for living.

Any competitor eligible to compete shall be registered with his national federation. Unless otherwise allowed by the competitor's national federation, any financial advantage, which a competitor gains based on athletic fame and/or competitive results must be approved, administered, and controlled by his national federation. Such financial advantage shall not be available to the competitor before the end of his competitive career except for approved expenses.

INTERNATIONAL RELATIONS

Member shall not admit to its membership any club affiliated to another Member. A competitor of one Member joining a club of another Member.

A competitor of one Member joining a club of another Member and participating in the competitions of the latter shall be regarded as coming within the jurisdiction of the latter. No team shall be designated by the title of a Country or Sport Country unless the competitors have been selected by the Member of the Country or Sport Country. When a competitor represents country or Sport Country in a competition, he shall be a citizen, whether by birth or naturalization, of the nation he represent, provided that a naturalized citizen shall have lived in that country for atleast one year prior to that even and further, that any competitor changing his affiliation from one national governing body to another must have resided in the territory of and to under the jurisdiction of the latter for at least twelve months prior to the aforesaid event.

For International competitions, the competitors who have two nationalities according to the laws of the respective nations must choose one "sport nationality" to be under the control of only one affiliated Member.

If a competitor competed in an International meet representing a nation, it is to be considered that he choose that "Sport nationality" and he will be under the control of the Member according to and cannot represent another Member until he officially changes his affiliation and resides in the territory under the jurisdiction of the latter at least twelve months after change of affiliation and prior to the event mentioned above.

TOURS IN FOREIGN COUNTRIES

A competitor competing at a meet in a foreign country shall be a member of an affiliated Member or of a club affiliated thereto. This section shall apply equally to judges, officials, trainers, and coaches.

All competitions must be sanctioned by the Member where the competition takes place, and all competitors or clubs must have permission from their respective Member.

UNAUTHORIZED RELATIONS AND MISBEHAVIOUR

No affiliated Member shall have any kind of relationship with a non affiliated or suspended body.

The exchange of competitors, administrators, directors, judges, officials, trainers, coaches, etc., with non-affiliated or suspended bodies is not permissible. The holding of demonstration and/or exhibitions, clinics, training, competitions, etc., with non-affiliated or suspended bodies is not permissible.

Bureau may authorize rotations with non-affiliated or suspended bodies as in rules through. Any individual or group violating this Rules shall be suspended by the affiliated Member for a minimum period of one year, up to a maximum period of two years. FINA relation this right to review the suspension made by the affiliated Member and to increase it up to the maximum of two year in accordance with the circumstances involved. The affiliated Member shall abide by any such increase made on review. In the event that such individual or group has resigned its membership with the affiliated Member or is not a Member, it shall not be allowed to affiliate with that Member or is not a Member, it shall not be allowed to affiliate with that Member for a minimum period of three months up to a maximum period of two years. FINA retains the right to review any such sanction imposed by the affiliated Member and to increase it up to the maximum of two years in accordance with the circumstances involved. The affiliated Member shall abide by any such increase made on review.

In every case where a permit to hold a meeting is granted, each Member agrees to see that the Rules governing eligibility are strictly enforced and each affiliated Members concerned shall insist that in the advertisements, entry forms, programmes, and all other official notices, it shall be stated that the competitions will be held, and ensure that they actually are held, under the rules of the relevant Member.

The competitors individually or as a group including the team officials of Member representatives, participating in any FINA event, who are guilty of any or all of the following offenses, shall be disciplined by the FINA Bureau.

— Refuse to carry out their obligations as true sportsmen.

— Withdraw from an event for political reasons.

— Or in any other way display non-cooperation with the authorities of the Organizing Committee of the competition, engendered by political views.

— Any sanction imposed on a competitor or group by a Member shall be recognized and complied with by all Members, subject to reconsideration by the Bureau on appeal.

RIGHT TO PARTICIPATE

Any competitor may join as many clubs as he wishes, but he is allowed to represent only one at a time. Any competitor who temporarily or permanently changes his residence to another country may join a club affiliated to the respective Member in the new country.

Any competitor who wishes to represent a club in another country must make a written declaration of his intention to his former club and to the new club. The right to represent the new club may be allowed after a minimum of one month following the request.

COSTUMES

The costumes of all competitors shall be in good moral taste and suitable for the individual sports discipline.

All costumes shall be non-transparent. The referee of a competition has the authority to exclude any competitor whose costume does not comply with this Rule.

ADVERTISING

Technical equipment worn when in the water

The competitor is not permitted to wear any visible form advertising exceeding 18 square centimetres in area each.

POOL DECK EQUIPMENT

Towels and bags may carry two advertisements. Track suits and Officials' uniforms may carry two on the top and two on the trousers or skirt. The logo of the manufacturer or sponsor may be repeated, but the same name may be used only once on each article or garment. Body advertisement is not allowed in any way whatsoever. No advertisement may be florescent or be of a colour which adversely effects television.

DISQUALIFICATION AND WITHDRAWAL

In all competitions except Water Polo, a competitor of team not wishing to take part in this final in which qualification was earned shall withdraw within thirty minutes following the preliminary in which the qualification took place.

In Swimming, Diving, and Synchronized Swimming, where a competitor who competed in the finals is disqualified for any reason, including medical control, the position he would have held shall be awarded to the competitor who finished next and all the lower placing competitors in the finals shall be awards, the awards shall be returned and given to the appropriate competitors applying the foregoing provisions.

If a team (i.e., national team, regional team, club team, etc) withdraws from a FINA competition within less than two months of the first day of the competition, a fine of 6,000 Swiss France shall be paid to the Organizer. This Rule shall not apply to a withdrawal following a change in date or venue.

SMOKING BAN

At all international competitions, no smoking shall be permitted, in area designated for competitors, either prior to or during competitions.

GENERAL RULES FOR FINA COMPETITIONS

Organization

FINA alone shall have the right to organize World Championships and FINA events for Swimming, Diving, Water Polo, Synchronized Swimming, and Open Water Swimming. The words World and FINA may not be used in connection with any Swimming, Diving, Water Polo, Synchronized Swimming or Open Water Swimming event without the consent of FINA.

The national flags of the countries of the competitors placed, 1st, 2nd, and 3rd shall be raised and the national anthem of the country of the champion in the individual and team competitions shall be played. This Rule does not apply to Masters Championships.

The Bureau is empowered to formulate all rules and regulations for the conduct of such competitions. All regulations set by the Bureau must be announced and published one year prior to the opening day of the competition.

WITHDRAWALS

Except as provided in GR 8.1 any withdrawal from heats or finals in Swimming, diving, or Synchronized Swimming events, at any international competition under the management of FINA, including the Olympic Games, the respective Member to which such competitors belong, shall pay without any excuse, to the Honorary Treasurer of FINA, the sum of thirty Swiss Francs for each competitor on individual events, and the sum of sixty (60) Swiss Francs for each team in team events.

If a team withdraws from of FINA Water Polo

event any time after the draw has been concluded, and without the approval of the Management Committee, then that team will be sanctioned by the Bureau with an economic sanction of 8,000 Swiss Francs, from which 6,000 Swiss Francs goes to the Organizer, and suspension from all competitions for a minimum period of three months up to a maximum period of two year.

If member qualified for the World Cup in Synchronized Swimming withdraws after having submitted its entry in the competition, the Member shall be sanctioned with a line of 4,000 Swiss France from which 3,000 Swiss Francs goes to the Organizer.

PROTESTS

Protests are possible

If the rules and regulations for the conduct of the competition are not observed; If other conditions endanger the competitions and/or competitors; or Against decisions of the referee; however, no protests shall be allowed against decisions of fact.

PROTEST MUST BE SUBMITTED

To the referee; in writing; by the responsible team leader only; together with a deposit of 50 Swiss Francs, and within 30 minutes following the conclusion of the respective event or match.

If conditions causing a potential protest are noted prior to the competition, a protest must be lodged before the signal to start is given.

All protests shall be considered by the referee. If the rejects the protests, he must state the reasons for his decision. The team leader may appeal the rejection to the Jury of Appeal whose decision shall be final. If the protest is rejected, the deposit will be forfeited to the management body of the competition. If the complain is not accepted, a formal protest may be made.

JURY OF APPEAL

For Olympic Games and World Championships, the Jury of Appeal shall be composed of the Bureau members and Honorary Members present with he President, or in his absence of Vice-President, as Chairman. For all other FINA events, the Jury of Appeal shall have one vote, except as provided hereunder, and in case of equality of voting, the Chairman has a casting vote.

A jury member is allowed to speak, but not to vote, on a case in which the interest of his own federation is involved. A jury member having acted as an official is not allowed to vote on a case if there is a protest against his decision or on his interpretation of a Rule. In case of urgency, the jury may vote on a matter even if it has not been possible to call all the members. The decision of the jury is final.

MANAGEMENT COMMITTEE

For Olympic Games, World Championships and FINA events, the FINA Bureau shall appoint a Management Committee. For other competitions, a Management Committee may be appointed by the responsible body for the competition in question.

The Management Committee shall be responsible for the entire management of the competition.

OLYMPIC GAMES AND WORLD CHAMPIONSHIPS

Management Committee

The actual management of all Olympic Games and World Championship contests shall be under the control of FINA.

The Management Committee shall be Bureau of FINA. The Committee shall have the power, if they think it advisable, to add to their numbers by the addition to one representative of one country holding the Olympic Games or World Championships. The Management Committee shall be responsible for the entire management of the contest, including the arrangement of the programme of events, appointment of officials, and adjudication of protests.

Should any member of the Management committee be absent from the Olympic Games or World Championships, the remaining members shall have the power to appoint substitutes, if necessary. Nine members shall constitute a quorum. When the Management Committee is acting as Jury of Appeal, Rule GR 10.4 Shall apply.

COMMISSIONS

For each discipline a commission shall be appointed consisting of the respective technical delegate and the Chairman and the honorary Secretary of each respective Technical Committee. Subject to the supervision of the FINA Bureau, the Commissions shall be responsible for

— the control of all pool equipment and all technical installations, in due course prior to and during the event.

— the conduct of the competition in the respective discipline,

— making daily rosters for acting officials, and investigating cases of protest as preparation for the Jury of Appeal.

OFFICIALS

The Bureau will sand to all Members application forms for judges to act at the Olympic Games or World Championships. These forms must be signed by the president or Secretary of the Member and all candidates must have been fully certified by the respective Technical Committee of FINA.

FACILITIES

Olympic Games and World Championships Rules FR 3, FR 6, FR 8 and FR 11 shall apply. At Olympic Games and World Championships approved Automatic Officiating Equipment shall be provided and used. All pools shall be available for use by entered competitors before the competition begins. Swimming, Water Polo, Synchronized Swimming 5 days prior, Diving-8 days prior.

During the competition days the pools shall be available for training when competitions are not in progress. Diving training shall be permitted during Swimming heats in separate pool in the same area. Seating positions along the side of the pool shall be provided for all competitors, team officials and unassigned technical officials, from which they may properly observe training and competitions.

ENTRIES

At least 10 days before the commencement of the

Olympic Games or the World Championships, the Secretaries of the Members sending competitors shall forward to the Organizing Committee of the Country hosting the competition a list of any competitors entered who are not starting, so that the non-starters any be eliminated from the entries.

For Olympic Games, entries shall be made on officials forms signed by the Secretary of the respective national Olympic Committee and delivered to the Organizing Committee of the Country holding the Games, on or before the date determined by the International Olympic Committee. The Honorary Secretary of FINA or his deputy shall claim these entries at least even days before the start of the first contest.

For World Championships, entries shall be made on official entry forms signed by the Secretary of the respective Member and delivered to the Organizing Committee on or before the date determined by FINA. The Honorary Secretary of FINA or his deputy shall claim these entries at least five days before the start of the first competition.

SWIMMING

For each individual event at the World Championships, each member may enter a maximum of 2 competitors, regardless of standards. For each individual event at the Olympic Games, each Member may enter one competitor, regardless of standards. If a second competitor is entered, then both competitors must meet the qualifying time standards as set by the Bureau.

For each relay event each Member may enter only

one team. All swimmers entered can be used in relays. The composition of a relay team may be changed between heats and finals of an event.

The names of swimmers actually swimming on a relay must be submitted at lest one hour before the start of the session in which the event is to take place, in the order in which they are to swim. The names of swimmers in medley relay events must be listed for their respective strokes.

Each Member may enter a maximum number of 26 men and 26 women swimmers. The heats and finals shall be arranged in accordance with rule SW 3, under the supervision of the Technical Swimming Committee.

The heat list shall be published at least four have before the first day of competition.

In every event, including 800 m freestyle for women and 1500 m freestyle for men, competitors shall be seeded for the heats in accordance with the times submitted on the official entry form. Swimmers shall be advanced to 'B' and 'A' finals on the basis of their placing in the heats.

DIVING

For each Diving event at the World Championships, each member may enter a maximum if 2 competitors, regardless of standards. For each Diving event at the Olympic Games, each member may enter one competitor, regardless of the standards. If a second competitor is entered, then, both competitors must meet the qualifying standard established by the Bureau.

Each Member may enter a maximum number of 4

men and 4 women divers. At the Olympic Games and at the World Championships, in spring board and platform Diving contests there shall be executed the dives prescribed by the FINA Rules for Diving and not other dives may be added.

WATER POLO

For Water Polo, any entry of a maximum of thirteen players may be accepted. Any team member can be freely interchanged during each round of competition.

Qualification for Olympic Games- Men

Automatically the first 6 teams from the previous World Championships plus the host. If the host is in the first 6 teams, then the 7th team to is to be included.

The other 5 (or 6) teams are to come from the Olympic Games Qualification Tournament.

Qualification for Championship-Men

The competitions shall be between teams selected in the following manner; The ten highest ranking teams from the preceding Olympics, one team from the host country, one team from each of the five continents to be selected through a qualifying tournament of continental championships.

The highest qualifying team from the continental qualifying tournament or continental championships shall be entitled to represent that continent; if this team does not accept, then the next highest ranking team willing to accept and participate in the World Championships shall qualify.

If the host country is already included in the ten highest ranking teams from the preceding Olympics, then that entry position shall be filled from the next team form the continent of the host country. If another one of the ten highest ranking teams from the preceding Olympics does not enter, then that position shall be filled from the next team from that team's continent.

If there is then, for any reason, a vacancy, that vacancy will be filled from the host continent.

Qualification for World Championships- women

The competition shall be between a maximum if twelve teams to be chosen by selection process. The bureau has the authority to with to Continental Organizer in which way and at what me the tournament will take place. The bureau has the right to Incorporate members in Qualification Tournaments of different continental region.

SYNCHRONIZED SWIMMING

In Synchronized swimming, each Member may enter not more than ten competitors, in accordance with events approved by the I.O.C. in Olympic Games or by FINA in World Championships.

Each member may enter one solo, one Duet, and one Team in the World Championships, and subject to I.O.C. approval in the Olympic Games. Competitors entered for Diving, Water polo, and Synchronized Swimming cannot swim relay events, and those entered for Swimming, Diving, and Synchronized Swimming cannot be used a Water polo reserves, with the proviso that one and the same swimmer could compete in Water Polo as well as other Swimming events, if officially entered for such events.

Once fixed, the standard daily programme of events may be altered only by FINA Management

Committee, and then under exceptional circumstances. Notice of any alteration must be posted on the Officials Bulletin Board at least Twenty-four hours before the alteration is to come into operation. The competitions at the Olympic Games shall take place during a period of fourteen days, the dates to be fixed by the I.O.C and FINA jointly.

There shall be morning, afternoon and evening sessions. The competitions at the World Championships shall take place during a period of ten days, the dates to be fixed by the FINA Bureau. There shall be morning, afternoon and evening session.

Exhibitions or displays outside the usual Olympic Games or World Championships programmes are not desirable and may not be held during these Swimming contests, unless authorized by FINA.

AWARDS

Medals; Gold, Silver and Bronze medals shall be awarded to the first three places in individual and team final events at the World Championships.

Diplomas: At World Championships, diplomas are awarded to all sight finalists in individuals events and to the first six finalists in team events.

SCORES

Only in World Championships point are awarded to all finalists, according to the following point distribution:

Swimming

Individual

"B" finals 9,7,6,5,4,3,2,1 points

"A" finals 18,16,15,14,13,12,11,10 points

Relay

"B" finals-18, 14,12,10,8,6,4,2, points

"A" finals- 36,32,30,28,24,22,20 points

A special FINA Trophy should be given based upon the following;

First Place	5 points
Second Place	3 points
Third Place	2 points
Fourth Place	1 point

Individual world Record 2 Points for each record broken. if there is a tie, performance will be compared with the World Records and a decision made by the Swimming Commission.

Diving

18,16,14,12,10,8,6,5,4,3,2,1 points

Water Polo

No points, Rated 1st, 2nd, 3rd, etc.

Synchronized Swimming

Sole, 9,7,6,5,4,3,2,1, points

Duet 18,14,12, 8, 4, points

In the case of a tie, the points for each place involved in the tie shall be added together and divided equally among the competitors of teams involved in the tie.

WATER POLO COMPETITIONS

Olympic Games Tournament

Draw: The draw for the Olympic Games tournament

will be on the last day of the Olympic Games qualification Tournament as follows:

— For the Preliminary Round, all qualifying teams will be drawn into two groups, either A to B

— First and first and second place teams from the previous World championships will be drawn one into A, the other into B.

— Next, the third and fourth place teams from the previous world Championships will be drawn one into A, the other into B.

— Next, the fifth and sixth place teams from the previous World Championships will be drawn one into, a, the other into B.

— If the host country is in the first through sixth places from the previous World Championships, the draw will continue as follows:

— First and second place teams in the Olympic Games Qualification Tournament will be drawn, one into A, the other into B.

— The third and fourth place teams in the Olympic Games Qualification Tournament will be drawn, one into A the other into B.

— The fifth and sixth place teams in the Olympic Games Qualification Tournament will be drawn, one into A, the other into B.

— If the host Country is not in the first through sixth, places in the previous World Championships, the draw will continue as follows:

— First and second place teams in the Olympic Games Qualification Tournament will be drawn, one into A, the other into B.

— The third and fourth place teams in the Olympic Games Qualification Tournament will be drawn, one into A, the other into B.

— The fifth place and host country will be drawn, one into A, the other into B.

If two teams shall have equal points, further classification shall be established as follows:

— Precedence shall be given to the team winning the match in which they have played against one another.

— In the event of the match in which they have played against one another having ended in a tie score, a further classification shall be established on goal difference, i.e.., the team with the largest difference between goals scored for and against shall be given precedence. for the purposes of.

— In the event of goal difference being equal, then the team having scored the highest number of goals shall be given shall be given precedence.

— In the event of further equality, the tie shall be resolved by each team shooting six penalty shorts at their opponent's goal in alternate succession; and then the other team shall take its first penalty shot, etc., If a tie shall exist after that procedure, each team shall again be awarded six penalty shots in the seem manner and if a tie still exists, the procedure shall continue to be repeated until it is broken. Any member or members of a team may shoot the penalty shots, if not being necessary that any single member shoot all six penalty shots or that different members shoot each shot. The procedure shall be conducted one half four following the completion of the final game of that round.

— If more than two teams have equal points, a second classification shall be established on goal difference, i.e., the team with the largest difference between goals scored for an against shall be given precedence.

— In the event of goal difference being equal, then the team having scored the highest number of goals in games involving only those teams tied in points shall be given precedence.

— In the event of still further equality, precedence shall be given to the team winning the match in which they have played against one another.

— In the current of a further quality, the tie shall be resolved by each team shooting six penalty shots at their opponents goal in alternate succession; and then the other team shall take again be awarded penalty shots in the same manner, and if a tie still exists, the procedure shall continue to be repeated until it is broken. Any member of the team may shoot the penalty shots, in not being necessary that any single member shoots the penalty shots, or that different members shoot each shot. This procedure shall be conducted one half hour following the completion of the final game of that round.

— In case a team taking part in the water Polo Tournament declares a forfeit, or is disqualified for one or more matches, the match or matches shall be awarded to the opponent with the goals score of 5-0.

— *Withdrawal:* if, for any reason, qualified teams do not wish to participate in the draw, the next ranking team(s) will than be taken in order from their placing in the Olympic games Qualification Tournament.

For the Final Round

— First and Second place teams in Group A and in Group B from a Group C of four teams.

— Third and Fourth place teams in group A and in Group B form a Group D of four teams.

— Fifth and Sixth place teams in Group A and in Group B form a Group E of four teams.

— Games played in the Preliminary Round will not be repeated in the Final Round with two exceptions.

Classification of teams placed 5-12 will be made on points namely, two points for each match won, one point for each match drawn and zero points for each match lost.

Medal Round

Day 1

1A vs 2B

2A vs 1B

Day 2

Day 1 losers will play for the bronze medal, and Day 1 winners will play for the gold, even if they might have played previously; and since a definite winner is required, it may be necessary to invoke the Rule regarding extra time play in the Water polo Rules.

World championship Tournament

Schedule of Games for 16 Teams

PRELIMINARY ROUND

— For groups of four teams each from Group A, Group B, Group C, and Group D.

— In each group the teams play a single Round Robin.

SEMI-FINAL ROUND

— The first and second place teams in Group A and in Group 3 form a new group, Group E, which consists of four teams.

— The first and second place teams in Group C and in Group D form a new group, Group F, which consists of four teams.

— The third and fourth place teams in group A and in Group B form a new group, group G, which consists of four teams.

— The third and fourth place teams in Group C and in Group D form a new group, group H, which consists of four teams.

FINAL ROUNDS

— The third and fourth place teams in Group G and H play for places.

— The first and second place teams in Group G and H play for places.

— The third and fourth place teams in Group E and F play for places 5 to 8.

— For the first Four places

The first and second place teams of Group E and Group F play for places 1 to 4.

Day 1

2E vs 1F

1E vs 2F

Day 2

Day 1 losers will play for the bronze medal and Day 1 winners will play for the gold medal, even if they might have played previously; and since a definite winner is required; it may be necessary to invoke the Rule regarding extra time play in the Water Polo Rules.

WORLD CUPS

General Rules

FINA may conduct World Cups in each discipline be accordance with FINA Rules and in particular the Rules set forth in this Rule.

— The World Cups shall normally beconduced in odd number years.

— All World Cups shall be conducted with doping control in accordance with MED 4.

— At all World Cups the Management Committee shall be the members of the appropriate Technical Committee present at the Event, with the Bureau Liaison as Chairman who shall have a casting vote, if necessary.

— Judging selections shall be determined by the appropriate Technical committee, subject to approval by the Bureau or the Executive.

DIVING

The Diving World Cup shall be conducted as a team

competition and as a individual competition for both men and women on the 1 metre springboard, the 3 metre springboard and the 10 metre platform.

For each event, each federation may enter one diver regardless of standard, or two divers provided that both divers meet a minimum qualifying standard for the event, which shall be the 12th place points for the event in the team competition at the previous Diving World Cup rounded down to the even 10 points. The qualifying standard must be attained in a recognized international, continental or national championship competition, during the two year period preceding the Diving World Cup. The minimum qualifying standards shall be announced by publication in the FINA News not later than September of the year preceding the competition.

Placement points shall be awarded such diver in the team competition on the following basis:

— Ist place in team competition 50

— 2nd place in team competition 48

— 3rd Place in team competition 47

— 4th place in team competition 46, and

— reducing by 1 point for each placement position.

The 12 divers earning the highest aggregate score in each team competition event shall qualify for the Diving World Cup individual competition in that event.

Each individual event in the Diving World Cup shall be determined by match play tournament competition, matching divers in groups of four. The four diver earning the highest aggregate scores in the team competition shall earn a bye in the quarter-final round. The first quarter-final round shall be comprised of the sixth, eight, tenth and twelfth place finishers from the team competition, and the second quarter-final round shall be comprised of the fifth, seventh, ninth and eleventh finishers. The two divers earning the highest point total in each round will advance to the next round. The second and fourth finishers in team competition shall compete in the first semi-final round against the first two finishers in the first quarter-final, and first and third finishers in the team competition shall compete in the second semi-final round.

If there is a test for 12th place in a team event, all divers so place shall qualify for the individual event and shall compete in the first quarter final.

Where a qualified diver is unable for any reason to commence a quarter final round, the thirteenth placed diver in the team competition shall compete in the quarter final. If the thirteenth diver is unavailable then the next available diver shall complete the tournament field of twelve divers. If a diver shall be left vacant and shall not be filled by any other diver.

If there is a tie for fourth place in the team competition the diver to touch the bye shall be the diver earning the highest total points on a single dive.

If there should be a tie for second place in the quarter final or semi-final then each diver so placed shall compete in the next round.

If there should be a tie for any other place, the position of the divers in the tournament, draw shall be determined by a blot.

In each round of tournament competition the divers shall dive in reverse order of their placing in team competition.

The diver may make changes to his dive list before the commencement of any round in the tournament provided the amended list is lodged with the tournament secretary within on hour of the completion of the team competition or the previous session of the tournament, if a new list of divers is not submitted by the diver, within the time provided, the diver shall perform the same dives he performed in the previous session.

The 1 metre springboard and the 3 metre springboard individual events for men and women shall be held separately; however, the platform tournament event for men and women shall be combined. The first round of women's divers shall begin at the end of the second round of men's dives.

The Diving World Cup team champion shall be determined for men, women and combined team by accumulating points (See GR 12.2.4) earned on 1 metre springboard, 3 metres springboard and 10 metre platform by each team member.

WATER POLO

There shall be eight teams in both the men's and Women's Cups.

For the Men's Water Polo World Cup the team from the host country and the top seven (or eight, if the team from the most country is among them) teams from the immediately preceding Olympic Games or World Championships shall be qualified. If any on the first eight reams do not compete, the next placing team from the immediately preceding Olympic Games or World Championships shall take the position in the World Cup.

For the Women's Water Polo World Cup in the year following the World Championship, the eight teams shall be selected as set forts.

For the Women's Water polo World Cup in the year following the Olympic Games (until such time as the event is place don the Olympic programme), the eight teams shall be selected by the TWPC with approval of the Bureau or Executive.

Qualified federations must declare their intention to send a team to the World Cup at least six months prior to the event. The draw shall be held approximately four months prior to the event.

The teams shall be drawn into two Groups A or B, based upon the results of the immediately preceding Olympic Games or World Championships, as follows:

— First and second in prior events shall be drawn between A1 and B1

— Third and fourth in prior event shall be drawn between A 2 and B 2.

— Fifth and Sixth in prior event shall be drawn between A 3 and B 3.

— Seventh and Eight in prior event shall be drawn between A 4 and B 4.

Semi-Final round:

Third in A will play Fourth in B.

Fourth in A will play Third in B.

First in A will Play Second in B.

Second in A will play First in B.

Final round

Losers of Games 13 & 11 play for seventh and eighth place.

Winners of Games 13 & 16 Play for fifth and sixth places.

Losers of Games 15 & 16 play for third and fourth places.

Winners of Games 15 & 16 play for first and second places.

Games 13 through 20 must be played to conclusion

SYNCHRONIZED SWIMMING

The first eight finishers from the previous Olympic Games or World Championships shall qualify to enter the sole, Duet and Team events. In addition, if the host federation is not so qualified, they shall automatically be allowed to enter the event. In such cases, there will be a maximum of nine entries in said event(s). If the qualified entries are not complete, the next rankings in order will be accepted.

The World Cup held in the year prior to the Olympic Games may be an open event which may serve as a qualifying event for the Olympic Games.

Eligibility for the World Cup held in the year after the Olympic Games shall be as follows:

— Team Event-Based on the Olympic Games.

— Solo and Duet Events-Until these events are reinstated into the Olympic Games, eligibility shall be based on the result of a specific competition designated shall be named by the Technical Synchronized Swimming Committee one year in advance.

THE POOL

Specifications for pools for the conduct of Olympic Games and World Championships, Regional Games and all international competitions.

Length--50.00 metres. When touch panes of electronic timing equipment are used on the starting end, or additionally on the turning end, the pool must be of such length that ensures the required distance of 50.00 metres between the two panels.

Dimensional Tolerances.

Against the nominal length of 50.000 metres, a tolerance of plus 0.03 metres; 0.3M above and 0.8M below the surface of the water. This applies to both end walls at all points.

These measurements should be certified by a surveyor or other qualified official appointed or approved by the governing body of the Country.

Width--21.0 metres.

— Depth 1.8m over all for Olympic Games and World Championships.

Walls

— Shall be parallel and vertical.

— End walls shall form right angels with the surface

of the water, and shall be constructed of solid material, with a non slip surface, extending 0.8M. below the water surface, so as to enable the competitor to touch and push off in turning without hazard.

— The minimum measurement of the electronic touch pads shall be 240 cm x 90 cm X 1 cm and shall extend 30 cm above and 30 cm above and 60 cm below the surface of the water.

The electronic equipment for each lane must be connected independently, so that they may be controlled individually. The surface of the touch panels must be of a bright colour and must bear the line markings approved for the end walls.

— Rest ledges along the pool walls are permitted; they must be not less than 1.2M below the water surface, and may be 0.1 to 0.15M wide.

— Cutters-may be placed on all four walls of the pool. End wall gutters if installed must a allow for attachment of touch panels to the required 0.3M. above the eater surface. They must be covered with a suitable grill or screen.

Gutters should all be equipped with adjustable shut-off values, so that the water may be kept at a constant level.

Number of lanes-8

Width of lanes-2.5M. each, with 2 spaces each of 50 cm; width outside of lanes and 8. There must be a lane rope separating these spaces from lanes 1 and 8 respectively.

Lane Ropes-shall extend the full length of the course, secured at each end wall to anchor brackets recessed into the end walls. Each lane rope will consist of floats placed and to end having a minimum diameter of 5cm. to a maximum of 11 cm. The colour of the floats extending for a distance of 5.0 m. from each end of the pool shall be distinct from the rest of the floats.

Starting platforms—The height of the platform above the water surface may be from 0.5 m. to 0.75 m.

The surface area- minimum 0.5 m. x 0.5 m.

Surface to be covered with non slip material.

Maximum slope-not more than 10 degrees.

Handgrips for backstroke start-must be placed within 0.3 m. to 0.6 m above the water surface horizontally and vertically. They must be parallel to the surface of the end wall and must not protrude beyond the end wall.

Numbering—Each starting block must be distinctly numbered on all 4 sides, clearly visible to the judges, No. 1 being on the right hand side when facing down the course.

Backstroke turn indicators—Flagged ropes suspended across the pool 1.8 m, above the water surface from fixed supports or stands, shall be set 5.0 m. from each end wall.

False Start Rope—shall be suspended across the pool from fixed standards placed 15.0M. in front of the starting end. It shall be attached to the standards by a quick release mechanism.

Water—Temperature— +24 Centigrade. Minimum. + 77 Fahrenheit. Minimum.

Level—During competition the water in the pool must be kept at a constant level, with no with no appreciable movement.

Lighting—Light intensity over starting platforms and turning ends must not be less than 100 foot candles.

Lane Markings: shall be of a dark contrasting colour, placed on the floor of the pool in the centre of each lane.

Each lane shall end 2.0 m. from the end walls of the pool with a distinctive cross line 1.0 m long and of the same width as the lane line.

The distance between the centre points of each lane line shall be 2.50 m.

Target lines must be placed on the end walls or on the electronic timing pads, in the centre of each lane of the same width as the lane lines.

They shall extend without interruption from the deck edge, to the floor of the pool. A cross line 0.5 m. long shall be placed 0.6 m. below the water surface, measured to the centre point of the cross line. The cross line on the touch pad shall be place 0.3 m. below the water line.

Distance separating swimming pool from diving well-minimum-5.0 m.

MANAGEMENT OF COMPETITIONS

The Management Committee appointed by the

governing body shall have jurisdiction over all matters not assigned by the rules to the referee, judges consistent with rules adopted for conducting any event.

At the Olympic Games, World Championships and World Cups, the FINA Bureau shall appoint the following minimum numbers of officials for the control of the competitions:

Referee (1)

Judges of stroke (4)

Starters (2)

Chief inspectors of turns (2, 1 at each end of the pool)

Inspectors of turns (1 at each end of each lane)

Chief recorder (1)

Recorder (1)

Clerks of course (2)

False start rope personnel (1)

Announcer (1)

For all other international competitions, the governing body shall appoint the same or fewer number of officials, subject to the approval of the respective regional or international authority where appropriate. Where Automatic Officiating Equipment is not available, such equipment must be replaced by chief timekeeper, 3 timekeepers per lane, chief finish judge and at least one finish judge per lane.

The swimming pool and the technical equipment for Olympic Games and World Championships shall be inspected and approved in due course prior to the Swimming competitions by the FINA Delegate together with a member of the Technical Swimming Committee.

Where underwater video equipment is used by television, the equipment must be operated by remote control and shall not obstruct the vision or path of swimmers and must not change the configuration of the pool or obscure the required FINA markings.

OFFICIALS

Referee

The referee shall have full control and authority over all officials, regulations related to the Competitions. He shall enforce all rules and decisions of FINA and shall decide all questions relating to the actual conduct of the meet, and event or the competition, the final settlement of which is not otherwise covered by the rules.

The referee may intervene in the competition at any stage to ensure that the Fina regulations are observed, and shall adjudicate all protests related to the competition in progress.

The referee shall ensure that all necessary officials are in their respective posts for the conduct of the competition. He may appoint substitutes for any who are absent, incapable of acting or found to be inefficient. He may appoint additional officials if considered necessary.

At the commencement of each event, the referee shall signal to the swimmers by a short series of whistles inviting them to remove all clothing except for swimmer, followed by a long whistle indicating that they should take their positions on the back of the starting platform. When the swimmers and officials are prepared for the start, the referee shall gesture to the starter with a stretched out arm, indicating that the swimmers are under the starter's control,

The referee shall disqualify any swimmer for any violation of the rules that he personally observes or which is reported to him other authorized officials.

Starter

The starter shall have full control of the swimmers from the time the referee turns the swimmers over to him until the race has commenced.

The starter shall report a swimmer to the referee for delaying the start, for willfully disobeying an order or for any other misconduct taking place at the start, but only the referee may disqualify a swimmer for such delay, willful disobedience or misconduct. Such disqualification shall not be counted as a false start.

The starter shall have power to decided whether the start is fair, subject only to the decision of the Referee. If the starter believes the start is not fair, he shall recall the swimmers after the signal of start has been given, except after a false start has occurred, when the starter shall not recall the swimmers after the signal of start has been given.

When starting an event the starter shall stand on the side of the pool within approximately five metres of the starting edge of the pool where the timekeepers can see the starting signal and the swimmers can hear the signal.

Clerk of Course

The clerk of course shall assemble swimmers prior to each event.

Chief Inspector of Turns

The chief inspector of turns shall ensure that inspectors of turns fulfil their duties during the competition.

The chief inspector of turns shall receive the reports from the inspectors of turns if any infringement occurs and shall present them to the referee immediately.

Inspectors of Turns

One inspector of turns shall be assigned to each lane at each end of the pool

Each inspector of turns shall ensure that swimmers comply with the relevant rules for turning, commencing from the beginning of the last armstroke before touching and ending with the completion of the first armstroke after turning. Inspectors of turns at the finish end of the pool shall ensure that swimmers finish their race in accordance with the relevant rules.

In individual events of 800 and 1500 metres, each inspector of turns of the turning end of the pool shall record the number of laps completed by the swimmer in his lane and keep the swimmer informed of the remaining number of laps to be completed by displaying "lap cards".

Each inspector at the starting and shall determine, in relay events, whether the starting swimmer is in contract with the starting platform when the preceding swimming touches the starting wall. When Automatic Equipment which judges relay take- offs is available, it shall be used in accordance. Inspectors of turn s shall report any violation on signed cards detailing the event, lane number, the swimmer's name and the infringement delivered to the chief inspector of turns who shall immediately convey the report to the referee.

Judges of Stoke

Judges of stroke shall be located on each side of the pool.

Each judge of stroke shall ensure that the rules related to the style of swimming designated for the event are being observed, and the infringement.

Chief Timekeeper

The chief timekeeper shall assign the seating positions for all timekeepers and the lanes for which they are responsible. There shall be three timekeepers for each lane. There shall be two additional timekeepers designated, either of whom shall be directed to replace a timekeeper whose watch did not start or stopped during an event, or who for any other reason is not able to record the time.

The chief timekeeper shall collect from each timekeeper a card showing the time recorded and, if necessary, inspect their watches.

The chief timekeeper shall record or examine the official time on the card to each lane.

Timekeepers

Each timekeeper shall take the time of the swimmers in the lane assigned to him a accordance. The watches shall be certified correct to the satisfaction of the meet Management Committee.

Each timekeeper shall start his watch at the starting signal, and shall stop it when the swimmer in his lane has completed the race. Timekeepers may be instructed by the chief timekeeper to record times at intermediate distances in races longer than 100 metres.

Promptly after the race, the timekeepers in each lane shall record the times of their watches on the card, give it to the chief timekeeper, and if requested present their watches for inspection. They shall not clear their watches until they receive the 'clear watches' signal from the chief timekeeper or the referee.

Unless a video backup system is used, it may be necessary to use the full complement of timekeepers even when Automatic Officiating Equipment is used.

Chief Finish judge

The chief finish judge shall assign each finish judge his position and the placing to be determined.

After the race, the chief finish judge shall collect sighed result sheets from each finish judge and establish the result and placings which will be sent directly to the referee. Where Automatic Officiating Equipment is used to judge the finish of a race, the chief finish judge must report the order of finish recorded by the Equipment after each race.

Finish Judges

Finish judges shall be positioned in elevated stands in line with the finish where they have at all times a clear view of the course and the finish line, unless they operate an Automatic Officiating device in their respective assigned lanes by depressing the 'push-button' at the completion of the race.

After each event the finish judges shall decide and report the placing of the swimmers according to the assignments given to them. Finish judges other than push-button operators shall not act as timekeepers in the same event.

Desk Control

The chief recorder is responsible for checking results from computer printouts or from results of times and placings in each event received from the referee. The chief recorder shall witness the referee's signing the results.

The recorders shall control withdrawals after the heats of finals, enter results on official forms, list all new records established, and maintain scores where appropriate.

Officials shall make the their decision autonomously and independently of each other unless otherwise provided in the Swimming Rules

SEEDING OF HEATS AND FINALS

The starting station for all event in Olympic games, World Championships, Regional Games and other FINA competitions shall be by seeding as follows:

HEATS

The best competitive times of all entrants for the preceding twelve months shall be submitted on entry forms and listed in order of time by the Management Committee. Swimmers who do not submit times shall be considered the slowest and shall be placed at the end of the list. Placement of swimmers with identical times or of more than one swimmer without times shall be determined by draw. Swimmers shall be placed in lanes according to the procedures set forth in below. Swimmers shall be placed in trail heats according to submitted times in the following manner:

If one heat, the fastest swimmer shall be seeded in the second heat, next fastest in the first heat, next fastest in the second heat, next in the first heat etc.

If three heats, the fastest swimmer shall be placed in the third heat, next fastest in the second, next fastest in the first. The fourth fastest swimmer shall be placed in the third heat, the fifth in the second heat, and the sixth fastest in the first heat, the seventh fastest in the third heat, etc.

Exception: When there are two or more heats in an event, there shall be minimum of three swimmers seeded into any one preliminary heavy but subsequent scratches may reduce the number of swimmers in such heat to less than three.

Except for 50 metre events, assignment of lanes shall be (number lane being on the right side of the pool when facing the course from the starting end) by placing the fastest swimmer or team in the centre lane in pool with a odd number of lanes, or in lane 3 or 4 respectively in pools having 6 or 8 lanes. The swimmers having the next fastest time is to be placed on his left, there alternating the others to right and left in accordance with the submitted times Swimmers with identical times shall be assigned their lane positions by draw within the aforesaid pattern.

When 50 metre events are contested, the races may be swum, at the discretion of the Management Committee, either from the regular starting end to the turning end or from the turning end to the starting end, depending upon such factors as existence of adequate Automatic Equipment, starter's position etc. The Management committee should advise swimmers of their determination well before the start of the competition. Regardless of which way the race is swum, the swimmers shall be seeded in the same lanes in which they would be seeded if they were both starting and finishing at the starting end.

Finals

Where no preliminary heats are necessary, lanes shall be assigned in accordance with above. Where preliminary heats have been held, lanes shall be assigned as in based, however, on times established in such heats.

In the event that swimmers from the same or different heats have equal times registered to 1/100 second for either the eighth place or sixteenth place, there shall be swim-off to determine which swimmer shall advance to the appropriate finals. Such swim- offs shall take place not less than one hour after all involved swimmers have completed their heat.

Where one or more swimmers scratch from a final event, substitutes will be called in order of classifications in heats. The event or events must be re-seeded and supplementary sheets must be issued detailing the changes or substitutions, as prescribed.

In other competitions, the draw system may be used for assigning lane positions.

THE START

The start in Freestyle, Breaststroke and Butterfly races shall be with a dive. On the long whistle from the referee the swimmers shall step onto the back surface of the starting platform with both feet the same distance from the front and remain there. On the starter's command "take your marks", they shall immediately take up starting position with at least one foot at the front of the starting platforms. When all swimmers are stationary, the starter shall give the starting signal.

The start in Backstroke and Medley Relay races be from the water. At the referee's long whistle the swimmers shall immediately enter the water and return without undue delay to the starting position When all swimmers have assumed their starting positions the starter shall give the command "take your marks". When all swimmers are stationary, the starter shall give the starting signal.

In Olympic Games, World Championships and other FINA events the command "Take your marks" shall be in English and the start shall be by multiple loudspeakers, mounted one at each starting platform. The sound of three loudspeakers shall be sufficiently loud that repetition of the signal will give adequate recall signal for a false start.

The starter shall call back the swimmers at the first false start and remind them of not starting before the starting signal. After the first false start any swimmer starting before the starting signal has been given shall be disqualified. If the starting signal sounds before the disqualification is declared, the race shall continue and the swimmer or swimmers shall be disqualified upon completion of the race. If the disqualification is declared before the starting signal, the signal shall not be given, but the remaining swimmers shall be called back, be reminded by the starter of the penalties, and start again.

The signal for a false starts shall be the same or the starting signal but repeated along with dropping of the false start rope. Alternatively, if the referee decides that the start is false he shall blow his whistle, which shall be followed by the starter's signal and dropping of the false start rope.

If an error by an official follows a fault by a swimmer, the fault by the swimmer is expunged.

FREESTYLE

Freestyle means that in an event so designated the swimmer may swim any style, except that in individual medley or medley relay events, freestyle means any style other than backstroke, breakstroke or butterfly.

Some part of the swimmer must touch the wall upon completion of each length and at the finish.

BACKSTROKE

The swimmers shall line up in the water facing the starting end, with both hands holding the starting grips. The feet, including the toes, shall be under the surface of the eater. Standing in or on the gutter or bending the toes over the lip of the gutter is prohibited.

At the signal for starting and after turning the swimmer shall push off and swim upon his back throughout the race. He must be on his back at all times except when executing a turn. The normal position on the back can include a roll movement of the body up to but not including 90 degrees from horizontal. The position of the head is not relevant. "Except when executing a turn" means any deviation from the normal backstroke position in order to execute a continuous turning action.

Some part of the swimmer must break the surface of the water throughout the race, except it shall be permissible for the swimmer to be completely submerged during the turn end for a distance of not more than 15 metres after the start and each turn. By that point the head must have broken the surface.

During the turn the shoulders may be turned over the vertical to the breast but the swimmer must have returned to a position on the back upon leaving the wall. When executing the turn there must be a touch of the wall with some part of the swimmer's body.

Upon the finish of the race the swimmer must touch the wall while on the back.

BREASTSTROKE

From the beginning of the first armstroke after the start and after each turn, the body shall be kept on the breast and both shoulders shall be in line with the normal water surface.

All movements of the arms shall be simultaneous and in the same horizontal plane without alternating movement.

The hands shall be pushed forward together from the breast on, under, or over the water, and shall be brought back on or under the surface of the water. The hands shall not be brought back beyond the hip line, except during the first stoke after the start and each turn.

All movements of the logs shall be simultaneous and in the same horizontal place without alternating movement.

The feet must be turned outwards during the propulsive part of the kick, A scissors, flutter or downward dolphin kick is not permitted. Breaking the surface of the water with the breast is allowed unless followed by downward dolphin kick.

At each turn and at the finish of the race, the touch shall be made with both hands simultaneously at, above, or below the water level. The shoulders shall remain in the horizontal plane until the touch has been made. The head may be submerged after the last arm pull prior to the touch, provided it breaks the surface of the water at some point during the last complete or incomplete cycle preceding the touch.

During each complete cycle of one arm stroke and one leg kick, in that order, some part of the swimmer's head shall break the surface of the water, except that after the start and after each turn the swimmer may take one arm stroke completely back to the legs and one leg kick while wholly submerged. The head must break the surface of a water before the hands turn inward at the widest part of the second stroke.

The body must be on the breast at all times, except when executing a turn. The shoulders shall be in line with the water Surface from the beginning of the first armstroke, after the start and after each turn and shall remain in that position until the next turn or finish. It is not permitted to roll onto the back at any time.

Both arms must be brought forward together over the water and brought backward simultaneously.

All movements of the feet must be executed in a simultaneous manner. Simultaneous up and down movements of the legs and feet in the vertical plane are permitted. The legs or feet need not be at the same level, but no alternating movements are permitted.

At each turn and at the finish of the race, the touch shall be made with both one arm pull under the water, which must being him to the surface.

INDEX